The M & E Higher Business Education Series

Financial Accounting

Raymond Brockington
BCom MSc(Econ) FCA
Lecturer in Finance and Accounting
University of Bath

Macdonald and Evans

Macdonald & Evans Ltd
Estover, Plymouth PL6 7PZ

First published 1983

© Macdonald & Evans Ltd 1983

British Library Cataloguing in Publication Data

Brockington, Raymond
Financial accounting.—(Higher business education
series)
1. Accounting
I. Title   II. Series
657'.48   HF5635

(Paperback) ISBN 0-7121-0639-1
(Case) ISBN 0-7121-0644-8

Text set in 11/12pt Linotron 202 Times
printed and bound in
Great Britain at
The Pitman Press, Bath

The M & E Higher Business Education Series

Financial Accounting

General Editor

Dr Edwin Kerr
*Chief Officer, Council for National
Academic Awards*

Advisory Editors

K. W. Aitken
*Vice-Principal, South East
London College*

P. W. Holmes
*Director, Regional Management
Studies Centre, Bristol Polytechnic*

Other titles in the same series:
Practical Business Law
Quantitative Approaches in Business Studies

Foreword

In recent years business practice has been undergoing major and fundamental changes for a variety of economic, social and technological reasons. In parallel with these changes the developments of education for business at all levels have also been extensive and far-reaching. In particular this is true at the advanced levels for courses leading to (a) the first degrees of the Council for National Academic Awards and of the universities, (b) the higher awards of the Business Education Council and its Scottish equivalent, and (c) examinations of the relevant professional bodies. Many such courses are now offered in educational institutions which include the polytechnics, the universities, the colleges and institutes of higher education, the further education colleges and the Scottish central institutions. In addition to these developments in curricular design there have also been important advances in educational and teaching methods.

Macdonald and Evans already has a large involvement in meeting needs of students and staff in Business Education through its BEC BOOK series and its HANDBOOK series. It has now decided to complement these series with its Higher Business Education series.

The series is intended to be one of major educational significance which will cover all important aspects of Higher Business Education. It will be designed for student and staff use with all of the advanced courses at all of the educational institutions mentioned above. Each book will have both a planned part in the series and be complete in itself and, in it, a thematic and problem-solving approach will be adopted, thus bringing a body of theory to bear on business problems—a major feature of the whole series.

The editorial team have chosen authors who are experienced people from technological institutions and from professional practice and will collaborate with them to ensure that the books are authoritative and are written in a style which will make them easy to use and will assist the students to learn effectively from such use.

The editorial team will welcome criticisms on each of the books so that improvements may be made at the reprint stages to ensure a closer achievement of the objectives of the books and the entire series.

Edwin Kerr
General Editor

Preface

A problem faced by any accounting educator, whether he be lecturer or author, is that of how to blend his course so that it contains the appropriate mix of theory and practice. What is appropriate depends on the nature and aspirations of his audience. If this consists of students with strictly vocational aims seeking a skill in financial processes of immediate use in their daily work, then the development of practical expertise is rightly to the fore. If it is made up of qualified accountants seeking further insight into the fundamentals of their subject, then a theoretical approach is likely to be correct.

The audience for this book is made up of first degree and higher diploma students of business studies (whether they are specialising in financial accounting or not) and the problem therefore takes on particular dimensions. These students are likely to be highly motivated by well-structured career aspirations although not necessarily predominantly in the financial area. At the same time they are studying within the context of a multi-disciplinary course having its own designed educational objectives to which financial accounting makes an important but not exclusive contribution.

The right blend of theory and practice is not here easy to find. It is necessary to provide a theoretical structure for the subject which will allow the proper intellectual development of the student and the integration of financial accounting with concurrent subjects of study, typically law, economics, behavioural sciences and quantitative methods. There is also a need to give sufficient technical content to satisfy career demands. A too-theoretical course will produce that despair of the professional accountant's office—an apparently relevant graduate, glib in ideas, but who cannot do any of the things which an accountant is supposed to do. A too-practical course will be sterile and ultimately boring to an enquiring student, making a fulfilment of the educational aims of the course impossible and imparting, at best, a few skills which may be of very short term usefulness in a rapidly changing world.

This book describes in adequate, though not exhaustive, detail what an accountant does and why he does it. It examines the implicit frame of reference within which accounting currently operates and thus constructs a theoretical underpinning to practice. It explores the possibilities and merits of adopting quite different frames of reference and investigates the consequences for practice of so doing. It is thus hoped that conflicts between theory and practice are used as a gateway to understanding rather than as a barrier to progress.

Although this depends to an extent on the syllabus and general design of the course which the student is following, it is anticipated that this book will serve as a basic text for the whole of the first year of study of this subject and for a substantial part of the second. Thereafter it will fill the role of an introductory and supporting text which will need to be supplemented increasingly by specialist reading. Because this will be individual to each separate course, it is left to the teacher to recommend reading and no references to further reading are made here.

The format of the book is intended to give a logical progression to study although many chapters, particularly the later ones, may be taken out of order. Chapters 1 and 2 define the subject and establish its theoretical foundations. Chapters 3 and 4 then show how the two basic financial accounting statements, the balance sheet and the profit and loss account respectively, are derived. These chapters are followed by an important section, embracing Chapters 5 and 6, which develops double entry book-keeping, first in principle and then in considerably more practical detail. Chapters 8 to 10 show the important new accounting problems posed by those different but both important forms of organisation, the partnership and the limited company. Chapters 11 and 12 develop further accounting techniques of specific relevance to limited companies and Chapter 14 shows the importance of the interpretation of financial accounting figures and how this is supported by the calculation of ratios. Chapter 15 is a vital one discussing the detailed legal requirements imposed on companies' published accounts. The problem of the measurement of income and the associated problem of accounting within an inflationary environment are dealt with in Chapters 16 and 17. Chapter 18 is on Accounting Standards and Chapter 19 takes a speculative look at the future.

Each chapter is preceded by a statement of its contents and is followed by a summary of its important points. This should be helpful to the efficient planning of study and to revision. There is also a selection of test questions covering both theoretical and practical matters at the end of each chapter. At the end of the book there is an appendix containing essay topics which will provide ample material for course assignments. Another appendix consists of six substantial practical exercises. These will provide practice in the use of accounting techniques and could also be used as case studies for class consideration and discussion.

1983

                                                                    RBB

Contents

CHAPTER 1

Financial Accounting Defined

OBJECTIVES

In this chapter we shall deal with the following important topics:

(*a*) a definition of the subject;
(*b*) the contexts in which it is used;
(*c*) the limitations of financial accounting;
(*d*) the need to define the purposes for which accounts are being prepared;
(*e*) the functions of financial accounting.

1. INTRODUCTION

To give an account of something is to describe and explain it. Thus financial accounting must be defined as that subject dealing with the description and explanation of financial matters. A very important part of all of human activity is concerned with the optimisation of our standard of life, given the resources we find about us. The way in which we do this is the area of study of the subject known as Economics. In a developed society it is an essential feature of such optimisation that it requires specialisation of function and an appropriate mechanism for the exchange of goods and services. Money is the medium by which such exchanges take place and has therefore become the unique measure of one person's indebtedness to another, of the quantity of resources devoted to a particular enterprise and of the success or otherwise of their use. Financial matters thus come to be equated with economic matters and financial accounting comes to be seen as a description and explanation of economic activities.

Every one of us is involved in economic activity in some way or another. This is true whether we be the chief executive of a multi-million pound enterprise or a pensioner seeking to make a small fixed income go as far as possible. Accounting thus affects every one of us. It helps us to organise and manage our own affairs in an appropriate fashion and it helps to assure that part of the quality of life which derives from the efficient operation of the businesses which supply us, the government which controls us and the social services with which we are provided.

Most of this book will be concerned with the financial accounting of business organisations, that is of organisations set up with the object that they should earn a profit on behalf of their proprietors. We might debate as an exercise in philosophy whether this profit is to be seen as a just reward for efforts made and for risks taken or whether it is the fruit of the exploitation of the weak or the ill-informed. This is not important to our present purpose which is to develop techniques whereby we can record what has happened and provide an analysis of its implications so that informed action can be taken in making progress towards a goal.

2. TYPES OF BUSINESS

Businesses are organised in many different ways and these differences may be important to the accounting process. One business might be established by a single individual providing his own capital, labour and management expertise. Such a person we would describe as a sole trader and businesses of this kind are very common. They tend to be small and to operate in fields where relatively little capital but much specialised skill is required. The small shop on the corner, the window cleaner and the landscape gardener are often operated by sole traders. They will usually be given the name of the proprietor, e.g. John Smith or, perhaps, to make them sound bigger, John Smith and Co., or they may adopt some appropriate business name like Toytown General Store.

Another business might operate as a partnership. The distinction between this and the sole trader is merely that, in a partnership, two or more people set up in business in common jointly providing the inputs which in the case of the sole trader come from one person. Partnerships are often formed in the case of businesses providing professional services such as accountants, doctors and solicitors. A partnership would have some such name as Smith, Brown and Jones or Roberts and Sons.

A third important form of business organisation is the limited company. Here the capital is provided jointly by a body of people, which may be very large, known as the shareholders or members of the company, while the management is provided by a small group of people employed for the purpose and known as directors. Companies frequently operate very large businesses and are most common where amounts of capital beyond the resources of an individual or small group of individuals are needed. A company will carry some such name as Arkville Manufacturing Company plc or McTavish Garden Centre plc.

3. BUSINESS ACCOUNTS

These forms of business organisation all have one thing in common. They assemble factors of production and organise them with a view to making a profit. They may be very successful in this endeavour or only moderately successful. They may even fail totally, ending up by making a loss. Although normally any profit is made for the exclusive benefit of the ultimate proprietor, it should not be overlooked that highly profitable businesses can afford to pay good wages and to offer good value for money to customers, i.e. that the benefits of successful operation may be widely spread. Similarly, although a loss falls apparently on the providers of capital, it may also lead to the loss of jobs by employees and to the cutting of the range of choice offered to customers.

The accounts which are prepared for each type of business will be similar in so far as they relate to the basic business activity but will have important differences when they deal with proprietorship matters. So far as the former is concerned the accounts will powerfully reflect the profit motive and the necessity to maintain an appropriate assembly of resources for continuance of the activity. So far as the latter is concerned the accounts will reflect the relative rights and entitlement of the proprietors. Thus we shall receive accounts from time to time which will tell us that during a particular period a business has made a certain profit and that it now stands in a certain position from which there is a potential for earning more profit in the future. They will also show who is to share in current profit and who has a stake in the current position and in what proportions these shares are held.

Important though business accounts are it should not be overlooked that financial accounting is important also to other forms of organisation. Nationalised industries, local authorities, charities and sports and social clubs are examples of different kinds of organisation where the conventional profit motive is absent. They do, however, have objectives and the use of scarce resources is involved in achieving those objectives. The objective of a nationalised industry is to provide efficiently some commodity or service on a commercial basis while breaking even, making neither profit nor loss, in the long run. A local authority has to spend its rates income in the way which optimises the benefit which ratepayers receive from the services which it provides. A charity will be concerned to do as much good as it can within its budget. We cannot judge the extent to which these objectives are met without information on which to base such a judgment. Such information will be provided by processes falling within the field of financial accounting.

4. PURPOSE OF ACCOUNTS

No one who gave more than a moment's thought to the matter could possibly suppose that all of the effects of economic activity, still less of the whole of human activity, could be quantified in terms of money. Financial accounting may tell us what value of our product a particular customer has bought in the past. It will not tell us what goodwill has thereby been generated and thus what we might anticipate that he will buy in the future, although this is crucial to our continuing success and survival. Again it will tell us what we have spent on the wages of our employees and on providing them with amenities such as a canteen and a sports field. It will not tell us the value of a contented, well-motivated workforce which again is as important to us as is cash in the bank. It will show us how much we pay our chief executive but will not directly reveal the benefit we receive from his personal enthusiasm and special flair for the job. We must be quite clear, therefore, that financial accounting explains money matters and only money matters. We shall be misled if we conclude that a complete explanation of a financial situation is the same thing as a complete explanation of an economic situation.

Accounting does not exist in a vacuum. It is essentially a conveyance of information from one person to another for a particular purpose and all of these components are important. The author of this book is explaining certain matters to his readers so that they can pass examinations in the subject and can then use what they know in their work. A naughty schoolboy will explain his conduct to the headmaster seeking to persuade the head not to punish him. A newspaper will explain events to its readers so that they may be informed for their own interest and for the creation of what is known as public opinion.

We do not have to look far for examples of how an account depends not merely on its underlying facts but on its originator, its intended recipient and on the context and purpose of the communication. Here is a novelist's description of a house: "It was a friendly house. Even as I approached it its windows seemed to twinkle with delight and its front door to open into a smile. Once I had entered it wrapped me in a warm embrace and seemed to tell me that I belonged and made it somehow complete". An estate agent might describe a house as follows: "Four bed det. res., 2 recep., 2 bath, hall, kitch., util., gas c.h., mature gdn." Each of these quotations describes a house and yet their form and content depends completely on the purpose for which they are given and they are in no way interchangeable.

The purposes of financial accounting may usefully be categorised under three headings. These are (*a*) administrative, (*b*) regulatory and (*c*) decision-informing.

Administrative

Any organisation will require a considerable amount of financial information of a routine nature if it is to operate in an effective and businesslike fashion. The techniques for providing this kind of information are of a very simple nature but important because they must make it as accessible, clear and free from error as possible.

A few examples of administrative information and how it might be provided will immediately make its nature clear. Many businesses sell to some or all of their customers on credit terms. This means that goods are supplied as required on the understanding that they will be paid for at some future time, e.g. following a statement provided at the end of the month. It will be necessary to keep a record to show the value of the goods so supplied and any amounts paid so that we can ensure that all amounts due are eventually collected. An account such as the following would serve very well.

ACCOUNT WITH A CUSTOMER FOR JUNE

	(*Goods supplied*)			(*Amounts paid*)	
11th June	144 notebooks	£12.00	30th June	Cash	£17.60
12th June	50 pkts envelopes	5.60		Balance (amount	
15th June	10 boxes paper	22.80		still owed)	22.80
		£40.40			£40.40
1st July	Balance	£22.80			

From this it can readily be seen that at 1st July our customer still owed us for ten boxes of paper. It can also be seen that this amount has been outstanding for 15 days.

When we take delivery of goods on credit we shall need to keep a similar record of goods and cash to ensure that we pay what we owe at the agreed time. Another example of administrative information is where we keep an account of cash to show how much has been received or paid and what now remains in hand. Without such records debts would be uncollected, bills would be unpaid or paid twice and it would be impossible to check bank statements for accuracy or know how the business stood for cash.

Regulatory

Certain requirements for information are imposed on businesses by contract, by the law of the land or in some other regulatory way. Perhaps the best example is the statutory requirement imposed on all limited companies under the Companies Acts to produce an annual balance sheet and profit and loss account. Copies of these must be sent to each shareholder and deposited with the Registrar of Companies where they are available for public consultation. The purpose of these accounts is to monitor the company to ensure that it is being operated honestly and in accordance with law and with the instruments (articles and memorandum of association) setting it up. The Stock Exchange requires the provision of accounting information over and above that which the law demands as a condition of offering companies a listing (i.e. the facility of having its shares dealt in on the Stock Exchange). Partnership accounts may be required under the agreement between the partners in order to enable profits to be calculated and correctly divided. The Inland Revenue has the legal power to compel financial disclosure as part of its duty to assess and collect tax. Nationalised undertakings are compelled under the individual Acts of Parliament establishing them to prepare and publish annual accounts. We must establish procedures whereby this sort of information can be correctly and promptly provided.

Decision-informing

Financial accounting has a third function and this is to provide information to those who need it for the purpose of making decisions. People who come into this category obviously include the providers of capital, actual and potential shareholders in the case of a limited company. It may also include lenders (such as banks) and those considering advancing credit to the business, e.g. the suppliers of goods. Some would argue that it includes employees who need to make decisions based on the ability of the business to meet wage demands and on the basic security of their employment. It may also include customers who may need information enabling them to decide whether they are being exploited (as evidenced by too high a profit) and members of the public at large who have an interest in the activities of any organisation with the power to change their environment.

The extent to which this decision-making requirement should be met will depend, in the absence of specific regulations, on the degree of responsibility which is accepted by the business in this connection. It has been argued that responsibility should go hand in hand with power and any centre of economic activity has power, although the degree of this will vary with size and other factors. The proprietor of a small corner shop has the power to inconvenience his customers by closing at awkward times or to serve them badly by selling low-quality goods at high prices. This power, however, is limited to a local area and can be avoided by most customers who can travel elsewhere. On the other hand, a giant international manufacturing concern can hold power over millions of people who look to it as an employer, a supplier or a customer.

5. CONCLUSION

Financial accounting is a developing subject with plenty of opportunity for new techniques to be devised to replace those which have outlived their usefulness. The administrative function is probably the most stable, but any business which grows in size will find that the administration becomes more complex throwing greater burdens on the accounting system. Branch accounts and disaggregated trading and profit and loss accounts are examples of this kind of development. The regulatory aspects of financial accounting must change in response to new legislation and to new Accounting Standards and the rate of change in this area is quite high. Decision information needs will change and develop as ideas change on what information is relevant to a particular type of decision.

SUMMARY

1. Financial accounting is that subject dealing with the description and explanation of financial matters.

2. It is of use to a wide variety of organisations whether or not concerned with business. Important forms of business organisations are the sole trader, the partnership and the limited company.

3. Accounting is the conveyance of information from one person to another. It must have regard to the needs of its users as well as to the facts of the situation on which it is based.

4. The purposes of financial accounting may be usefully categorised as (a) administrative, (b) regulatory and (c) decision-informing. Each of these is important.

QUESTIONS

1. "A business should concentrate its efforts on the activity which makes it its profits. Time spent on the mere keeping of records is wasted". Discuss.

2. The sole trader, the partnership and the limited company are three different kinds of business organisation. Why should variety in the form of organisation exist?

3. Give examples of the use of accounting under the three headings, administrative, regulatory and decision-informing.

4. "In preparing accounts a knowledge of the use to which they

are to be put is just as important as a knowledge of the facts which are to be conveyed." Discuss.

5. As a student of both management accounting and financial accounting, what do you see as being the essential differences between them?

CHAPTER 2

The Fundamental Concepts

OBJECTIVES

In this chapter we shall deal with the following important topics:

(*a*) the importance of the conceptual basis of financial accounting;
(*b*) the generally accepted concepts:
    (*i*) entity,
    (*ii*) proprietorship,
    (*iii*) going concern,
    (*iv*) objectivity,
    (*v*) money measurement,
    (*vi*) conservatism;
(*c*) the working principles:
    (*i*) realisation,
    (*ii*) consistency,
    (*iii*) cost,
    (*iv*) matching,
    (*v*) materiality.

1. INTRODUCTION

Before we start on a study of its techniques we need to examine some of the main ideas on which financial accounting is based. These provide the theory which will guide and give a logical structure to practice. These ideas are often referred to as accounting's *basic concepts*. Perhaps the best way to define a concept is to say that it is a viewpoint which sets the parameters within which a situation is understood. The matter is very important because the interpretation of a situation may depend as much or more on the concepts used in describing it than on the facts of the situation itself. An important danger is that concepts are often taken as self-evident, and thus not subject to challenge, so that it is not apparent that they do in fact impart a particular slant to the information.

Here is a very simple example of this. The statement "John was travelling to London accompanied by his wife" is, apparently, a simple statement of fact which would pass without comment. There is, however, contained within it an implicit concept of female subservience. We gain the impression that John is the traveller with the important business and that his wife is merely a passive follower. This can quite clearly be seen by considering the subtle change in meaning which would be conveyed if the statement was amended to "Betty was travelling to London accompanied by her husband".

Now here is a financial example showing the importance of concepts used in that context. The facts are these: "John bought a motor vehicle, which he believed to be worth £500, for £480. He used it to drive a total of 1,000 miles and then sold it for £400 although he believed it then to be worth £450." The facts are simple and have the result that John started with £480 and ended with £400. The way in which we account for these events, however, may depend on our point of view and we will take, by turns, several different ones.

Let us supposed first that John is a dealer in motor vehicles seeking to buy and sell them at a profit. The facts set out above will be accounted for as follows:

Sale of vehicle	£400
Less Cost	480
Loss on transaction	£80

The enterprise is seen to have made a loss and will therefore be judged to be an unsuccessful one. Its object (to make a profit) was not achieved.

Now let us suppose that John is a traveller seeking to minimise the cost of his travel. It would have cost him (say) 20p per mile to hire a car to travel the 1,000 miles and the temporary use of the car he bought was an alternative. He would account for it as follows:

Value of travel obtained: $1,000 \times 20p$		£200
Cost of vehicle	£480	
Less recovered on sale	400	80
Gain on transaction		£120

Using this different concept the transaction has been successful.

Next we will make the whole affair more complicated and suppose that John sees himself having, by turns, three different roles. He is first a buyer of motor vehicles, then a traveller and then a seller of motor vehicles. Here are his accounts:

As a buyer:

Value of car bought	£500
Less Cash paid	480
Gain on buying	£20

John has therefore been successful as a buyer.

As a traveller:

Value of travel		£200
Value of car before travel	£500	
Value of car after travel	450	
		50
Gain		£150

He has been successful as a traveller

As a seller:

Proceeds of sale	£400
Value of car sold	450
Loss	£50

He is unsuccessful as a seller of the vehicle.

These different understandings of the situation may lead to important consequences if John uses his accounts to guide his actions. As a dealer in motor vehicles he is a failure—the inference is that he should avoid this activity in the future. As a traveller he has been successful—the inference is that this activity could be repeated in the future. Where there are seen to be multiple roles John is successful at buying vehicles and in travelling at low cost but unsuccessful in selling vehicles. The inference is that he should employ a salesman to do his selling for him.

We have learnt from this example that the concepts employed are very important to the understanding of a situation. We have also learnt that if an inappropriate concept is used we are likely to be misled by our accounts and to take the wrong action. If John's accounts are prepared on the basis that he is a dealer when in fact he sees himself as a traveller, the signal given by the accounts that the activity is unsuccessful will mislead him.

In this example we have taken great care in selecting concepts which are supposedly tailor-made to John's situation. Most financial accounts prepared for businesses are not tailor-made but are based on very broad generally accepted concepts of wide applicability. This is necessary if they are to be useful to a wide range of different people. By giving a universal "grammar" to financial accounts this makes them easy to understand and more or less comparable between one business and another. It inevitably means, however, that they do not fit perfectly the requirements of any individual case and we are likely to be misled if we adopt a very literal interpretation of figures without understanding the point of view from which they are prepared. Shortly we will look at these basic universal concepts, often referred to as generally accepted accounting principles, but first we must make a very important point about them.

Accounting concepts do not emanate from any ultimate authority on such matters. They have developed, to an extent spontaneously, as accounting practice has developed. It would be reassuring to be able to assume that they derived from experience and that having stood the test of time they were the most appropriate which could be adopted. In some cases this may be true. In others, however, we have to admit that they derive from our cultural environment or that they survive from a resistance to change or that they suit the convenience of a particular vested interest. Examples of all of these can easily be given. The fact that we live in a capitalist society with a considerable reverence for property and for rights over it has profoundly affected the shape of accounts. The fact that admittedly imperfect measures of value based on historic cost survive undoubtedly owes something to a resistance to change. The demands of the tax authorities for information on which they can base tax computations according to current law is an example of a particular interest serving to maintain quite large areas of current accounting practice.

2 BASIC CONCEPTS

We will now look at some of the more important of the basic concepts embodied in current accounting practice.

The entity concept

When accounts are prepared they relate to some defined focus of activity. This may be an individual person, a business, a social club, a charity or any one of a whole range of like possibilities. Some of these have a physical, tangible existence or are recognised in law as though this were the case. One person, for example, has a physical existence quite separate from that of other persons. He or she has important legal rights and obligations. A limited company is recognised in law as a person and thus, for accounting purposes, is much the same thing. The business of a sole trader, however, and that of a partnership have no physical or legal existence separately from the persons who make them up. Nevertheless, it is convenient for accounting purposes to presume that they have. To do this focusses our attention on the object of our interest and thus excludes much extraneous information. It also makes our objective sufficiently compact for us to be able to deal with it.

Since the entity concept is an important one and has some significant practical consequences we will explore it a little further. Mr X runs a small retail business which is his only occupation and provides the income on which he lives. Not surprisingly the business takes up a great deal of his time and he is often thinking about it or doing some work for it when he is ostensibly occupied with something else. For example, when out on a pleasure trip with his family he will sometimes stop off to make deliveries of goods to his customers.

For a number of reasons it will be useful for Mr X to account for his business activity separately from his private life even though, in fact, they are inextricably mixed. For one thing he needs to know how efficiently his business activity is being conducted. Again he needs to assure himself that he has committed to the business the right quantity of resources to ensure its long term survival, but that at the same time it is not wastefully overprovided. He will need to provide information on business profits to the Inland Revenue for tax purposes. The entity concept makes the separation possible. The business is thereby given recognition as having an existence separate from that of Mr X even though we know that this is just a convenient fiction. It follows from this that Mr X may have dealings with his own business. He will supply it with capital in the first place and it will remit to him the profits which have been earned from the use of that capital.

The proprietorship concept

This concept is an extension to the entity concept. If a business is an entity but is not a real person it must be an entity which is acting on behalf of a real person or persons. This is because only real people can ultimately obtain satisfaction from the consumption of resources. To these people go the benefit of the entity's successful operation and they are the sufferers if it fails. It is a matter of philosophical argument as to who the business ought to be working for. Is it for the community at large? Is it for its own workforce? Is it for the suppliers of capital? Is it for its customers? The view which we take will profoundly affect the form of the accounts. The concept very clearly contained in current accounting practice is that a business works on behalf of its proprietors, i.e. those who provide it with its risk capital. The proprietorship concept thus states that the function of the business entity is to act on behalf of its proprietors, reporting to them on its activities and aiming to fulfill their objectives (usually regarded as the maximisation of profit).

The going concern concept

It is fairly easy to evaluate the outcome of an activity when that activity is wholly complete. A business is, however, normally a succession of activities which persist over a very long period. Accounts cannot wait until the end of the life of the business if they are to be of any use but must be prepared at relatively frequent intervals. Accounting at the end of an activity when everything is known and nothing is left over is quite different from accounting at an interim point when many outcomes are uncertain and many matters fall to be carried forward. The presumption adopted when periodic accounts are prepared during the lifetime of a business are that the lifetime extends indefinitely into the future. This is very helpful, as we shall presently see, to the making of our valuations. It can be contrasted with the possible alternative idea that the business has no life beyond the immediate accounting period. This might be termed a single venture concept.

Let us look at a simple example to show the effect of this. Mr Y purchased 100 pounds of apples at 10p per pound. He set up a stall by the roadside on a certain day and sold 70 pounds of apples at 20p per pound. A single venture concept would account for this as follows:

Sales (70 lbs @ 20p)	£14
Less Costs (100 lbs @ 10p)	10
Profit	£4

A going concern concept would recognise a future opportunity to sell the remaining 30 pounds of apples and would regard the outcome of that opportunity as being of no concern to this account. It would therefore show:

Sales (70 lbs @ 20p)	£14
Less Costs (70 lbs @ 10p)	7
Profit	£7

Exceptions are found in practice to the use of the going concern concept. The main examples are where it is in fact known that the business is closing down or where, for other reasons, the saleability of residual stocks is seriously in doubt.

The concept of objectivity and auditability

This concept is that what is included in accounts should be objective, i.e. determined independently of the observer, and thus auditable, i.e. capable of independent verification. This concept is useful in that it keeps accounts as free as possible from the risk of manipulation by the unscrupulous, but it is inhibiting in that it can exclude from consideration some information which might be extremely relevant and useful.

Consider a case in point. Mr Z is considering the purchase of a second-hand bookcase but does not have any idea as to what he ought to offer for it. The only objective information about its value is that the present owner paid £200 for it when it was new three years ago. Although capable of verification (by looking at the original bill) this information is not very useful. The bookcase is now partly worn and, in any case, the general level of furniture prices has altered considerably since it was bought. The vendor expresses the opinion that the bookcase is worth £150 at the present time. This subjective information is potentially useful as it is given with a knowledge of current circumstances. Mr Z cannot, however, place too much confidence in the valuation because it is given by a person with an interest in persuading him to pay as much as possible. A friend of Mr Z who is a dealer in furniture, says that the bookcase is worth £120. This is again subjective information but Mr Z might properly regard it as a very useful guide. Regardless of one's intuitive feelings on the matter conventional accounting practice would disregard both of these subjective valuations and would favour the objective, although, outdated figure.

The money measurement concept

This concept is that all relevant matters may be evaluated in terms of money. This is a clear limitation of the kind of things which will appear in our financial accounts. A business may have the services of a hard working and energetic proprietor with a flair for seeing and exploiting business opportunities. This will give it great advantages over a business with a less able proprietor. This advantage cannot, however, be valued in terms of money and will thus be disregarded by accounting.

The concept of conservatism

This is sometimes called the concept of prudence. There is built into accounting practice the notion that caution is a good thing and that it is thus better to be pessimistic than optimistic. This is presumably based on the experience that the probability of survival is thereby increased. It does, however, necessarily build a permanent bias into our accounts. This is how it operates. A business holds some stock for which it paid £2 per unit but it expects to sell it for £3 per unit. On the principle of not counting chickens before they are hatched (prudence) this will conventionally be valued at £2 per unit. Another lot of stock cost £5 per unit but has proved to be a bad buy. It is expected that it can only be sold if the price is dropped to £2 per unit. Conservatively, therefore, it will be valued at £2 per unit. The effect of this concept is that where we give a valuation to something we are saying that it is worth at least that amount. When we state a profit we are saying that the profit earned is at least that amount. In each case the actual situation is possibly better than that reported.

Although prudence is a fundamental concept it will be interesting to see, as we shall in Chapter 17, that inflation has made a nonsense of it and it has become possible for accounts pessimistically prepared nevertheless to convey a wildly optimistic impression. For now, however, let us note merely the problem of consistent bias.

3. WORKING RULES

Most modern books on accounting list and discuss its fundamental concepts as has been done here. What is confusing to the student beginner, however, is that no two lists of concepts are exactly the same. The reason for this is that all concepts are to be implied from the way in which accounts are actually prepared and that there is no ultimately authoritative list to which we can refer. In order to give some assistance in a reconciliation we refer below to certain working rules of accounting which can be shown to derive from the concepts referred to above. Some authors would list these working rules as though they were separate concepts.

The principle of realisation

This means that generally we shall never take account of a profit until it is actually turned into cash or into something (such as a debtor) which is very near to being cash. We may, for example, hold stock which we are quite confident will be sold at a profit to us of £5 for every unit held. This profit will not be recorded, however, until a buyer has been identified and has actually paid for the stock or has firmly agreed to do so. The principle of realisation arises out of two concepts—those of conservatism and of objectivity. It is more conservative to delay the recognition of a profit until all events contributing to it (including ultimate sale) have been completed. The existence of the profit can be verified objectively only when the record is complete that the transactions have occurred.

The principle of consistency

This says that where differing accounting treatments of a particular type of transaction are legitimately available then one shall be selected and adhered to. It will not generally be permissible to vary the treatment between one case and another. The wisdom of this is plain. If the bases of accounting treatment vary between one period and another this will invalidate any comparisons which might be made and make conclusions drawn from them misleading. The principle derives from the concept of objectivity and auditability, as without it the methods used could vary arbitrarily.

The concept of conservatism and the principle of consistency sometimes come into conflict. For example, conservatism demands that we value stock at the lower of its cost or its selling value but consistency would demand that we always use one or the other. Where this occurs the rule is that the concept of conservatism will prevail over the principle of consistency.

The principle of cost

The valuation of resources at their cost is sometimes put forward as a concept of accounting. It merely states that the value of anything will normally be measured in terms of what it originally cost. It is suggested, however, that cost measurement derives directly from the concept of objectivity since, unlike most other bases of valuation, direct documentary evidence of it can always be obtained. It is interesting to note, in passing, that the principle of cost valuation is now seriously under challenge. This, however, is a matter to which we shall return later.

The principle of matching

This states that, in computing profit, all expenditure will be matched against the revenue to which it relates. This is a manifestation of the going concern concept. In the example we gave under that heading the cost of 70 pounds of apples was matched against the revenue from the sale of 70 pounds of apples leaving the cost of the remainder to be matched against other revenues in the future. It is the going concern concept which leads to the presumption of future revenues against which this expenditure can be matched.

The principle of materiality

Accounts are not generally drawn up on a hair-splitting basis. Trivial matters which do not make any significant difference to the reported figures are disregarded or dealt with on a broadly approximate basis. For instance, a business might spend 25p on a packet of paper-clips which lasts for five accounting periods. A strict adherence to the matching principle would dictate that 5p of this expenditure should be attributed to each period. The principle of materiality would say that it is not worth the trouble and would attribute the whole of the expenditure to the period in which it occurs.

SUMMARY

1. Financial accounting is based on certain concepts which provide a structure of theory for the guidance of practice. The concepts used are fundamental to the understanding which the accounts impart.

2. Accounting concepts do not emanate from any ultimate authority but may be deduced from the collection of practices which has grown up over time.

3. The important, currently accepted, concepts are:

(a) the entity concept—that accounts relate to a defined focus of activity;

(b) the proprietorship concept—that a business operates on behalf of its proprietors, i.e. those who provide its risk capital;

(c) the going concern concept—that the business has a life extending indefinitely beyond the end of the accounting period;

(d) the concept of objectivity and auditability—that what is included in accounts should be objectively verifiable;

(e) the money measurement concept—that only matters capable of measurement in the form of money shall be included;

(f) the concept of conservatism (prudence)—that accounts should be based on a cautious (pessimistic) view of profits and valuations.

4. There are in addition certain important working rules or principles. These are:

(a) the principle of realisation—that no profit is to be recognised until actually turned into cash or near-cash (e.g. debtors);

(b) the principle of consistency—that similar items shall be treated similarly as between one occasion and another; (Note that where the principle of consistency conflicts with the concept of conservatism, as it might, the latter is to prevail.)

(c) the principle of cost—that resources should be valued, normally, at what was originally paid to acquire them;

(*d*) the principle of matching—that, in computing profit, all expenditure will be matched against the revenue to which it can be related;

(*e*) the principle of materiality—that trivial matters will not be dealt with in a pedantically correct fashion where the effort of so doing is unwarranted by its effect on the figures.

QUESTIONS

1. List the six concepts mentioned in the Chapter. State in each case an alternative concept which *might* be adopted regardless of whether you believe that to do so would be useful.

2. Why are concepts and principles important to financial accounting?

3. Summarise the advantages and disadvantages of the concept of conservatism.

4. "The money measurement concept ties accounts to a very narrow view of the world. Released from this it could achieve much more." Discuss.

5. Granny Smith bought a hundredweight (112 lbs) of apples for £20 the lot. She sold 56 lbs at 40p per lb and gave 6 lbs to her grandchildren to eat. She says that she is £12.40 better off after all this. She has calculated this as follows:

Sales 56 lbs @ 40p		£22.40
Cost of 112 lbs apples	£20	
Less value of 6 lbs eaten and 50 lbs retained	10	
	——	10.00
		£12.40

What accounting concepts and principles has Granny Smith used in compiling these figures?

CHAPTER 3

The Balance Sheet

OBJECTIVES

In this chapter we shall deal with the following important topics:

- (*a*) the balance sheet defined;
- (*b*) assets and liabilities;
- (*c*) valuation methods;
- (*d*) classification;
- (*e*) the dual nature of transactions.

1. INTRODUCTION

In this chapter we bring together the theoretical structure which we have developed and the generally accepted accounting principles which we have examined and give them practical expression by looking at the preparation and use of the balance sheet. The balance sheet is a basic and very important accounting document. Historically it can be regarded as the oldest form of accounting statement and early company legislation required its production but not that of the profit and loss account. Today it remains central to the accounting process and critical to the understanding of how an enterprise stands. An investor considering the investment of funds, a banker processing a loan application or a manager concerned about the financial health of his business will all look to the balance sheet as an important source of information.

2. THE BALANCE SHEET

What then is a balance sheet? Its name does not help us much. It is certainly a sheet which balances, i.e. it contains two columns of figures which sum to the same total, but this is a purely technical description of one of its features giving no clue as to its actual accounting function. This function depends on one's point of view. To one person it is a statement of solvency, of the ability to meet financial obligations. To another it is a statement of economic potential, of resources awaiting profitable exploitation. To a third it is a statement of accountability, of explanation of the use of entrusted funds. We shall perhaps be best served by regarding the balance sheet simply as a statement of financial position.

This emphasises a very important feature of the balance sheet which is that it is prepared at a particular date and therefore relates to a position at an exclusive moment in time. When a ship radios its position this gives valuable information but says nothing about where it has come from nor where it will go to next. Similarly, a balance sheet shows how the business stands now without indication of how this has been achieved nor of what it will achieve in the future. Just as, however, a ship positioned amongst icebergs, near rocks or in the path of a storm is in danger and one in calm water is not, so inferences might be drawn from a balance sheet as to the underlying health or otherwise of the enterprise to which it relates.

A balance sheet very clearly embodies several of the concepts and principles which we developed in the last chapter. One of these is the entity concept of the enterprise. A balance sheet is always prepared for a particular entity. This may be identifiable with an actual person, as in the case of a sole trader, with an entity created by statute, as with a limited company, or an entity which is a convenient fiction, as with a partnership. This entity is represented as being capable of owning tangible valuables and of gathering about it valuable rights. It is also subject to the exercise of rights against it by others and can thus incur obligations to them. Later we shall see that the balance sheet embodies other concepts as well.

3. ASSET VALUATION

The first important part of our statement of position will be an inventory and evaluation of those valuable things to which the business can lay claim. In technical accounting language these are known as its assets. Assets may formally be defined as things, capable of being valued in money terms, which are owned by the business entity. It should be noted that assets come in various kinds. Some have physical existence, such as buildings and equipment, whilst some are in the form of rights over others such as a debt owed by a customer or a bank balance evidenced by a figure on a bank statement. It should also be noted that "capable" of being valued in money terms does not necessarily mean easily valued in those terms. Although we shall need to elaborate on this problem later it will be useful if we now stop to consider this matter of valuation and of what it means.

There are certain characteristics of things which are intrinsic to them and which can be objectively determined and unequivocally stated. A certain object, for example, may be discovered to have a mass of three kilograms and, once this has been established, it will be true at all times and in all places for all observers. Value, however, is not such a characteristic and depends on how badly a thing is desired and on how scarce it is. Both are matters which can and do vary over time and space and between observers. Although the term is sometimes used there is no such thing as intrinsic value and many examples could be cited to illustrate this fact. A bag of sand would have no value at the seaside because there is plenty of sand about and everyone has as much as he requires. In the High Street DIY shop, however, it may command quite a high price. Again, what is regarded as a piece of junk fit only for throwing away one day may become a prized and valuable part of an antique collection on another. All this means that there is no test for the value of anything which does not involve recourse to the idea of a market whereby such things are exchanged for other things, e.g. money. It will suffice for present purposes if we refer to the two main concepts of value competing for attention in the accounting world today. These are *historic cost* and *current value*.

Historic cost

Under the historic cost principle all assets are valued at a level established by their most recent submission to the market, i.e. generally the price which was paid for them when they were bought. Where an asset is demonstrably being consumed over time that consumption, measured as accurately as possible, will be allowed for.

Here are some examples of historic cost valuation. A building was bought in 1921 for £10,000 and in 1981 was still valued by its owner at that figure. A motor vehicle was bought three years ago for £6,000. It is expected to last for five years in all. It is, therefore, deemed to be three-fifths consumed and is valued at £6,000 × 2/5 = £2,400. Goods for resale have just been acquired for a total of £8,000. Half of them have already been sold. The rest are valued at 1/2 × £8,000 = £4,000.

There are two main modifications to the historic cost principle commonly associated with its use in practice. The most important is that where it is believed that current realisable value is below cost, then that realisable value is substituted for cost. This is an application of the principle of conservatism. Here is an example. Goods for resale were purchased for £5 per unit. Demand for these has fallen off and it is thought that the goods will have to be marked down to £1 each to clear them. They are, therefore, immediately valued at £1.

The other modification is that where an asset has been held for so long that historic cost has become wholly unrealistic a current valuation may be substituted. Thus the owner of the building referred to above may choose in 1981 to obtain a professional up-to-date valuation. He may then use this rather than the 1921 historic cost as his valuation. As in our example this is most commonly done in the case of buildings which tend to appreciate in value as the years go by.

The overwhelming advantage of historic cost as a method of valuation is its complete objectivity. By maintaining careful records it is easily made capable of independent verification. It thus relates to our principle of auditability. It conforms to the prudence principle because no increase in valuation, and hence no profit, is reported until assets have actually been sold (revaluation is a special case).

It has, of course, several disadvantages. One is that valuations are not up-to-date. This may not be so grossly conspicuous as to demand attention as with the case of freehold buildings but may nevertheless give a misleading view to someone trying to assess the business's current position. Another disadvantage of historic cost is that valuations are not homogeneous. Some are established in a market of many years ago (like buildings), some in a market of a few months or years ago (like motor vehicles) and some very recently (like stock for resale). Another failing is that historic cost automatically excludes from consideration assets which were not acquired through a market and thus have no identifiable cost. Examples of these are a valuable patent arising from research done within the business and goodwill built up over a long period of reliable trading.

Current value

The main rival to historic cost as a basis of valuation is current value. Under this principle assets are valued at what they are currently worth to the business. In most cases (and we shall consider this in more detail later on) this means what the asset would cost if purchased currently. In the case of a partially consumed asset, like our motor vehicle, this is interpreted in a particular way. Where two-fifths of the vehicle's life remains it would be valued at two-fifths of the current cost of a similar new vehicle. The principle of consistency demands that reference is always made to the new market and does not move to a succession of second-hand markets.

Current cost valuation has the important advantage of being up-to-date. It also provides the possibility (not always in practice realised) of giving a valuation to assets which have not been acquired by purchase in a market, so long as they are capable of being so acquired. Its disadvantage is that it contains an element of subjectivity, varying in degree from one asset to another, and is thus less susceptible to independent confirmation.

4. CONSTRUCTING THE BALANCE SHEET

Having briefly discussed these two principles of valuation we shall construct our balance sheet. We shall elect to do so using the historic cost convention because this is still the most widely used in practice, because it is essential that this be understood as a foundation for our later studies and because it will lead us naturally into our consideration of the double-entry method of financial recording.

Our example will concern the retail business of a Mr Smith who we shall follow as he makes a complete inventory of his business assets. First of all he owns a building in which the business is conducted and this is used solely for business purposes. He bought it ten years ago for £10,000. Although he believes it would probably fetch £25,000 if sold now he has never had any formal professional revaluation. He will, therefore, record his building at its original cost: Building £10,000. The building is equipped with furniture and specialised fittings. These were bought at the same time and are about half way through their useful life. Their total original cost was £6,000. Allowing for the portion "used up" to date we shall record them as: Furniture and fittings £3,000. There is a delivery van bought four years ago for £3,000 when it was expected to have a useful life of five years. We shall record this as: Delivery van £600. Stored in the building are goods which are the subject of Mr Smith's trade. They cost him a total of £7,500 and all are expected to be sold at prices in excess of cost except for one line which cost £500 and which will have to be cleared at a sale price totalling £200. We shall record all this as: Stock £7,200.

All the assets so far referred to have a physical existence and can be directly observed. As we indicated earlier, however, rights against others can equally be assets. Mr Smith has two assets in this category. His customers owe him a total of £1,000 for goods already supplied and he has a balance of £500 with his bank. These will be recorded as: Debtors £1,000 and Bank £500. Debtors are defined as those who owe one money. Finally Mr Smith holds £25 in cash in his till.

The complete tally of assets is as follows:

Building	£10,000
Furniture and fittings	3,000
Delivery van	600
Stock	7,200
Debtors	1,000
Bank	500
Cash	25

5. ARRANGEMENT OF INFORMATION

We shall take a short diversion at this point for a brief word on the classification or arrangement of financial information. Although not directly adding to the information itself, the way in which it is arranged can nevertheless be of great importance to its usefulness. An extreme example will easily make this point. A dictionary has its words arranged in alphabetical order and this enables us to look up the definitions we require. If its words were jumbled up randomly there might well be precisely the same information in the dictionary as there had been before but it would be inaccessible and of very little use to us.

Fixed and current assets

There are two ways of arranging lists of assets which have logic and have been found to be useful. One is to classify the assets according to whether they are *fixed* assets or *current* assets. Fixed assets are defined as those assets which are held, usually long term, for the purpose of obtaining the benefit of the service which they provide. Current assets are those held, usually short term, for the purpose of circulation and conversion in the ordinary course of business. In our example the building, the furniture and fittings and the delivery van are fixed assets while the stock, the debtors, the bank balance and the cash are current assets. An appreciation of the relative proportions of fixed and current assets is important to an understanding of the basic financial structure of the business.

Liquidity

The other useful classification is based on the degree of *liquidity* of the assets, that is to say the readiness with which they may be converted into cash. At the two extremes a bank balance is a very liquid asset while a building, though possibly much more valuable, is very illiquid. This has a bearing on the short-term solvency of the business. Obviously if one can pay the electricity bill by drawing on a bank balance this has quite different implications for solvency than if one has to sell a building in order to do so.

Both of these classifications are normally used, assets being categorised as either fixed or current and then arranged, within these categories, in order of liquidity. This is shown below. The words in brackets are explanatory and would not normally appear on a balance sheet.

	Fixed assets		
(Least liquid fixed asset)	Building		£10,000
	accessories Furniture and fittings		3,000
(Most liquid fixed asset)	Delivery van		600
			13,600
	Current assets		
(Least liquid current asset)	Stock	£7,200	
	Debtors	1,000	
	Bank	500	
	Cash	25	
(Most liquid current asset)			8,725
			£22,325

We now have a complete, classified, list of Mr Smith's business assets. We have inserted subtotals for the amounts respectively of fixed and current assets and a grand total for all assets at the end.

We should give pause for thought as to the significance of this final figure. At first consideration it seems obvious that it is the total value of the resources held for business purposes. We have, however, arrived at it by adding together things which are not by any means homogeneous. There is a building with a valuation established under market conditions of ten years ago and there is stock whose value was established a few weeks ago. There is in any case no obvious resemblance between a building and stock. Our addition is a bit like the 4 apples + 3 pears = 7 fruit type. This would be outlawed in algebra but is a commonplace in accounting. We would be wise to note, however, that algebraic illegitimacy is not just a technicality and if we are not careful we might sometimes mislead ourselves by this kind of calculation. For the moment, with this reservation noted, we will take it that we have established a fair total valuation for the resources committed to the business.

6. LIABILITIES

We now need to look at the other side of the picture—that is we need to recognise that there are various claims against the business's resources. Such claims are known as *liabilities*. Liabilities are obligations which can be evaluated in terms of money. They do not present the same problems of valuation as do assets because they are in the form of rights which other people have over the business and are usually evidenced by a contract in which their value is clearly stated.

We will suppose that Mr Smith's business is partly financed by a long-term loan of £7,500 from his friend Mr Brown. We will also suppose that it owes £2,300 for goods recently supplied to it and for other unpaid bills. These latter would be described as creditors. Against a fund of assets of £22,325 we have identified liabilities totalling £9,800. The difference between the two figures—what is left over—is the amount which the business holds on behalf of its owner. This is a liability of a special kind and it is known as the owner's equity or as his capital. Its special nature is that its value is always determined as a residue of the fund embodied in the assets after the other liabilities have been deducted from it. The use of a figure for capital in the balance sheet is a manifestation of the proprietorship concept.

7. SETTING OUT THE BALANCE SHEET

We are now in a position to set out a balance sheet. This consists of a list of the liabilities (including capital) side by side with a list of the assets. It should be noted that liabilities are generally arranged in order of their degree of permanence starting with capital and moving through long-term loans to creditors. Liabilities which are expected to be settled soon after the balance sheet date are referred to as current liabilities.

MR SMITH'S BUSINESS BALANCE SHEET AS AT . . .

		Fixed assets		
Capital	£12,525	Building		£10,000
Loan from Mr Brown	7,500	Furniture and		
		fittings		3,000
		Delivery van		600
				13,600
Current liabilities		*Current assets*		
Creditors	2,300	Stock	£7,200	
		Debtors	1,000	
		Bank	500	
		Cash	25	
				8,725
	£22,325			£22,325

It is obvious that a balance sheet will always necessarily balance because of the insertion of capital as a balancing figure.

The balance sheet can be regarded in two ways. Reading from left to right we might say that it shows the sources from which the total finance of £22,325 has been obtained and then shows how it has been deployed. Reading from right to left we might say that a certain fund is owned and then we see who is entitled to the benefit of this.

There are other ways of arranging a balance sheet which are often used. In the USA, for example, assets would be on the left and liabilities on the right. Again a common form of presentation used in the published accounts of companies in this country is the so-called *vertical* form.

Mr Smith's balance sheet is redrafted in vertical form below.

MR SMITH'S BUSINESS BALANCE SHEET AS AT . . .

Fixed assets		
Building	£10,000	
Furniture and fittings	3,000	
Delivery van	600	
	———	£13,600
Current assets		
Stock	£7,200	
Debtors	1,000	
Bank	500	
Cash	25	
	———	
	8,725	
Less Current liabilities: Creditors	2,300	
	———	6,425
		———
		20,025
Deduct Loan from Mr Brown		7,500
		———
		£12,525
		═══
Financed by:		
Capital		£12,525
		═══

All these forms of balance sheet convey the same information. It is just a matter of opinion as to which is the most easily assimilated and styles can come and go in these matters.

8. THE EFFECT OF TRANSACTIONS

As we have explained a balance sheet shows a static picture of a business. It reports on its financial position at some particular point in time. When prepared, as we have illustrated, on the historic cost principle it also has the characteristic that it is *transaction based*. This means that all of its figures have been determined by some accounting event, i.e. transaction. A transaction is merely an occurrence of a type which would be recorded in the financial accounts. Obvious examples of transactions are purchases and sales of goods, purchases of fixed assets and payments of previously incurred liabilities. All of these are transactions between the business and some outside party. There may also be transactions between the business and its own proprietor. Examples of these are the withdrawal of profits by the proprietor or the introduction, by him, of new capital. Transactions can also take place wholly within the business. This occurs, for example, where fixed assets are reduced in value by use and the passage of time or when a building is revalued in line with an independent professional opinion.

Not only do these transactions lie at the foundation of the figures in the balance sheet, however, but they are also what gives accounting its dynamic dimension. Transactions are the outward manifestation of the taking place within the business of the processes which ultimately earn its profit. It is important that a careful record of all transactions is kept.

Here is a simple example which will convey a very important feature of the recording system which we are going to develop. Mr X set aside £5,000 for business purposes, placing it in a special bank account. His business's balance sheet then appeared as follows:

Capital	£5,000	Bank	£5,000

On behalf of the business Mr X then purchased £3,000 worth of stock for resale, paying for it by a cheque drawn on the business bank account. The business thus acquired a second asset, stock, but only at cost of the diminution of the existing asset, bank. After this transaction the balance sheet appeared as follows:

Capital	£5,000	Stock	£3,000
		Bank	2,000
	£5,000		£5,000

The important point illustrated is the dual nature of all transactions. No figure in the balance sheet can be altered by a transaction without a corresponding alteration elsewhere. Technically this arises from the fact that a balance sheet balances and must continue to do so. Conceptually it arises from the idea that a transaction consists of a flow of value. Value does not appear out of thin air nor does it disappear without explanation. It must always have both a source and a destination. This is plainly so in the case of each of the two transactions so far described. The first is a flow of value *from* the proprietor (Capital) *to* the bank account. The second is a flow of value *from* the bank account *to* the stock of goods for resale.

It will be interesting and instructive to see what happens when some of the stock is sold at a profit. We will suppose that some stock, which had cost £1,000, was sold for £1,500 which was received in the form of a cheque and paid into the bank. Here there is a flow of value back from the stock and into the bank but in the process some value has been added to the goods so that a profit has been made. It will be obvious from what has already been said about the construction of the balance sheet that this added value will have to find its way to capital for a balance to be retained. Thus:

Capital	£5,500	Stock	£2,000	(£3,000 − £1,000)
		Bank	3,500	(£2,000 + £1,500)
	£5,500		£5,500	

It is important to visualise the logic of this. When we buy something from a shop we know perfectly well that we are being charged more than the shopkeeper paid for it in the first place. The reason we are willing to pay this price is that we believe that along with the goods we are receiving a service. This may take a variety of forms. It may be the advantage of being able to buy in small quantities, of having a choice of different brands of the product displayed in one accessible place or of having advice on our choice, to mention some possibilities. Whatever the service may be its source is the business itself (this is, after all, from the customers' point of view the sole reason for the business's existence) and hence ultimately its proprietor. The flow into the bank may be seen, therefore, as a flow partly from the stock (the goods) and partly from the proprietor (the attached services).

Use of worksheets

It will be useful if we set up a worksheet to show what is happening. On it we shall indicate flows of value by showing a negative (−) at their source and a positive (+) at their destination.

	Capital £	Stock £	Bank £
Introduction of capital	−5,000		+5,000
Balance sheet (*i*)	−5,000		+5,000
Purchase of stock		+3,000	−3,000
Balance sheet (*ii*)	−5,000	+3,000	+2,000
Sale of stock	−500	−1,000	+1,500
Balance sheet (*iii*)	−5,500	+2,000	+3,500

Note some interesting features of this worksheet. Each transaction is represented by one line in which the values, adding pluses and minuses across, sum to zero. This signifies that both parts of the dual nature of each transaction have been properly dealt with and it provides a record of the effects of the transaction. The alternate lines (i.e. subtotals) give all the figures required for the balance sheet. Negative amounts are interpreted as liabilities and positive amounts as assets.

We will record a few more representative transactions below to show further how this works. These are:

(*a*) a further consignment of stock is purchased for £2,000, this time on credit;

(*b*) The proprietor takes £800 in stock for his own use (i.e. the business hands over an asset in part settlement of its obligation to him);

(*c*) stock which had cost £750 is sold for £1,150 to a credit customer (debtor);

(*d*) £1,500 is paid to the creditors in part settlement of the amount owed to them;

(*e*) £650 is received from a debtor.

The worksheet up to date is as follows:

	Capital (£)	Stock (£)	Bank (£)	Creditors (£)	Debtors (£)
As above	−5,500	+2,000	+3,500		
(*a*) Stock purchased		+2,000		−2,000	
Balance sheet (*iv*)	−5,500	+4,000	+3,500	−2,000	
(*b*) Proprietor	+800	−800			
Balance sheet (*v*)	−4,700	+3,200	+3,500	−2,000	
(*c*) Stock sold	−400	−750			+1,150
Balance sheet (*vi*)	−5,100	+2,450	+3,500	−2,000	+1,150
(*d*) Creditors paid			−1,500	+1,500	
Balance sheet (*vii*)	−5,100	+2,450	+2,000	−500	+1,150
(*e*) Debtor pays			+650		−650
Balance sheet (*viii*)	−5,100	+2,450	+2,650	−500	+500

The final balance sheet can easily be constructed from the last line of the worksheet.

Capital	£5,100	Stock	£2,450
Creditors	500	Debtors	500
		Bank	2,650
	£5,600		£5,600

The worksheet style which we have adopted above has several advantages. It provides a running record of all transactions. It provides figures for a balance sheet whenever these are required. It has an important self-checking feature which should reduce the risk of error. Every line should contain figures which sum to zero and this can readily be checked if a difference is revealed on the final balance sheet. All of this comes from reading the worksheet line by line. It is also useful when read column by column. The column headed Capital, for example, gives an account of what has happened to the proprietor's interest in the business. The column headed Bank gives the story of what has happened to our money in the bank. Each column is termed an account.

Our worksheet does have certain disadvantages. One is that we have needed to calculate new subtotals on the occasion of each transaction—a major task when hundreds of transactions are involved. Another is that the worksheet becomes physically cumbersome when a large number of accounts are involved as would be the case in a real business situation. In Chapter 5 we shall look at the way in which the idea contained in the worksheet can be developed into a procedure for recording transactions which is of considerable flexibility and thus useful in a very wide variety of situations.

SUMMARY

1. A balance sheet is a document which portrays the financial position of an entity at a specified point in time.

2. It consists of a list of assets and a list of liabilities of equal total amount. The principle is that total claims on a fund of assets must precisely exhaust that fund.

3. The proprietor's interest in a business, termed his capital, is a residual one. He is entitled to whatever is left after all other claims have been met.

4. The main method of valuation in accounting is that based on

historic cost. Broadly, this implies that assets are valued at the amount originally paid for them.

5. An alternative method of valuation is current value.

6. The classification of assets and liabilities is useful as an aid to the understanding of the balance sheet. Assets are normally classified as fixed or current. Fixed assets are those held for the service which they provide to the business. Current assets are held for the purpose of circulation and conversion in the ordinary course of business.

7. A transaction is an event causing a change in the position revealed by a balance sheet. The effect of a series of transactions can conveniently be shown in the form of a worksheet.

QUESTIONS

1. The following information relates to the business of Mother Hubbard at 31st December. Prepare her balance sheet on an appropriate basis.

(a) She held a freehold building bought in 1920 for £5,000. A professional revaluation made in 1980 estimated its value then at £50,000.

(b) She owns a motor vehicle which had cost £5,000 two years ago. It has an expected useful life of five years. It could currently be sold for £3,000 but would cost £3,500 to replace with a similar second-hand vehicle. A similar new vehicle would cost £6,000.

(c) She owns stock which had cost £3,000 but which is certain to be sold for £5,000. A further lot of stock cost £2,000 but it is not expected to sell for more than £1,500.

(d) The business is owed £2,000 by its customers. A customer owing £200, and included in that total, has recently gone abroad without leaving a forwarding address.

(e) There is cash of £500 and bills owing of £3,500.

2. For each of the assets referred to in 1.(a)–(e) above, discuss alternative bases of valuation which you might have used and justify the choice which you made.

3. Prepare a worksheet recording the following transactions and hence draw up a balance sheet at their conclusion.

(a) Roebuck placed £10,000 in a special bank account preparatory to starting up in business.

(b) He purchased fixed assets costing £7,500. These were paid for in cash (i.e. from the bank account).

(c) He bought stock costing £5,000, paying £2,000 cash and taking the rest on credit.

(d) He sold stock which had cost £3,000 for £4,000 allowing credit to his customers.

(*e*) He received £3,000 from customers in cash. Goods which had been supplied at a price of £400 were returned as unsuitable but it is expected that they can be resold.

(*f*) He paid creditors £1,500 of the amount owing.

4. Interpret the following:

(*a*) a capital account on the assets side of a balance sheet;

(*b*) a reduction in stock accompanied by a reduction in capital (this time a liability);

(*c*) an increase in freehold buildings accompanied by an increase in capital—no building has been purchased nor has any money been spent on the existing buildings;

(*d*) a reduction in creditors accompanied by a reduction in cash;

(*e*) a reduction in creditors accompanied by an increase in capital;

(*f*) a reduction in creditors accompanied by a reduction in debtors.

5. "A balance sheet perfectly represents the position of a business at a particular point in time." Discuss.

CHAPTER 4

The Profit and Loss Account

OBJECTIVES

In this chapter we shall deal with the following important topics:

(a) the profit and loss account;
(b) the recognition of revenues and the matching of expenses;
(c) gross profit and net profit;
(d) proprietor's drawings.

1. INTRODUCTION

Just as the balance sheet is a statement of position so the profit and loss account is a statement of progress. In any activity, of which business is one, where there is implicitly a movement towards a goal reports on progress as well as the present point of arrival will be useful and complementary to one another. We saw, however, in the case of the balance sheet that it is no simple matter to construct a universally valid statement of position and that many assumptions had to be made before we were able to do so. Exactly the same is true of the profit and loss account, which, like the balance sheet, is based on certain underlying concepts. In a later chapter we shall discuss what is meant by the concept of profit itself, the limitations on its measurement and the ultimate usefulness of the figures we produce. In this chapter we are concerned with the present state of the art and we shall describe how profit and loss accounts are in practice prepared and how, at a practical level, some of the inherent problems are resolved. For this purpose we shall adopt a very simple definition of profit and a similarly simple idea of the purpose of a business enterprise. We shall define a profit as an increase in the value of the assets to which the proprietor of the business can lay claim. This is in accordance with our proprietorship concept of accounting. We shall further assume that the aim of a business is to make as big a profit as possible on behalf of its proprietor. A poor rate of profit will be seen as a failure to achieve the main objective of the business and a loss will be seen as a very bad failure to do so.

2. THE NATURE OF PROFIT

A profit arises where an activity creates a revenue which exceeds the cost of the activity. One case of this is where goods are sold at a price greater than that for which they were bought. Suppose that goods which had cost £1,000 were sold for £1,500. The asset stock, valued at £1,000, is exchanged for the asset cash (or debtor) worth £1,500 and the consequent increase in the total value of assets, being attributable to the proprietor, is the profit. There have been two separate transactions making this up. One was the inflow of £1,500 and the other the outflow of £1,000. There may easily be a gap in time between the two transactions. It would, however, be misleading to regard them separately, seeing them as first a profit of £1,500 followed by a loss of £1,000. This would imply the nonsensical conclusion that being paid for things you supply was a successful occurrence but that paying for what you use is an unsuccessful one. Clearly these transactions cannot be separated in this fashion and we should calculate or "report" a profit only when we have gathered together all the related bits and pieces making up the activity. The inflows relating to an activity we describe as its revenues and the outflows relating to an activity we describe as its expenses. A profit is the surplus of revenues over expenses. A simple account will represent the example we have used:

Revenue (Sales)	£1,500
Less Expenses (Cost of sales)	1,000
Profit	£500

The words in brackets indicate the particular kind of revenue and expense with which we are dealing on this occasion. The revenue is the money we have paid for the goods which have been sold ("Sales" for short). The expense is money we have paid for the goods which have been sold ("Cost of sales" for short). The example used here to illustrate the terms revenue and expense also illustrates two very important principles in the construction of a profit and loss account. One of these is the matter of *revenue recognition* and the other is the *principle of matching*. These were referred to as principles arising out of basic accounting concepts in Chapter 2.

3. REVENUE RECOGNITION

The matter of revenue recognition may seem to be a very obvious one but closer consideration will show that it does present some theoretical difficulties. A sale is the end of a process which may have been a fairly short one extending over only a few days or may have been much longer lasting even for several years. The time at which we include the revenue from this activity in our profit and loss account (this is what is meant by *recognising* it) is the time at which we shall calculate the profit or loss which has been made. Consider, however, the chain of events involved up to the sale of even a simple single item. An example is the case of a man's suit sold by a clothing shop.

The suit was at some stage chosen by the shop's buyer as something likely to appeal to customers and it was brought for stock. It was taken to the shop and displayed for sale. A number of customers enquired about it and their enquiries were dealt with by sales staff. Eventually the suit was bought by a certain customer who required certain alterations to be made to it. These were completed and the suit was delivered to the customer. He was allowed credit terms and paid for the suit some time after it had been delivered. All the links in this chain of events represent activity by the business which absorbs resources. The profit on sale is the eventual reward for the commitment of these resources and for the management which organises them.

The whole process may extend over several weeks and will not necessarily be confined to one accounting period. It could plausibly be argued that the total profit should be regarded as being earned over the same period that the activity proceeds. Part, it could be said, is earned after the buyer has made a skilful choice of stock; part when shop space, lighting and materials are used to display the suit; part as the assistants measure customers and allow them to try on the suit; part when the alterations are carried out and part while the shop waits for the money it has earned to be paid. However theoretically defensible and however useful the information might be in judging the relative effectiveness of different parts of the business's operations, it is not feasible for us to break the profit up in this way. We cannot tell how much profit has been made at each stage partly because the stages are difficult to define exactly and partly because we do not know the ultimate outcome. The sensible practical rule we follow is to recognise revenue when two conditions are met. One is that the series of activities generating the revenue is substantially complete and the other is that the ultimate amount of revenue has become known with certainty by us. It can be observed that this practice is supported by our concepts of realisation and of objectivity.

In our example, applying the criteria, the revenue from the sale would normally be recognised when the customer agreed to buy the suit and became a debtor for its price. Note that this could mean that revenue is recognised in one accounting year (e.g. in respect of something sold on 1st January) even though almost all the activity involved in earning the ultimate profit took place in a previous year. This is another case where theoretical perfection bends to practical feasibility.

4. THE PRINCIPLE OF MATCHING

The other profit and loss account principle is that of matching. This says that once revenue has been recognised there will be matched against it all the relevant expenses in order to determine the profit or loss. The reported profit for a particular year, therefore, is not the revenues of the year less the expenses of the year but the revenues *recognised* in the year less the expenses related to that revenue.

Matching is not always easy and has to be done as best it can. There are three main methods. These are matching by *association*, matching by *time* and matching by *allocation*. They are given here in order of preference. Matching by association is "best" and should be used whenever possible. If matching by association is impossible then matching by time may be used. Failing that matching by allocation will clear up all that is left. We will look at each of these and its implications carefully.

Matching by association

This means that we match against revenues expenses which can be directly associated in some way with the object of the transaction giving rise to the revenue. One example of this is the cost of materials actually incorporated into a manufactured product. Another is the amount paid by a retail business for the goods which it is selling.

Here is an illustration. Mr X set up in business as a second-hand car dealer. In his first month he bought two cars, A and B, for £1,000 and £1,500 respectively. In his second month he bought car C for £1,200 and car D for £950. He sold A for £1,600 and C for £1,300. In the third month he sold B for £1,800 and bought E for £600.

In terms of cash flows Mr X's transactions can be represented as follows:

	Month		
	1	*2*	*3*
Received for sales	*Nil*	£2,900	£1,800
Spent on cars	2,500	2,150	600
Inflow/(outflow) of cash	(£2,500)	£750	£1,200

Mr X thus ends up £550 out of pocket, so far as cash is concerned, but owning two cars which together cost him £1,550 (D and E).

Let us now draw up monthly profit and loss accounts based on the principles of revenue recognition and matching. In Month 1 there is no revenue and therefore no "trigger" to the computation of a profit even though some activity (the purchase of two cars) relevant to the earning of profits has taken place. In month 2 the revenue is £2,900 which derives from the sale of cars A and C. The expenditure involved in buying these cars is matched against that revenue even though A was actually paid for in the previous month. The matched expenditure totals £2,200 and the profit is therefore reported at £700. In the third month revenue totals £1,800 and matched expenses total £1,500. Profit is therefore £300. The tabulated profit and loss accounts appear below:

	Month		
	1	*2*	*3*
Revenue	*Nil*	£2,900	£1,800
Less Expenses	*Nil*	2,200	1,500
Profit	*Nil*	£700	£300

Although materials used in manufacture and goods purchased for resale are the most obvious examples of expenses which can be matched by association there are others. Work done on repairing or servicing the cars for resale is a case in point, and so would be the direct labour involved in the manufacture of a product. The result which is produced by relating revenue and its directly associated expense is termed the *gross profit*. Even though there may remain other expenses to be matched in some other manner, gross profit is a useful figure to calculate because it provides an indication of the effectiveness of the basic profit earning process of the business. For this reason it is often calculated in its own section of the profit and loss account which would be called a *trading account*.

Matching by time

There are many types of business expense which, however necessary they may be, cannot directly be related to specific items of revenue. In the case of the men's clothing shop of our earlier example the cost of a specific suit can easily be matched to the revenue produced by its sale but the rent paid for the shop premises cannot. Other indirect items of a similar kind, to pick out a few at random, are the general advertising for the shop, electricity for heating and lighting and the salaries of the office staff. Such items may usefully be regarded as the expenses of providing an environment within which the profit making process—here buying and selling—can take place. These are the kinds of expense which are usually matched on the basis of time. They are matched against the revenues of the period for which they have provided a benefit. Note, however, that this is not necessarily the period in which they are paid for. This point will become clearer presently.

First here is another illustration. Mr Y sells books by mail order. They are sold for £10 each, carriage paid. He buys the books for £5 each and spends another £2 per volume for postage and packing. In a certain year he spent £1,000 to rent his warehouse, £100 to insure the contents and £800 as wages to a part-time assistant. He sold 1,000 books. The profit and loss account appears below and it should be noted that it has been split to reveal the gross profit before continuing on its way to give the final profit, a figure which is described as the *net profit*.

MR Y: PROFIT AND LOSS ACCOUNT FOR THE YEAR

Sales		£10,000	
Less Cost of sales	£5,000		(These expenses are matched
Post and packing	2,000		by association with revenue.)
	———	7,000	
		———	
Gross profit		3,000	
Less Other expenses:			
Rent	£1,000		
Insurance	100		(These expenses are matched
Wages	800		by time.)
	———	1,900	
		———	
Net profit		£1,100	

It was stated above that in matching by time the important factor was the time in which the benefit obtained from the expenses was felt and that this was not necessarily the same as the time at which the expenses were actually paid. Here is an illustration of what is meant by this. Suppose that our business has an accounting period coinciding with the calendar year. On 1st July, Year 1, a fire insurance is taken out giving cover for one year, i.e. up to 30th June, Year 2. The premium of £100 is, as is customary, paid immediately. This is an expense *paid* in Year 1, the *benefit* of which is felt in each of the two years 1 and 2. The expense should be matched, therefore, such that £50 is charged against the revenues of Year 1 and £50 against the revenues of Year 2. At the end of Year 1 the £50 worth of unexpired insurance would be described as a prepayment or a payment in advance (and would, in fact, appear on the balance sheet as a current asset).

A discrepancy between date of payment and period of benefit can also occur when payments are made in arrear. This is commonly the case for gas, electricity and telephone bills. Here quarterly accounts are rendered and paid some time after the end of the period to which they relate, which may itself straddle more than one accounting year. Consider the case of a business with a financial year coinciding, once again, with the calendar year. It pays its electricity bill when received at the end of February, May, August and November. By the end of December Year 1 electricity will have been paid for only up to the date of the meter reading in November. The electricity consumed from then up to 31st December will be an unidentifiable amount contained within a bill not due until February Year 2. Nevertheless because its benefit is felt in Year 1 the value of this electricity should be charged against the revenues of that year. It is ascertained either by taking a meter reading at the year end or, alternatively, by inserting an estimated amount. Such an amount is known as an *accrual*. As well as affecting the profit and loss account accruals will appear on the year end balance sheet amongst current liabilities.

The following data are given regarding electricity consumption and the payments for it in a certain year. Electricity has been taken to cost £5 per 100 units.

November 30	Meter reading	14,200	£200 paid
January 1	Meter reading	15,700	
February 28	Meter reading	18,600	£220 paid
May 30	Meter reading	23,200	£230 paid
August 31	Meter reading	26,900	£185 paid
November 30	Meter reading	31,100	£210 paid
December 31	Meter reading	32,500	
February 28	Meter reading	35,200	£205 paid

The meter readings in February, May, August and November will have been taken by the Electricity Board for billing purposes. The readings at 1st January and 31st December will have been made by the management of the business for accounting purposes. The total amount *paid* during our accounting year is £220 + £230 + £185 + £210 = £845. This, however, is not the correct figure to match against revenues because it includes (in the February payment) an amount relating to December in the previous year and omits (to be paid in the following February) an amount relating to December in the current year. A fairly straightforward calculation will give us a correct time matching.

Amount paid for electricity	£845	
Less relating to previous year	75	(1)
	770	
Add relating to this year		
not yet paid	70	(2)
Cost of electricity for the year to be matched against revenue for the year	£840	(3)

(1) $(15,700 - 14,200) \div 100 \times 5 = £75$ This was the accrual at the end of last year.

(2) $(32,500 - 31,100) \div 100 \times 5 = £70$ This is the accrual at the end of this year.

(3) This tallies with the actual value of electricity consumed in the year as can be checked:

$$(32,500 - 15,700) \div 100 \times 5 = £840)$$

Matching by allocation

Matching by allocation is done where expenses cannot directly be attributed either to a specific revenue earning activity or to a specific time period. It may be done on a wholly arbitrary basis but more usually it is done by applying reasonable estimates to produce an approximation to the matching that might have been achieved by one of the other methods. It typically occurs where substantial but irregular expenditure is incurred on fixed assets or on programmes of promotion or development. In these cases the benefit of such expenditure will extend over a number of accounting periods. The devices whereby matching is achieved are known as *depreciation* and *amortisation*. The terms are not quite interchangeable. Depreciation normally implies that there is some underlying rationale to the allocation of the expenditure. Amortisation often implies that the allocation is arbitrary.

We should look at illustrations of each case. A business purchased for £10,000 a motor vehicle for use in delivering its goods to customers. The benefit of this will obviously last over several accounting periods and the cost needs somehow to be matched against the revenues of those periods. Although we may not know precisely how long the vehicle will last it is not difficult to make a realistic estimate. Let us say that the life is estimated to be five years. We may now allocate the total cost of the vehicle by charging £10,000/5 = £2,000 in each year's profit and loss account. This amount will be described as depreciation and the method we have used, which allocates a cost in equal instalments, is known as the straight line method. Depreciation is an important topic and this method, along with others, will be discussed more fully in Chapter 7.

Here is an illustration of a slightly different matching problem. A business spent £100,000 in developing and promoting a new product. For this sum it did not acquire anything tangible. There was no additional building or piece of machinery to point to and certainly nothing which could be sold so that the expenditure could be recovered. What did exist was a valuable product idea, the know-how to exploit it and a receptiveness in the public mind which would ensure that a reasonable market share would be obtained. We have to decide how to match the expenditure of £100,000 against the revenues presumed to benefit from it. At one extreme we could argue that the future benefit from the expenditure is so nebulous that we should charge the whole amount in the current year's profit and loss account. This would, however, considerably distort the reporting of profit in this year and, paradoxically, imply that the business was worse off for having incurred this expenditure. At the other extreme we could say that the benefit from the expenditure is everlasting and thus spread over an infinite number of years so that the annual charge is nil. If we do this the outlay remains as a permanent asset. This, however, is in conflict with the principle of conservatism which makes us very reluctant to attach a value to anything incapable of being realised. The compromise usually adopted is to amortise or allocate the expense over a reasonable number of years probably determined in part by a view as to what the profit will stand. Thus there might appear, say, ten instalments of £10,000 in successive profit and loss accounts. The number ten is chosen quite arbitrarily and is justified only on the ground that it is convenient.

5. PROFIT AND LOSS ACCOUNT EXAMPLE

Let us now look at a more complicated illustration which incorporates all of the profit and loss account problems we have discussed to date. It will clearly demonstrate the use of the important rules of revenue recognition and expense matching which will guide us through the complications.

A and Co. commenced trading on 1st January in a certain year. A summary of its cash receipts and payments during the year up to 31st December is as follows.

Cash received		*Cash paid*	
Capital paid in by proprietor	£25,000	Cash paid to suppliers	£21,290
Received from sales	47,200	Rent and rates	8,100
		Electricity	1,950
		Insurances	2,520
		Purchase of fixtures	
		and fittings	25,000
		Wages	8,200
		Miscellaneous expenses	760
		Cash in hand at year end	4,380
	£72,200		£72,200

This summary tells us that, of the £25,000 in cash advanced to the business by its proprietor, £4,380 is now left in that form. It is not possible, without the addition of further information and analysis, to see whether the business has or has not made a profit. This other information now appears below.

At the year end there were debtors totalling £4,600 and creditors totalling £2,100.
Stock at the year end was valued at £2,670
The payment for rent and rates included £2,700 in advance for next year and that for insurance £630 in respect of next year.
Electricity used by the year end but not yet billed or paid for was £350.
The fixtures and fittings were expected to have a five year life.

First of all we will determine the revenue to be recognised in the year. Receipts from sales were £47,200 but the business was also entitled to receive a further £4,600 from its debtors. Both of these amounts fulfil our criteria that the activity generating them is complete and that the ultimate amount receivable has become certain. Thus:

Cash	£47,200
Add Debtors	4,600
Total sales	£51,800

Against this revenue we must now match the relevant expenses. Only the actual cost of sales can be matched on the basis of direct association. This figure cannot, however, be read directly from the information given. It is determined as follows.

Cash paid to suppliers	£21,290
Add Creditors	2,100
Total cost of goods acquired	23,390
Less Stock not yet sold	2,670
Cost of sales	£20,720

Other expenses must be matched on a time basis.

Rent and rates paid	£8,100
Less paid in advance	2,700
	£5,400
Insurances paid	£2,520
Less paid in advance	630
	£1,890
Electricity paid	£1,950
Add accrued not paid	350
	£2,300

Wages and miscellaneous expenses, where there are no payments in advance or accruals, are equal to the total amounts actually paid in the year.

Finally we come to the expenditure on fixtures and fittings. Using the straight line method of depreciation this would mean an expense of £5,000 in each year of their life, including the present year.

Putting all this together:

A AND CO. PROFIT AND LOSS ACCOUNT FOR THE YEAR ENDED 31ST DECEMBER

Sales		£51,800
Less Cost of sales		20,720
Gross profit		31,080
Less Expenses:		
Rent and rates	£5,400	
Insurances	1,890	
Electricity	2,300	
Wages	8,200	
Miscellaneous	760	
Depreciation	5,000	
		23,550
Net profit		£7,530

This account tells the proprietor of A and Co. that the business has earned him £7,530 during the year—a fairly handsome return of around 30% per cent per annum on his original investment.

It may be of interest also to look at the year end balance sheet of A and Co. It should in particular be noticed how this "keys in" with the profit and loss account.

A AND CO. BALANCE SHEET AT 31ST DECEMBER

Capital	£25,000	*Fixed assets*		
Add Profit for the year	7,530	Fixtures and		
		fitting		£20,000
	32,530			
Current liabilities		*Current assets*		
Creditors and accruals	2,450	Stock	£2,670	
		Debtors and pay-		
		ments in advance	7,930	
		Cash	4,380	
				14,980
	£34,980			£34,980

6. MANUFACTURING ACCOUNT

So far all our examples of accounting entities have been retailing businesses. The item "cost of sales" in the trading account is thus determined by the buying price of the goods which are bought for resale to customers. In the case of a manufacturing business, however, the composition of this item is much more complex. Such a business will purchase a variety of raw materials and will employ labour and other resources to convert them into a saleable product. The manufacturing account is a statement which shows, for a manufacturing business, the detailed composition of the item "cost of sales". Its construction requires us to consider two important matters which will otherwise give us problems. These are, firstly, the way in which manufacturing costs are classified and, secondly, the way in which the more complex position over stocks is dealt with.   ∧ OVERHEADS

The classification of costs which is found by experience to be the most useful divides them under three broad headings which are *material, labour* and *factory expenses* (sometimes called *overhead*). The classification is based on a certain logical concept of the manufacturing process. This is that all manufacturing requires that some material is worked on by labour within the environment provided by the expenditure associated with the factory.

It is important to note that the classification of a cost, under this method, depends on its function rather than its nature. To be classified as material the expense must be for materials actually incorporated into the product. Other materials, such as those used in maintaining machinery or in repairing the factory building, would be classified as factory expenses. Similarly, labour means the cost of work directly applied to the material in making the product. The cost of other work, such as that of supervisory personnel or maintenance staff, is again to be regarded as part of the cost of the general environment of production, i.e. factory expenses. Material and labour put together, because both can be seen to be directly incorporated into the product, are termed *prime cost*. Prime cost has the characteristic that its total will vary more or less proportionately with the level of production. Factory expenses are often fixed over a wide range of levels of production (this is an important source of the economies of high output). It is worth noting that the classification of manufacturing expenditure described here is fundamental to many of the cost statements produced by the management accountant.

For a manufacturing business there are three points in the process between purchase and sale where value can be held (i.e. stocks) as opposed to one in the case of a retailing business. Thus there will be stocks of raw materials awaiting use; there will be stocks of material and other resources held in a partially completed state in the middle of the manufacturing process (described as work in progress) and there will be stocks of finished goods awaiting sale. These are dealt with separately but each in a similar manner.

Having established these initial ideas we are in a position to look at an illustrative example.

Example of a manufacturing account

Beer is a manufacturer of soft drinks. The following values, amongst others, appeared on his balance sheet at 1st January 19—.

Stocks of raw materials	£36,392
Work in progress	£102,667
Stocks of finished goods	£74,661

During the year ended 31st December 19— the business's sales totalled £1,171,739.

Expenditure relating to manufacturing (allowing for all accruals and prepayments) was:

Wages:	Direct labour	£292,112	
	Supervisory	65,779	
	Maintenance	58,470	
			£416,361
Purchases:	Materials for production	256,852	
	Materials for maintenance	43,853	
			300,705
Rent and rates of factory			80,397
Insurance of machinery			41,600
Miscellaneous factory expenses			3,654

Additionally £72,000 is to be provided for depreciation of machinery. Balance sheet values at 31st December 19—included:

Stocks of raw materials	£38,483
Work in progress	£118,218
Stocks of finished goods	£77,215

The manufacturing account based on this information and the trading section of the profit and loss account appear below.

BEER

MANUFACTURING ACCOUNT FOR THE YEAR ENDED 31ST DECEMBER 19—

Stock of raw materials at 1st January	£36,392	
Add Purchases	256,852	
	293,244	
Less Stock of raw materials at 31st December	38,483	
Material		£254,761
Direct labour		292,112
Prime cost		546,873
Factory expenses		
Rent and rates	£80,397	
Supervisory wages	65,779	
Maintenance wages	58,470	
Maintenance materials	43,853	
Insurance	41,600	
Depreciation of machinery	72,000	
Miscellaneous factory expenses	3,654	
		365,753
Factory cost		912,626
Less Increase in work in progress		15,551
Cost of goods finished in year		£897,075

TRADING ACCOUNT FOR THE YEAR ENDED 31ST DECEMBER 19—

Sales		£1,171,739
Less Cost of sales:		
Stock of finished goods at 1st January	£74,661	
Add Manufacturing cost of goods finished in year	897,075	
	971,736	
Less Stock of finished goods at 31st December	77,215	
		894,521
Gross profit		£277,218

7. PROPRIETOR'S DRAWINGS

Since it is a function of the profit and loss account to establish what a business has achieved on behalf of its proprietor it is important that no payment to the proprietor himself should ever appear in it. Such payments are described as the proprietor's drawings and they are properly regarded as a disposal of the profit after it has been earned and calculated.

An example will make this principle clear. Miss Thrift invested £1,000 with a building society. During the ensuing year she withdrew £80 for various purchases which she wished to make. At the end of that year she had £1,050 left in the account. She wishes to know how much was earned by her investment during the year. It would obviously be wrong to give the answer £80. The amount withdrawn is no indication of interest earned as she could, if she had wished, have withdrawn the whole amount. It would equally be wrong to give the answer £50 on the basis that the balance on the account had risen by that much. This would ignore the benefit which she had received but spent. The correct answer is £130. The figure of £130 is analogous to a business's profit and the figure of £80 to the drawings of its proprietor. If £80 of the profit is withdrawn it follows that £50 (£130 − £80) is retained and this is the correct interpretation of the increase in the balance on the account.

SUMMARY

1. The profit and loss account is a statement of progress and this covers a particular period of time, commonly one year.

2. A profit arises from activities which create resources greater than the expenditures which they absorb. The identification of revenues and expenses is therefore of critical importance to the measurement of profit.

3. Revenues are recognised, i.e. reported in the profit and loss account, when two conditions are met. One is that the series of activities generating the revenue is substantially complete, and the other is that the ultimate amount of the revenue has become certainly known.

4. Expenditure is matched against the revenue to which it relates. Matching is done in one of three ways: (*a*) by association, e.g. direct material costs; (*b*) by time, e.g the rent of the factory; and (*c*) by allocation, e.g. the depreciation of fixed assets.

5. A profit and loss account is often drawn up in such a way that gross profit is reported as a separate figure. Gross profit is the result arising from the basic profit earning activity of the business.

Other expenses, such as selling and administrative expenses, are then deducted from this to give the ultimate, *net*, profit. The section of the profit and loss account showing the calculation of the gross profit is termed the trading account.

6. In computing the profit of a business it is most important to exclude from the account any payment made by the business to its own proprietor. Such a payment, the proprietor's drawings, is properly to be regarded as a distribution of profit and not as an expense.

7. A manufacturing account shows, for a manufacturing business, the detail of how the item cost of sales is made up.

QUESTIONS

1. Mr Spanner set up in business on 1st January as a secondhand car dealer. His cash payments during the first three months of trading were as shown below:

	January	February	March
Advertising	£200	£150	£100
Rent of premises (for 3 months)	600		
Wages of mechanic	200	200	200
Purchases of vehicles: A	500		
B	200		
C		300	
D		600	
E			400

The mechanic was employed on servicing the vehicles before sale and he spent approximately the same amount of time on each one. Sales were:

January	A £750
February	B £300 and D £800
March	C £500

Prepare profit and loss accounts for each of the three months.

2. Redraft the following profit and loss account for proper form.

PROFIT AND LOSS ACCOUNT FOR THE YEAR ENDED 31ST DECEMBER

Sales: For cash	£122,000	
On credit	12,500	
Orders to be fulfilled later	6,800	
		£141,300
Wages[1]	15,400	
Goods for resale: Sent to customers	51,800	
Still in warehouse	15,200	
On order	3,200	
Furniture and equipment[2]	10,000	
Rent and rates[3]	5,000	
Light and heat[4]	9,000	
Drawings by proprietor	20,000	
		129,600
Profit		£11,700

Note that:

(1) £500 is owed for wages not included in this figure;

(2) this furniture and equipment is expected to last for four years;

(3) rent and rates includes £1,000 paid in advance;

(4) £2,000 is owed for light and heat and not included in this figure.

3. Mr B. Wildered has come to you with a problem which he states as follows:

"(*a*) my business bank balance has increased by £5,000 this year so that must represent my profit;

(*b*) my capital account has gone up by £2,000 so surely that ought to be the profit;

(*c*) I have drawn £8,000 from the business for my own living expenses. I could not have done that unless a profit had been earned of that amount;

(*d*) I always charge my customers what I paid for goods plus 50 per cent. As my sales this year have been £30,000 I must have made £10,000 in profit."

How can these different figures be reconciled?

4. Explain these terms:

(*a*) gross profit;   (*d*) drawings;

(*b*) depreciation;   (*e*) accruals.

(*c*) revenue;

5. In order to simplify his accounting procedures Jack Horner decides that he will, in future, calculate his profit as Cash Received less Cash Paid. Give a few simple examples to show ways in which this might turn out to be very misleading.

CHAPTER 5

Double Entry Book-keeping I

OBJECTIVES

In this chapter we shall deal with the following important topics:

    (*a*) double entry book-keeping—its operation and advantages;
    (*b*) debit and credit;
    (*c*) the trial balance;
    (*d*) preparation of final accounts and closing entries.

1. INTRODUCTION

In this chapter we are going to look at the operation of the double entry system of book-keeping (i.e. financial recording). This has a theoretical basis in the way in which a balance sheet is constructed but its importance is a practical one. It provides a very convenient method of collecting, categorising and assembling accounting information. We shall limit our discussion to its elements because in practice there is a wide variety of physical forms which the system might take. These range from the old-style leather-bound books still to be found in some old established small businesses to a modern computer-based system where the information is electronically stored.

The fundamental principle of double entry book-keeping is the one which we have already seen exemplified through the medium of the worksheet. This is that every transaction, every happening within a business with which financial accounting concerns itself, can be regarded as a flow of value from one station to another. This simple idea means that a very wide range of transactions can be recorded in a highly standardised manner which is yet sufficiently flexible to produce information in as much quantity and in whatever form is required. Such a system has the advantages that its maintenance can be reduced to a routine performed by clerical labour or electronically and that many checks can be built in to ensure automatic discovery of most types of error. Because the key to the system is very complete documentation and cross referencing of all transactions the system lends itself to methodical and thoroughgoing audit, thus conforming to this fundamental accounting concept.

2. ADAPTATION OF THE WORKSHEET

In order to set up a double entry system, the worksheet is broken up into its separate columns now known as accounts. Each account is then arranged in a certain way. Instead of the alternating + and − of our worksheet it has two sides to represent the inflows and outflows relating to the account. This means that there is no necessity to calculate a fresh total after every transaction. A total, or balance as it is called, is determined periodically when required as, for example, on the occasion of the preparation of a balance sheet.

Each account will appear as follows.

ACCOUNT FOR . . .

| This is known as the debit side. On it will be recorded all inflows to the account. | This is known as the credit side. On it will be recorded all outflows from the account. |

Within an account there is space not only for the money amount of the transaction but also for the date and for a brief description. Obviously this will enhance the value of the account as a permanent record of what has happened.

Below there appear the accounts required to record the transactions which appeared in worksheet form at the end of Chapter 3. Note carefully the way in which the balance is computed and inserted. This neatly closes off each account at the end of a financial period and leaves it ready to start the next one as well as determining and displaying the figure required for the balance sheet.

BANK

Capital introduced	£5,000	Purchase of stock	£3,000
Cash sale	1,500	Payment of creditor	1,500
Receipt from debtors	650	Balance	2,650
	£7,150		£7,150
Balance	£2,650		

CREDITORS

Bank	£1,500	Stock supplied	£2,000
Balance	500		
	£2,000		£2,000
		Balance	£500

CAPITAL

Stock supplied	£800	Bank	£5,000
Balance	5,100	Profit on sale	500
		Profit on sale	400
	£5,900		£5,900
		Balance	£5,100

STOCK

Bank	£3,000	Sales	£1,000
Creditor	2,000	Proprietor	800
		Sales	750
		Balance	2,450
	£5,000		£5,000
Balance	£2,450		

DEBTORS

Stock supplied	£1,150	Bank	£650
		Balance	500
	£1,150		£1,150
Balance	£500		

It should be clear from a careful examination of the above system of accounts that it retains all the desirable characteristics of the worksheet and possesses one or two additional ones of its own. One of these is that the system can be expanded without limit (by use of as many accounts as necessary) in order to provide what information is required. We can very easily cope with a longer list of assets and liabilities than appear in this example. We can also subdivide accounts if we wish to do so. Thus we might have several stock accounts representing different types of goods and several debtor's accounts, one for each customer.

3. REVENUE AND EXPENSE ACCOUNTS

We now need to see how this essentially simple system can be adapted so as to deal with out requirements for the profit and loss account as well as those for the balance sheet. One small development will achieve this. In the example just examined all profits were computed immediately they were earned and credited to the proprietor's capital account. In practice such frequent computations of profit would not be desirable even if they were practically possible. Whenever any transaction takes place containing elements which will have a bearing on the ultimate computation of profit these elements are marshalled by appropriate entries in special accounts. Unlike balance sheet accounts these record expenses and revenues rather than assets and liabilities but, as we shall soon see, this is a distinction which is unimportant and which cannot, in any case, be fully sustained.

A simple series of transactions will demonstrate this use of revenue and expense accounts. Mr K set up as a retailer of vegetables in a market. Over his first month's activity the following transactions took place.

(*a*) K made available £2,000 in cash to finance his venture.

(*b*) He paid £1,000 for stock for resale and £600 for three months' advance rent of his stall.

(*c*) He sold the initial stock for £2,000, being paid in cash.

(*d*) He bought more stock for £1,500. This time he paid £1,000 in cash and negotiated credit terms for the rest.

(*e*) He made further sales of £1,000, of which £200 was to a trusted customer who promised to pay in the following month and the rest was for cash.

(*f*) At the end of the month K paid £100 which is a monthly levy charged to each stallholder for the use of certain facilities provided by the market. He also found that he still held stock which had cost him £800.

Each of these transactions must be formulated in terms of flows of value and thus of debit and credit entries within our double-entry system.

(*a*) £2,000 has flowed from K into the business's cash float.
      DR Cash   £2,000:   CR Capital   £2,000

(*b*) £1,000 has flowed from the cash float into stock.
      DR Stock   £1,000:   CR Cash   £1,000
      £600 has flowed from the cash float into rent.
      DR Rent   £600:   CR Cash   £600

Note that, although part of rent is an expense of the month, we are at the moment treating it in the same way as we would the purchase of an asset. This is an essential feature of the marshalling process.

(*c*) The stock was sold for £2,000.
      DR Cash   £2,000:   CR Sales   £2,000

This is a profit-making transaction and previously we would have made an appropriate entry in the Capital account. Now, however, we shall open a Sales account to collect together items of revenue pending the eventual preparation of a full profit and loss account.

(*d*) There is a flow of value of £1,500 into stock. £1,000 of this is from cash and £500 from creditors.

DR Stock   £1,500:   CR Cash   £1,000
                            CR Creditors   £500

(*e*) There is an inflow of £1,000 from sales. £800 of this came into cash and the other £200 came into debtors.

DR Cash   £800:
DR Debtors   £200:   CR Sales   £1,000

(*f*) £100 flowed from cash to the services represented by the levy.

DR Levy   £100:   CR Cash   £100

These can now be recorded in double-entry account form. It is clear that eight accounts will be required. These are Cash, Capital, Stock, Rent, Sales, Creditors, Debtors and Levy.

CAPITAL

		Cash	£2,000

CASH

Capital	£2,000	Stock	£1,000
Sales	2,000	Rent	600
Sales	800	Stock	1,000
		Levy	100
		Balance	2,100
	£4,800		£4,800
Balance	£2,100		

STOCK

Purchases	£1,000	Cost of sales[1]	£1,700
Purchases	1,500	Balance	800
	£2,500		£2,500
Balance	£800		

(1) Cost of sales is a calculated figure (i.e. to make the account balance).

RENT

Cash	£600	

SALES

Balance	£3,000	Cash	£2,000
		Cash and debtors	1,000
	£3,000		£3,000
		Balance	£3,000

CREDITORS

	Stock	£500

DEBTORS

Sales	£200

LEVY

Cash	£100

4. THE TRIAL BALANCE

Note that in cases where there is more than one entry in an account we have calculated the balance standing on it at the end of the month. The balance is merely the ultimate net effect of the accumulation of entries put into the account up to that point in time. Since we have in all cases carefully observed the double entry rule it should now be that a list of debit balances will agree in total (or balance) with a list of credit balances. As this will test the balancing of the books such a list is termed a trial balance. The trial balance for Mr K's venture appears below.

K: TRIAL BALANCE AT END OF MONTH

Cash	£2,100	Capital	£2,000
Stock	800	Sales	3,000
Rent	600	Creditors	500
Debtors	200		
Cost of sales	1,700		
Levy	100		
	£5,500		£5,500

Although it balances, a trial balance is not the same thing as a balance sheet. A balance sheet contains assets and liabilities only whereas a trial balance contains these and other items as well. An examination of the trial balance will show that credit balances are either liabilities or revenues and that debit balances are either assets or expenses. Students sometimes find this hard to understand. They argue that liabilities are "bad" and revenues "good" and that it seems illogical to group them together. Similarly, assets are "good" and expenses "bad" so again do not sit happily together. It is, however, fallacious to think of particular balances as being of themselves either favourable or unfavourable. Credit balances *all* represent sources of value. Some of these sources, like creditors, need to be reimbursed and these are the liabilities. Others do not need to be reimbursed as they have been satisfied in the business process. These are the revenues, of which Sales is our only example here. A creditor could become a revenue, however, if for some reason he waived the amount owing. A sale could become a liability if for some reason, e.g. that we had provided faulty goods, a customer became entitled to his money back. Similarly, debit balances should be seen as the repositories of value. Some of this value still exists (the assets) while some has been consumed in the profit-making process (the expenses). As we have already seen some debit balances will represent assets which have become partially consumed since they were bought and thus are partly expense and partly asset. Depreciating assets, which we have already discussed, are the usual examples of this but in our present illustration the only instance is the £600 paid for rent. This is for three months' occupation of the stall. The matching principle requires that £200 of this be shown as an expenses in computing the current year's profit whilst the other £400 be carried forward as an asset to become the rent expense of the next two months in further equal instalments.

Preparation of accounts from a trial balance

It, perhaps, begins to become apparent that the trial balance, as well as providing a useful check on the accuracy of our book-keeping now comes into its own as a useful list of all the items required for preparation of both our profit and loss account and our balance sheet. Here is the trial balance again, marked up to indicate the destination of the amounts appearing in it.

Cash	£2,100	BS	Capital	£2,000 BS
Stock	800	BS	Sales	3,000 PL
Rent	600	{ PL £200 { BS £400	Creditors	500 BS
Debtors	200	BS		
Cost of sales	1,700	PL		
Levy	100	PL		
	£5,500			£5,500

Here now are the final accounts for Mr K's business for his first month of trading.

PROFIT AND LOSS ACCOUNT FOR THE MONTH

Sales		£3,000
Less Cost of sales		1,700
Gross profit		1,300
Less Expenses		
Rent	£200	
Levy	100	300
Net profit		£1,000

BALANCE SHEET AT END OF MONTH

Capital	£2,000	Stock	£800
Add profit	1,000	Debtors	200
	3,000	Payment in advance	400
Creditors	500	Cash	2,100
	£3,500		£3,500

It should be noted that all the figures here are drawn from the trial balance except for the net profit which is calculated within the profit and loss account and then provides a link between this account and the balance sheet. Effectively, then, the routine of preparing the profit and loss account and balance sheet (or final accounts as they are often termed) is a matter of allocating all figures in the trial balance to either the one document or the other (splitting between the two where necessary).

Closing entries

Although an invaluable working aid, this allocation conceals an important theoretical point which must be borne in mind. There is a fundamental difference in nature between the two documents making up the final accounts. The balance sheet is both the closing position of the first month and the opening position of the second. It thus provides a bridge between the two accounting periods. The profit and loss account, however, relates purely to the first month and has no relevance beyond that period. This means that although figures for assets and liabilities must remain in the trial balance (and hence in the underlying accounts) into the second month, expenses and revenues must not. If expenses and revenues did carry forward then they would, of course, appear again on a subsequent trial balance and could not be excluded from some future profit and loss account. It follows, then, that the trial balance at the beginning of the new period (i.e. a mirror image of the balance sheet) is different from the trial balance at the end of the preceding period. This difference is ensured by the making of what are known as closing entries to eradicate all spent balances. This is achieved by treating the profit and loss account, despite its very special importance, as just another account for book-keeping purposes. Its credits (i.e. revenues) require appropriate debit entries in another account and its debits (i.e. expenses) require appropriate credits. Completion of the double entry between the profit and loss account and other accounts will lead to the closure of accounts which represent pure revenues and expenses and lead to an amendment of accounts of mixed type. This is not demonstrated here but can very easily be verified by the reader if he completes the double entry as follows.

Entry in profit and loss account	*Consequent entry in other account*
Sales £3,000 (CR)	DR Sales £3,000 (closing it)
Cost of sales £1,700 (DR)	CR Cost of sales £1,700 (closing it)
Rent £200 (DR)	CR Rent £200 (amending balance to £400)
Levy £100 (DR)	CR Levy £100 (closing it)
Net profit £1,000 (DR)	CR Capital £1,000 (to show K's increased stake in the business)

The logic of the closing entries may be explained as follows. The profit and loss account, representing as it does the profit earning activity of the business, can be regarded as the ultimate source of all revenues and destination of all expenses. If these were recorded in the profit and loss account as they arose, however, it would lead this document to be a jumbled mass of unclassified and confusing entries, albeit giving the correct net profit in the end. The revenue and expenses accounts may thus be seen as temporary homes for the amounts placed in them. They are used to facilitate the collection and classification of the data.

SUMMARY

1. Double entry book-keeping has its theoretical basis in the balance sheet. It is a comprehensive routine whereby many different forms of financial transaction can be recorded in standard form.

2. It provides a convenient method of collecting, categorising and assembling accounting information. It has built-in checks and controls.

3. In double-entry recording every transaction is seen as a flow of value from one station to another. Each station is represented

by an account which is debited (left-hand side) with inflows and credited (right-hand side) with outflows.

4. A trial balance may be extracted from a set of books at any time. This (by balancing) provides a check on the accuracy of the records. When taken out at the year end it also provides a useful medium for the preparation of final accounts.

5. When final accounts are prepared from a trial balance, closing entries will be required in the books. These complete the the double entry for items which have been included in the profit and loss account.

QUESTIONS

1. State which accounts are to be debited and which to be credited in order to record each of the following.

(a) Stock costing £1,000 was bought. Payment was made of a deposit of 10 per cent, the balance being due in one month.

(b) Stock which had cost £500 was sold for £600 cash.

(c) The proprietor withdrew £250 from the business.

(d) A building which had cost £10,000 was revalued at £15,000.

(e) Credit customers paid £800 of what they owed.

(f) A supplier discovered that he had overcharged the business by £50. A reduction was therefore made to the amount owed which had not yet been paid.

2. Some types of recording error are automatically revealed when the trial balance fails to agree. Some are not revealed in this way. List six possible recording errors, three of which would be indicated by a failure to balance and three of which would not.

3. From the following trial balance prepare final accounts for the year ended 31st December. State what closing entries would be required.

X. WISEHEAD

TRIAL BALANCE AT 31ST DECEMBER

Administrative expenses	£1,000	Capital	£5,000
Bank	1,200	Creditors	800
Cash	700	Sales	10,000
Cost of sales	6,000		
Debtors	1,200		
Drawings	900		
Rent of premises[1]	2,500		
Stock	2,300		
	£15,800		£15,800

(1) Of this figure £500 relates to the following year.

4. The following is a list of closing entries made in the books of Don Quixote at the end of his financial year. From these reconstruct his profit and loss account showing gross and net profits.

Debits	
Sales	£52,100
Credits	
Capital	£750
Cost of sales	27,900
Depreciation	5,400
General expenses	590
Light and heat	2,600
Rent and rates	2,380
Wages	12,480

5. X records all of his financial transactions in the form of daily notes in a desk diary. Y uses a full double-entry system. State what advantages you would expect Y to gain over X.

CHAPTER 6

Double Entry Book-keeping II

OBJECTIVES

In this chapter we shall deal with the following important topics:

(*a*) cash transactions;
(*b*) bank transactions;
(*c*) sales on credit;
(*d*) purchases on credit;
(*e*) the journal;
(*f*) trial balance adjustments.

1. INTRODUCTION

Having looked at the essential features of the double entry system of recording financial transactions we need now to consider in a more practical way how it might be operated. Obviously there must be nothing haphazard about this process otherwise our records will be incomplete and of very little use. Because accounts are often used to establish rights as between individuals, to support applications for loans or to provide a basis for the assessment of taxation it is also necessary that they can easily be checked independently and evidence produced to support the correctness of all entries. This independent check, or audit, of accounts is frequently made, particularly in the case of limited companies where an annual audit is required by law. The linking documentary evidence which makes such an audit possible is termed the audit trail. Earlier we identified auditability coupled with objectivity as a fundamental accounting concept.

We can now usefully identify three objectives of any accounting system. These are:

(*a*) that it should be based on a routine process so that it can be readily and regularly maintained;

(*b*) that it should have built in checks so as to make error or fraud unlikely; and

(*c*) that it should provide auditability.

These objectives are achieved by a careful and appropriate documentation of all that occurs. This is illustrated by the systems which will now be described.

2. CASH TRANSACTIONS

The term cash in a business context is often used to cover not merely coin of the realm and banknotes but also bank balances. Thus if a businessman says he will pay cash for something he may actually mean that he is going to pay by cheque but immediately, as opposed to taking a period of credit. Nevertheless currency and bank balances present slightly different problems from an accounting and control point of view and so we will look at them separately.

Currency clearly presents a security risk. Anyone who handles a large amount of currency without having any control or check placed on them is subject to the temptation to misappropriate the money, to which a proportion of such people will eventually give way. Similarly if currency is physically lost or destroyed this is a loss which the business may find it very hard to recover even if insured. Most businesses minimise the risks and the recording problems associated with cash by arranging that, wherever possible, cash transactions are carried out through their bank account. As many payments as possible are made by cheque and money received, in whatever form, is paid into the bank as soon as possible.

The only type of business (other than those specialising in money such as banks or building societies) likely to handle large amounts of currency is a retail business. This is usually controlled by having a recording till which keeps a record of the amount paid into it and issues a receipt to be given to the customer. At least once a day, but possibly more often when turnover is high, the money in the till is checked against the running total recorded by the machine and then paid into the bank. Except for a small "float" or balance to enable change to be given the till should be kept as empty as possible. When the money is paid into the bank a permanent record is ultimately provided in the form of the bank statement which shows how much has been deposited.

It is interesting when going about one's daily life to observe the variety of ways in which cash receipts are controlled and recorded. These range from the recording till just described down to the laboriously written out bills, with carbon copies, which one is given in many drapers' or jewellers' shops. The apparently futile exercise of purchasing a ticket at the cinema only to have it torn up and discarded a moment later is another example of cash control. The number of tickets sold provides a record of cash received and the giving up of that ticket proves that the patron has paid. Errors are virtually eliminated by this system and fraud is only possible by collusion amongst cashier, usher and patron. This is unlikely to be feasible on any significant scale.

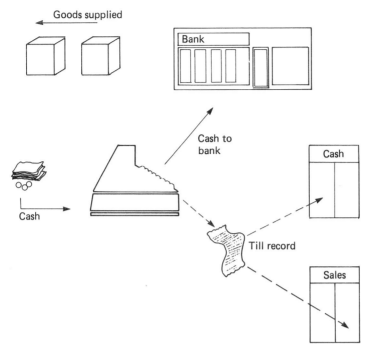

Fig. 1. *Sales for cash.*

Figure 1 illustrates in diagrammatic form the flow of cash and of information in a typical situation.

Petty cash payments

The only cash payments made by a business (except for wages which we shall consider separately) are likely to be very small amounts such as the weekly milk bill, the occasional packet of tea and a bus fare for a member of staff sent on an errand. These amounts are usually recorded in a special account for the purpose, which is given the self-explanatory name of petty (i.e. small) cash account. Petty cash is normally operated on an imprest system which provides a very simple and effective control. A small float is allocated to petty cash (say £20) and payments are made from this from time to time as required. Each payment must be evidenced by a voucher. This is merely a piece of paper describing the nature of the expense and signed by the person who incurred it on behalf of the business. Where possible there will be attached to the voucher further evidence of the payment such as a receipted bill or a used travel ticket. At any time the petty cashier should be able to produce cash and properly completed vouchers which together total to the original float issued. When the float runs low, or at predetermined regular intervals, the petty cashier hands over all vouchers in hand and is reimbursed by cash from the bank account to their total value. This means that his float is restored to its original level in readiness for the payment of further expenses. Under the imprest system the amount of cash held for petty cash can never rise above a preset maximum (the amount of the float), thus limiting the risk of loss. No expenditure can be made which is not authorised without the certainty of detection. Figure 2 shows how the system works.

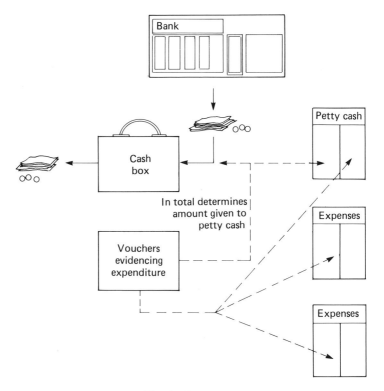

Fig. 2. *Petty cash.*

Wages

Although there is a growing movement towards the payment of wages by cheque or by direct credit to a bank account (and almost all salaries are paid in this way) many businesses still pay their weekly wages in the form of cash. It is usual to draw cash from the bank specifically for this purpose shortly before the time it is due to be paid. There are certain practical considerations relating to this which should be mentioned but which we need not consider for very long. One is that steps will need to be taken the determine what combination of notes and small change should be drawn from the bank so as to make it possible for the wage packets to be made up correctly. Another is that, as quite a large sum is normally involved, security precautions while the cash is in transit between the bank and the office and while the made up packets are being taken to the pay-out stations will be necessary. Finally some method of identifying workers will be necessary so as to ensure that the pay packet is handed to the worker entitled to it.

The recording of wages is made somewhat complicated by the fact that certain deductions have to be made from gross pay before the net amount due to the worker can be determined. Examples of these deductions are PAYE income tax, national insurance and pension fund contributions. The net amount only is drawn from the bank and the entry to record this is DR Wages and CR Cash with the total net wages. The figure for wages to appear in the profit and loss account, however, must be the total of gross wages as this is the cost to the business of employing labour. This is achieved by debiting to wages account the amounts of the separate deductions and crediting them respectively to PAYE, national insurance, pension fund, etc. All of these then become creditors for the amounts deducted on their behalf which will eventually be paid to them.

3. BANK TRANSACTIONS

Although we have given considerable attention to the matter of controlling and recording actual cash we have explained that in terms of total value most of a business's receipts and payments are likely to be in the form of bank money, i.e. cheques received or drawn. This is much easier to deal with than currency because the security risk is negligible and because the bank will maintain their own record of the business's account supplying it, from time to time, with a copy known as the bank statement. This does not mean, however, that it will not be necessary to maintain an account for bank money. There are several reasons why it is necessary. Firstly the bank may make a mistake and our record of transactions will enable this to be detected. Secondly this account can contain more narrative and other detail of the transactions than the bank will supply on its statement. Thirdly, because of delays in the banking process, the business's account will give a more up to date picture of the bank cash situation than will the statement. Fourthly the existence of an account in the books as a fully integrated part of the double entry system facilitates the proper working and balancing of that system. The account which records bank money transaction is usually known as the cash

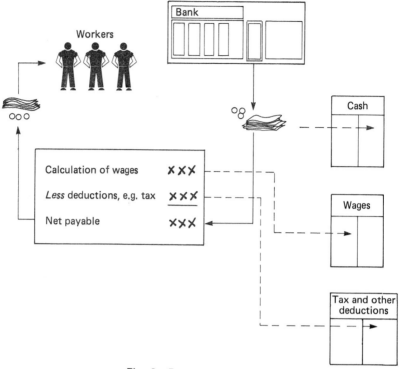

Fig. 3. *Payment of wages.*

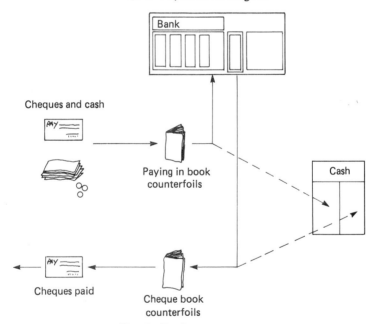

Fig. 4. *Bank transactions.*

account and, because of its bulk, is often kept, separately from the other accounts, in a cash book.

The documents which provide evidence of bank transactions for audit purposes are, for receipts, the counterfoils from the bank paying-in book and, for payments, the cheque counterfoils. The bank will also return paid cheques as further evidence if asked. For an overall check the bank statement is used. Figure 4 illustrates the bank cash recording process.

Below appears a typical page from the cash book of X and Co and the related statement from the bank.

CASH BOOK

1 Jan	Cash from till	£560	3 Jan	Blankshire Council (rates)	£340
2 Jan	Cash from till	225		White Supplies Co	295
	Cheque from Smith	25	4 Jan	Electricity Board	122
	Cheque from Jones	122		Telephone account	59
3 Jan	Cash from till	350		Goode Manuf. Co, plc	140
	Cheque from Robinson	98	5 Jan	Wages	800
4 Jan	Cash from till	420		Balance	214
	Cheque from McTavish	30			
	Cheque from Green	140			
		£1,970			£1,970
	Balance	£214			

BLANKSHIRE BANK PLC
STATEMENT OF ACCOUNT WITH X AND CO

		Debits	Credits	Balance
2 Jan	CSH		560	560
3 Jan	CSH + CHQS		372	932
	CHGS	30		902
4 Jan	CSH + CHQS		448	1,350
	972	295		1,055
5 Jan	CSH + CHQS		590	1,645
	975	140		1,505
	976	800		705
6 Jan	971	340		365

Key CSH = Cash CHQS = Cheques CHGS = Charges

A number of points should be noted concerning this bank statement. It is in a different form from X's own cash book. A bank normally calculates a balance after every transaction as shown here. This is helpful to many of its customers and also useful to its own monitoring process especially where overdrafts are concerned. The sides are reversed from the cash book. What X records as a debit the bank records as a credit and vice versa. This is because the bank looks at things, so to speak, from the other side of the counter. A balance in hand is, to X, an asset (a right to receive money) but to the bank it is a liability (an obligation to pay money). There is much less detail in the bank statement than in the cash book. Cheques paid are identified by serial number only and, where several amounts are paid in together, they are shown as one figure on the statement. Finally there is a discrepancy between the balance given by the bank statement and that given in the cash book. This arises because certain items are recorded in the one but not in the other. The most common example of this is what are known as unpresented cheques. When a business sends a cheque to a creditor it will record this as a payment immediately. The cheque must then go through the post to the recipient, be paid into his bank account when he has an opportunity to do so and ultimately be presented by that bank for payment to the business's bank. At any point in time that a balance is struck there are bound to be some cheques still in course of this process and thus recorded in the cash book but not on the bank statement. The present example also shows another source of discrepancy. The bank has made a charge for its services and debited the amount to the account. The appearance of this item on the statement will be the only notification of this charge to be given and it cannot therefore be recorded in the cash book until the statement arrives.

Bank reconciliation

It is useful from time to time to prepare a bank reconciliation in order to explain the difference between the cash book balance and the statement balance so ensuring that there are no errors but merely delays in the recording of certain items. A reconciliation appropriate to the given example appears below.

BANK RECONCILIATION

Balance according to cash book		£214
Less Bank charges		30
True balance of cash at bank		184*
Add Unpresented cheques	£122	
	59	
		181
Balance according to bank statement		£365

Note that the amount marked * would be the correct figure to appear on the balance sheet drawn up at this time. The bank charges would be debited to the profit and loss account (and would probably have formed the subject of an adjustment to the trial balance).

4. SALES ON CREDIT

A number of points require care in connection with sales on credit. Firstly, although it lies outside the direct scope of accounting, we must have some method of checking the credit worthiness of customers. One way of doing this is requiring them to provide bankers' or other references. Secondly we must be quite sure that when goods are supplied to a customer on credit that he is ultimately charged with the correct amount. Thirdly we must ensure that a record of outstanding debt is maintained and that steps are taken to follow up any debt which becomes overdue. In order not to endanger customer goodwill nor to risk losses through sloppy debt collection it will be necessary to have these records kept with great care. Error elsewhere may fairly readily be rectified. It is difficult, however, to mollify a customer threatened with legal action to recover a debt which he has in fact paid or to recover money from another customer who has been told that his account is clear.

To provide the necessary documentary basis for recording credit sales all sales of this kind should be accompanied by the issue of a sales invoice. This should be made out on a form printed with the name and address of the business and forms should be consecutively numbered by machine so that none will go astray. The business retains one copy of the invoice, issuing the customer with another. An invoice will typically describe the goods and show their quantity and price and show, finally, the total amount which is to be paid.

The copy invoices provide a prime record which then has to be entered into the ledger. The correct entry for each sale, as we have already seen, is a debit of the amount to the debtor's account and a credit to the sales account. We should now take a practical view of the form which that record will take. It will obviously be necessary to provide a separate account for each individual debtor and there may be a very large number of these. Because each is similar in form and in treatment they are usually kept together and a collection of all the accounts with individual customers is known as the sales ledger (or the debtors' ledger). There is no need to record sales individually in the sales account and the normal practice is to add together all the sales invoices for a particular period (e.g. one week or one month) and credit the total only to the sales account.

A diagrammatic representation of the process of accounting for sales on credit appears as Fig. 5.

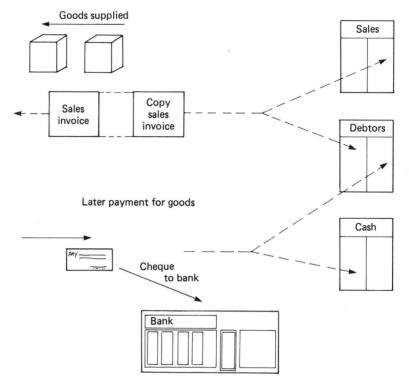

Fig. 5. *Sales on credit.*

Cash discount

Sometimes a business will offer a small discount (known as a cash discount) to customers who pay their accounts within a certain time. Thus its terms might be that payment is due within thirty days but that a discount of $2\frac{1}{2}$ per cent is offered for payment within seven days. This discount might be well worth its cost in terms of the improved cash flow which it creates. Where a customer claims the discount his cash payment will not completely clear the account. We must therefore transfer the amount of the discount to a discount allowed account where all other such amounts will be accumulated pending the preparation at the end of the financial period of a profit and loss account.

Bad debts

Occasionally a business will make a bad debt. This means that a customer fails to pay the amount due and that this becomes irrecoverable. If the amount is sizeable it will be worth making strenuous efforts to recover it having recourse to the courts if necessary. For small amounts or where it is known that the debtor is insolvent or has left the country this will not be worthwhile. In that event the unpaid balance on the debtor's account should be transferred to a bad debts account again pending ultimate charging in the profit and loss account.

5. PURCHASES ON CREDIT

The procedures associated with the recording of purchases on credit are the inverse of those relating to sales on credit. Care needs to be taken to ensure that such purchases are properly ordered (otherwise employees might be ordering things on their own behalf and leaving the business to pay) and that they have actually been delivered in good condition. The paperwork is fairly straightforward. Goods should be ordered by means of a written order of which a copy is kept. When the goods arrive they should be checked for quantity and quality against the copy order. The supplier of the goods will send his invoice just as we did to our customers. We shall describe this as a purchase invoice. Each invoice should be checked against the order and the record of correct delivery. When verified the relevant amount is posted to the credit of the appropriate suppliers account. The group of suppliers accounts is often known collectively as the purchase ledger (or creditors' ledger). As with sales individual invoices are posted to suppliers' accounts and batch totals to stock. As an additional refinement the initial debit may be to a purchases account. This merely collects all purchases for a period so that they can be taken in total, rather than piecemeal, to the stock account. Purchases on credit are represented diagrammatically in Fig. 6.

6. THE JOURNAL

So far we have considered only routine transactions and the way in which they are recorded. The common feature has been some activity evidenced and controlled by documentation which can then be used as a medium through which to write up, or post, the ledger. There will be some transactions which are not routine and which do not automatically create their own prime record. For these a journal is used. This is, in effect, a running record or diary of such transactions recorded in a form which provides full information on the transaction and sets out how it is to be recorded in the ledger. Examples of the kind of transaction for which a journal entry might be used are the rectification of an error,

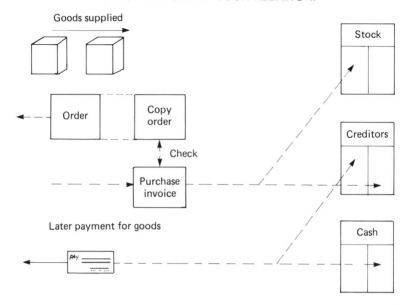

Fig. 6. *Purchases on credit.*

writing off depreciation and the revaluation of an asset. Let us use the last of these to provide an example.

A building owned by the business is professionally revalued at £40,000 which is £10,000 more than the figure currently appearing as a debit balance on the building account. The entry required to incorporate this revaluation in the books is a debit to buildings and a credit to capital of the £10,000 (not a credit to profit and loss account as this is not a "revenue" connected with the current year's trading). This entry could be recorded direct in the ledger and would lead to correct balances but in this form it would be difficult to verify as it would be impossible to make room for adequate explanation. From the audit point of view the verification of such one-off transactions, which may be quite sizeable, is of particular interest.

The journal entry below deals with the building revaluation of our example.

Journal

	DR	CR
Building	£10,000	
Capital		£10,000
Being implementation of the valuation of the building made by Messrs. Auctioneer and Agent on 23rd March as agreed at meeting on 5th March.		

It should be noted that a journal is no part of the double entry system any more than is a sales or a purchase invoice. Like them it is a prime record providing the basic information from which the double entry can then be made.

7. THE TRIAL BALANCE

As we have described it the book-keeping process has been reduced to a routine. Every transaction will generate its own documentation and, in due course, all ledger accounts will be written up from this information. We have already met a simple form of trial balance and have seen how the profit and loss account and balance sheet can be prepared from it. It is now time to look at a more realistically complicated example.

One of the possible complications is that in a real situation there are likely to be many more accounts than we have so far considered. This merely means that our work will take a little longer and our accounting statements will become more detailed. It is, therefore, easily dealt with. Another and more important complication is that because the recording system has been reduced to a routine it cannot be expected to think and we must do the thinking for it after the trial balance has been prepared. Extensive use of the journal before the preparation of the trial balance may obviate this necessity but in practice it is rare for this to be dealt with at that stage. This is because preparation of a trial balance is also a routine procedure which conveniently follows the others which we have described.

Adjustments

The routine procedures will have coped with all transactions where documentation is automatically created such as sales, purchases and payment of wages. It will not deal with things which do not create such a record and these will have to be inserted afterwards. These give rise to what are described as adjustments to a trial balance. Information on any necessary adjustments will have to be obtained before proper final accounts can be drawn up. Since adjustments arise from matters not covered by the formal recording system, it is obvious that their number will depend on how comprehensive the system is.

Some notes on what, typically, are likely to give rise to adjustments follow.

Stock

We have assumed so far that whenever stock was sold this gave rise to a book-keeping entry DR Cost of sales CR Stock with its cost. This will be how the matter is dealt with in a business of any size. A small businesss, however, may not be able or willing to record this detail and may content itself with recording purchases of supplies as they take place and then physically counting the stock at each accounting date. In such a case the trial balance will contain debit balances representing opening stock and purchases and there will be a note, given separately, of the closing stock. From this the cost of sales can easily be calculated, for example:

Stock at 1st January (from trial balance)	£21,560
Purchases in year (from trial balance)	136,900
Hence total stock made available to year	158,460
Less Stock at 31st December (given as adjustment)	24,290[1]
Hence amount used in year	£134,170[2]

(1) This figure appears in current assets in the balance sheet at 31st December.

(2) This figure appears as "Cost of Sales" in the Trading account for the year ended 31st December.

From an accounting point of view this method is quite satisfactory. It does, of course, leave something to be desired from a control point of view as there is opportunity for losses to occur which are not detectable until the next stock taking.

Proprietor's drawings
Again this is matter of most importance in the case of a small business. Since businesses exist to provide an income for their proprietors, it is usual for amounts to be drawn regularly by the owner rather than waiting until profits are finally ascertained at the year end. Properly these amounts should be recorded in the books as a credit to cash and a debit to capital (or drawings) and this will commonly be done where the drawings are made by cheque from the bank account. Sometimes, however, the proprietor will take regular amounts from the takings in the till (for the convenience of having this in cash) and may keep only a rough record of the amounts involved. Thus a trial balance may reveal bankings of, say, £20,000 from sales. If we are additionally informed that the owner regularly took £50 per week from takings before he banked the residue then true sales were £2,600 (52 × £50) higher than the recorded figure and an adjustment must be made.

Depreciation
Depreciation is an artificial transaction from the book-keeping point of view. Although the decline in the value of fixed assets as

they are consumed in the business process can be seen to occur it does not of itself generate any documentation. Often, then, no depreciation is calculated or recorded prior to the trial balance stage and this adjustment is made as the accounts are prepared.

Accruals and prepayments
We have already discussed the necessity to allow for accruals and prepayments. It will be obvious from their nature that routine recording processes will not provide the information and that a special adjustment will need to be made to trial balance figures.

Bad debts
Bad debts have already been referred to in connection with sales on credit. In their nature bad debts rarely signal themselves very emphatically and they are usually identified after examination of the debts owing at a particular balance sheet date. Some of the signs that a debt might be bad are that it has been outstanding for an unusually long time, that the customer disputes the amount owed or that the customer has moved without leaving a forwarding address. A judgment has to be made as to the amount of bad debts and this may have to be incorporated as an adjustment to trial balance figures.

8. EXAMPLE

Below is a worked example showing how final accounts are prepared from an annotated trial balance in the case of a sole trader carrying on a retail business.

Z AND CO

TRIAL BALANCE AT 31ST DECEMBER

Building	£50,000	Bank overdraft	£2,360
Debtors	1,605	Capital	75,200
Drawings (by cheque)	12,000	Creditors	9,080
Furniture	11,000	Sales	136,700
Insurances	2,000		
Light and heat	860		
Motor vehicles	7,200		
Miscellaneous	350		
Purchases	109,425		
Rates	3,500		
Stock (at 1st January)	19,200		
Wages	6,200		
	£223,340		£223,340

Note that:

(a) Z, the owner of the business, drew for his own personal use £1,000 per month from the bank (recorded in the books) and £500 per month in cash from shop takings (not recorded in the books);

(b) the value of stock at 31st December was £21,600;

(c) by the year end payments for rates included £700 paid in advance and insurances included £500 paid in advance;

(d) it was estimated that by 31st December a charge of £120 had accrued but had not been billed in respect of light and heat;

(e) interest on the bank overdraft totalling £290 had accrued by 31st December but had not been charged to the account;

(f) depreciation was calculated at £1,000 on furniture and £1,200 on motor vehicles; and

(g) on examining his debtors Z formed the opinion that an amount of £200 owing by a customer who had gone abroad should be regarded as a bad debt.

Let us now work through this. Because we are handling quite a lot of data and are working towards accounting statements that have to co-ordinate in a particular way it is absolutely essential to be methodical. We start from a balanced trial balance and therefore the production of balanced final accounts should be reasonably straightforward. Probably the best approach is to look at the notes leading to adjustments and to amend the trial balance figures to incorporate these. We must remember that we are in effect recording matters which have not been recorded before and we must follow the double entry rules carefully.

(a) £1,000 per month is already recorded and we can see £12,000 as a debit balance in drawings resulting from this. Another £6,000 (£500 × 12) must now be recorded as DR Drawings £6,000: CR Sales £6,000 (because this money was extracted from the takings). Thus the trial balance figures are amended to:

Drawings	£18,000	Sales	£142,700

(b) The closing stock figure of £21,600 does not of itself amend the trial balance but it tells us how to split the figures of opening stock and purchases.

	Trial balance	Total stock available	Accounts figures
Purchases	£109,425	£128,625	£21,600 Stock (BS)
Stock	£19,200		£107,025 Cost of sales (P and L)

(*c*) This note tells us that correct matching requires part of Rates and Insurance to be written off in the profit and loss account and part carried forward to a future period as a prepayment. Prepayments, in a balance sheet, are normally not shown separately but are added to debtors. The entry is therefore DR Debtors £1,200; CR Rates £700, CR Insurances £500. The new figures are:

Debtors	£2,805
Insurances	1,500
Rates	2,800

(*d*) Accruals are the complement of prepayments. Accruals are normally amalgamated with creditors. The adjusting entry here is DR Light and Heat £120: CR Creditors £120. The adjusted figures become:

Light and Heat	£980	Creditors	£9,200

(*e*) The interest charged by the bank will, when recorded, increase the overdraft on the bank balance and give rise to an expense to be charged in the profit and loss account. The entry is DR Bank interest £290: CR Bank £290 Trial balance figures become:

Bank interest (a new balance) £290		Bank overdraft	£2,650

(*f*) The figures for depreciation enable us to divide the values of fixed assets between the expired portion (for the profit and loss account) and the residual values (for the balance sheet). In book-keeping terms the adjustment is DR Depreciation £2,200; CR Furniture, £1,000 CR Motor Vehicles £1,200.

(*g*) This adjustment tells us that of the debtors, normally regarded as an asset, £200 has been lost and must thus be recorded as an expense: DR Bad debts £200; CR Debtors £200.

We can now draw up our final accounts from this adjusted trial balance. They appear on the following page.

The following features should be noted:

(*i*) the profit and loss account has been divided to show a figure for gross profit and so described as "trading and profit and loss account";

(*ii*) the capital account section of the balance sheet has been amplified so as to show clearly the linkage between the previous and current years' values.

Z AND CO

TRADING AND PROFIT AND LOSS ACCOUNT FOR THE YEAR ENDED 31ST DECEMBER

Sales		£142,700
Less Cost of sales		107,025
Gross profit		35,675
Less Expenses:		
Insurances	£1,500	
Light and heat	980	
Depreciation	2,200	
Miscellaneous	350	
Rates	2,800	
Bad debts	200	
Bank interest	290	
Wages	6,200	
		14,520
Net profit		£21,155

BALANCE SHEET AT 31ST DECEMBER

Capital at 1st January		£75,200	*Fixed assets*		
Add Profit for year		21,155	Building		£50,000
			Furniture		10,000
		96,355	Motor vehicles		6,000
Less Drawings		18,000			66,000
Capital at 31st December		78,355	*Current assets*		
Current liabilities			Stock	£21,600	
Bank overdraft	£2,650		Debtors	2,605	
					24,205
Creditors	9,200	11,850			
		£90,205			£90,205

SUMMARY

1. The accounting concept of auditability is given expression in the documentation and procedures used in any practical system of book-keeping.

2. *Cash transactions.* These present an obvious security risk. They should be kept to a minimum. They mainly occur in large amounts in connection with retail sales and with the payment of wages. Small cash payments are often dealt with on the imprest system whereby actual expenditure is regularly reimbursed so as to maintain a float of known amount.

3. *Wage payments.* Where these are made in cash great attention must be given to security. Deductions from wages must be carefully and appropriately calculated and recorded.

4. *Bank transactions.* Most of a business's so-called cash transactions will normally take place through its bank account. Since the bank maintains its own records of the account and supplies a statement of this from time to time, a close check on bank money is easily kept. Regular reconciliations between bank and business records should be a routine.

5. *Sales on credit.* Careful documentation is required to ensure the correct charging of amounts due from customers. A routine must be set up to ensure that debts are collected efficiently. A cash discount is sometimes offered to debtors who pay promptly. Bad debts, i.e. losses of amounts due because of non-payment, are, however, likely to occur occasionally.

6. *Purchases on credit.* A check has to be maintained that the business pays only for what it has ordered and received. Suppliers should be paid on the agreed date.

7. *The journal.* This is a record of prime entry in which a transaction is described and analysed before it is recorded in the double entry system. Nowadays its use is often confined to unusual or complicated transactions.

8. The trial balance gives the basic data required to prepare final accounts. Adjustments are often required in respect of (*a*) stock, (*b*) proprietor's drawings, (*c*) depreciation, (*d*) accruals and prepayments and (*e*) bad debts.

QUESTIONS

1. Doris extracted the following trial balance from her books on 30th June. From it, and the notes appended, prepare her profit and loss account for the year ended 30th June and balance sheet at that date.

Advertising	£13,242	Capital	£112,851
Cash	1,069	Creditors	20,879
Debtors	28,464	Sales	369,533
Drawings	20,000		
Electricity	6,946		
Fixtures and fittings	48,829		
Insurances	8,641		
Miscellaneous expenses	986		
Postage and stationery	3,280		
Purchases	239,690		
Rent and rates	9,740		
Stock at beginning of year	29,812		
Telephone	1,470		
Vehicles	39,060		
Wages and salaries	52,034		
	£503,263		£503,263

Note that:

(*a*) rent and rates for the month of July, amounting to £750, have been paid in advance;

(*b*) electricity accrued by the year end was £295;

(*c*) telephone charges accrued by the year end totalled £98;

(*d*) insurance paid in advance was £2,230;

(*e*) the stock at the end of the year was valued at £26,248;

(*f*) in addition to the drawings shown, Doris drew £2,000 in cash from takings before these were banked;

(*g*) of the debtors amounts totalling £218 are considered to be bad;

(*h*) depreciation is £6,900 on Vehicles and £4,200 on Fixtures and fittings; and

(*i*) included in Insurances was £120 which was paid on behalf of an employee and deducted from his salary.

2. Veronica has been in business for one year and wants accounts to enable her to judge the progress and position of the enterprise. She has not maintained full records but is able to give the following information.

(*a*)

SUMMARY OF BANK ACCOUNT FOR YEAR

Amount paid in to start business	50,000	Purchase of Building	£30,000
Received from customers	44,280	Paid to suppliers	46,710
		Modifications to building	5,000
		Wages to part time assistants	4,180
		Electricity	1,940
		Insurance	1,080
		Telephone	460
		Balance at year end	4,910
	£94,280		£94,280

(*b*) The amount still owed by customers at the year end is £6,110.

(*c*) The amount owing to suppliers is £4,080.

(*d*) Stock at the year end was valued at £8,650.

(*e*) Veronica drew £100 each week from the takings before banking them.

(*f*) Accrued electricity was £200.

(*g*) Insurance paid in advance was £100.

(*h*) £10 per week was paid out of takings for miscellaneous expenses.

Prepare accounts for the first year of trading.

3. What is meant by the term "audit trail". Give examples of where it occurs in a conventional accounting system and suggest how the auditor might use it.

4. Express the following transactions in the form of journal entries.

(*a*) The proprietor collected £1,000 from a customer while delivering some goods. He kept £170 of this for his own personal expenses, paid £500 of it to a creditor of the business and paid the rest into the business bank account.

(*b*) The business spent £1,200 on acquiring a new vehicle. This was made up as follows.

Cost of vehicle	£7,000
Road tax and fuel	100
	7,100
Allowance on old vehicle	5,900
	£1,200

(*c*) The business built its own extension to its office block. This cost £16,000 made up as follows.

Materials specially purchased	£2,500
Materials from stock	1,600
Wages of factory labour used on this work	11,900
	£16,000

5. The proprietor of a business is concerned that the figure for bad debts is increasing year by year. To what matters should he give attention in an attempt to reduce this figure?

CHAPTER 7

Depreciation

OBJECTIVES

In this chapter we shall deal with the following important topics:

(a) depreciation and its nature;
(b) methods of calculating depreciation;
(c) treatment of purchases and sales of fixed assets.

1. INTRODUCTION

By now we have several times encountered the idea of depreciation. It is an allocation of the cost of an asset to the profit and loss
accounts of the years which benefit from its use. In that sense it can
be regarded as representing the asset's decline in value through use
and the lapse of time. We have so far avoided the issue of how the
allocation is made by assuming equal instalments or by making use
of a given figure. Depreciation is, however, an important accounting problem and it will be worth some special attention.

Let us first make one or two preliminary observations about the
matter. It will be useful to look at a simple illustration. A certain
machine was bought for £8,000. It was expected to last for five
years and in each year would use raw materials and labour costing
£4,000 to produce product selling for £6,000. A profit and loss
account for each of the five years might appear as below.

Sales	£6,000
Less Cost of sales	4,000
Gross profit	2,000
Less Depreciation	1,600
Net profit	£400

Note the difference between net profit and the amount of cash
generated by operations. Since, broadly speaking, sales and cost of
sales are represented by cash inflows and outflows respectively,
gross profit will be matched by a net inflow of cash of approximately equal amount. Depreciation is not a cash expense and therefore

the cash position is unaffected by charging it in the account. Effectively, then, a year's operation generates £2,000 in cash of which £400 is declared to be available for distribution to the proprietor (by reporting it as a profit) and £1,600 is retained in the business as the proceeds of realisation of a portion of an asset.

This has led some writers to view depreciation as a device for retaining within the business funds for the replacement of the fixed asset concerned. There are several objections to this idea. One is that it unnecessarily sets depreciation apart from other types of expense. One could, with equal force, argue that, say, wages is charged in the profit and loss account so as to ensure that sufficient funds are available to meet the next round of wages. This would, however, seem a strange view. Another objection is that cash is rarely retained in liquid form in a well-run business. It will much more usually be used to invest in worthwhile projects as they become available than it will be retained for replacement of a specific asset. Thirdly, there is, in any case, no guarantee that any specific asset will, in fact, be replaced when it is worn out. It is just as likely that changing business needs will lead to the purchase of something else. It is, therefore, generally more useful to see depreciation merely as a device for allocating the amount spent on acquiring an asset to the periods which benefit from its use.

2. METHODS OF DEPRECIATION

A large number of methods have been devised for determining how this allocation should be done and we shall look at a representative group of them. Each of them is a rule based on what its advocates believe to be a logical idea. There is no consistency as between one and another and none can be said to be any more correct than the others.

Straight line method

This is the method which by implication we have used so far. The total cost of the asset is divided by the number of years of its life and that amount is charged as depreciation year by year. The value of the asset appearing year by year in the balance sheet, known as its "book" or "written down" value, is the original cost less all amounts of depreciation charged to date.

Here is an example. A motor vehicle cost £6,000 and is expected to last for five years. The table below shows the profit and loss account charge and balance sheet value for the vehicle for each year of its life.

Year	Depreciation charge	Balance sheet value at year end
1	£1,200	£4,800
2	1,200	3,600
3	1,200	2,400
4	1,200	1,200
5	1,200	Nil

A variant on this method is sometimes used where it is believed that an asset will have a substantial residual value at the end of its economic life. Here the depreciation is calculated to reduce the balance sheet value to scrap value at the end of that time. If, in the example just used, it were expected that the vehicle would have a value of £1,000 at the end of its five-year life the revised figures would be as follows.

Year	Depreciation charge	Balance sheet value at year end
1	£1,000	£5,000
2	1,000	4,000
3	1,000	3,000
4	1,000	2,000
5	1,000	1,000

The straight line method is very widely used in practice because of its simplicity. It also has the advantage that by remaining constant over the life of the asset the depreciation charge does not communicate irrelevant fluctuations to the profit and loss account. One disadvantage is that the balance sheet value of the asset is unlikely even to approximate to its market value. The method also relies very much on an accurate assessment of the asset's life. If this turns out to be inaccurate then anomalies will occur. Thus an asset might physically have ceased to exist whilst an undepreciated balance remained in the books or an asset might still be in use and providing a service after its cost has been fully written off.

Reducing balance method

Some would argue that it is erroneous to use a method of depreciation which attributes equal benefits to each of the time periods of an asset's life. A new asset, they would say, provides a better service than an older one and the periods which use it should be charged more accordingly.

The reducing balance method of calculating depreciation is one method which reflects this argument by causing a greater part of the total amount of depreciation to be written off early in the life of the asset. An appropriate percentage is selected and then applied annually to the residual book value of the asset to determine that year's depreciation. An example should make the principle clear. We will make use of the case of the same motor vehicle as referred to above and calculate depreciation at the rate of 30 per cent per annum which will reduce the book value of the vehicle to scrap value (approximately) as before.

Year	Depreciation charge (30% of value at previous year end —to nearest £)	Balance sheet value at year end
1	£1,800	£4,200
2	1,260	2,940
3	882	2,058
4	617	1,441
5	432	1,009

It should be noted that under the reducing balance method an asset would never become completely written off. The rate of depreciation selected must be such as to reduce the book value of the asset to its scrap value at the end of its economic life.

Advantages claimed for this method include that it gives a valuation for the asset in the balance sheet which is likely to approximate better to market value which commonly declines very rapidly for new assets and less rapidly thereafter. It is also seen as an advantage that if the life of the asset exceeds expectation it still (unlike with the straight line method) retains a value in the books from which a depreciation charge can be calculated. A further comment which is sometimes made is that the total cost of using an asset should be seen to be made up of a combination of depreciation and repairs and maintenance. Since repairs and maintenance are likely to increase as the asset gets older total cost is equalised if depreciation at the same time diminishes.

None of these arguments is very persuasive as, although the suppositions on which they are based might work out in practice, this would be largely a matter of chance and is not inherent in the method. A big disadvantage to the reducing balance method is a mathematical one and that is that for relatively short-lived assets the annual depreciation rate has to be very high. This means that the first year's profit and loss account charge is heavy. An asset costing £10,000 and having an expected life of three years would need a depreciation rate of 55 per cent under the reducing balance method to reduce its value to below £1,000 at the end of that life.

Sum of the year's digits

This method of computing depreciation, rather more popular in America than here, also has a decreasing charge over the life of the asset but on a basis rather different from that of reducing balance. Each year is given a number (or digit), these being in descending order. Thus for an asset with a five-year life the numbers would be 5, 4, 3, 2 and 1. The depreciation is then calculated as the year's number divided by the total of all the numbers multiplied by the cost of the asset. Thus:

Year	Proportion of value to be written off	Depreciation charge	Balance sheet value at year end
1	$\dfrac{5}{15}$	£2,000	£4,000
2	$\dfrac{4}{15}$	1,600	2,400
3	$\dfrac{3}{15}$	1,200	1,200
4	$\dfrac{2}{15}$	800	400
5	$\dfrac{1}{15}$	400	Nil

Again the method can easily be adapted to give a calculated scrap value if required.

Production unit method

This is a variant on the straight line method. Where that matches the cost of the asset against revenue on a strict time basis, the production unit method attempts to do so on the basis of direct association. The life of the asset is estimated in terms of the number of units of output which it will produce. In the case of our motor vehicle we might decide that it has an economic life of 100,000 miles and that it will be worth £1,000 at the end of that mileage. Depreciation is then provided at the rate of £5,000 ÷ 100,000 miles = 5p per mile so that in any year depreciation depends on the number of miles travelled. The table below shows depreciation year by year on that basis. Assumed mileages have been inserted.

Year	Mileage run	Depreciation charge	Balance sheet value at year end
1	18,900	£945	£5,055
2	22,200	1,110	3,945
3	19,300	965	2,980
4	20,200	1,010	1,970
5	19,700	985	985

Note that the actual miles run exceed those expected. This is not very important and will commonly occur.

3. THE ARBITRARY NATURE OF DEPRECIATION

The four methods of depreciation described above are the main ones used in practice. There are others, some of which use fairly complex formulae to evaluate the charge. It must be emphasised that there is a very high degree of arbitrariness involved in determining a depreciation charge. It is difficult therefore to argue that a more complicated method will lead to a more accurate figure. It should also be noted that many businesses take advantage of the arbitrariness of depreciation to adopt a prudent (as they would describe it) policy of accelerated depreciation. This means that they will write off an asset over a shorter period than the true estimated life. The motor vehicle, for example, believed to have a useful life of five years, may be written off over three years. Thus, although the basic concept of matching does underly depreciation it can become somewhat blurred in its actual operation.

A problem which often has to be faced is that of calculating depreciation on assets purchased part way through a financial year. Here is an illustration of the problem. A certain business has a financial year ending on 31st December. On 5th May it purchased for £10,000 an asset expected to last for four years at the end of which time it will have a scrap value of £2,000. The business uses the straight line method of depreciation. One full year's depreciation is easily calculated to be £2,000 but, by the end of the financial year in which it is purchased, it has not been used for a full year. Purists might argue that depreciation should be precisely apportioned so that the charge is:

$$\frac{\text{number of days held}}{365} \times £2,000 = \frac{240}{365} \times £2,000 = £1,315.$$

It is suggested, however, that this degree of precision in depreciation is a nonsense. A useful compromise policy might be for a business to provide for a half year's depreciation for every asset for the year in which it is bought. Many do, however, in fact provide a normal full year's amount even in the year of purchase.

4. DISPOSAL OF AN ASSET

We ought, finally, to give a thought to what happens when an asset is disposed of. Here all becomes known and any errors in the original estimates will have to be dealt with. Let us suppose that the motor vehicle of our favourite example is kept for four years and not the five which was originally expected. It was sold for £2,500. Assuming we are using the straight line method of depreciation its book value at the date of sale will be £2,000. The discrepancy between book value and the proceeds of sale is exactly like an ordinary profit—an asset worth £2,000 is exchanged for one worth £2,500. It might be argued that the profit of £500 could reasonably be transferred to the profit and loss account and there described as profit on sale of motor vehicle. This will have the effect, however, of boosting the reported profit with an item which is not relevant to current business operations. A preferred treatment is to bypass the profit and loss account and to transfer such amounts direct to capital. The same would apply to a 'loss" on sale. This treatment reflects that the discrepancy is seen as requiring a correction to earlier profit and loss accounts rather than affecting the current one.

SUMMARY

1. Depreciation is the process whereby the cost of an asset is allocated to the profit and loss accounts of the years which benefit from its use.

2. It is sometimes seen as a process of valuation or as a method whereby funds for the replacement of the asset may be retained within the business. Either view is likely to be misleading.

3. Different methods of calculating depreciation lead to quite different figures and there is no consistency as between one and another. There is, therefore, a large degree of arbitrariness in the figure eventually used.

4. Methods in common use are:
   (a) straight line method;
   (b) reducing balance method;
   (c) sum of the years' digit method;
   (d) production unit method.

5. Where an asset is acquired part way through a year exact apportionment of the depreciation charge gives a false precision and some simple rule, e.g. charging a half year's depreciation in the year of acquisition, is better.

6. When an asset is sold at a profit or loss relative to its book value, this should be transferred direct to capital, rather than included in the profit and loss account, as an item implying a correction to previous years' figures.

QUESTIONS

1. "Depreciation is of a fundamentally different nature from other expenses appearing in the profit and loss account." Discuss.

2. Grabbit and Co purchased an automatic packing machine for its product. The cost of the machine was £15,000 and it was expected to have a life of five years at its projected average usage of 2,000 hours per annum. Its scrap value was expected to be sufficient only to cover the cost of its disposal. Calculate the depreciation charge for each of the five years on each of the methods of depreciation described in the chapter.

3. Harry depreciates all his plant and machinery on the straight line basis over five years. In the year of purchase of any item he provides a half year's depreciation. His financial year runs to 31st December. His disposals of plant and machinery in the year ended 31st December 19–6 were as detailed below.

Item disposed of	Original cost	Date of purchase	Date of sale
Planer	£8,000	23/1/–1	15/6/–6
Honer	£10,000	15/7/–2	18/9/–6
Stretcher	£5,000	30/11/–3	2/11/–6
Fixer	£6,000	2/2/–4	13/12/–6

Suggest how these disposals should be recorded giving the actual figures to be used.

4. Robin has recently set up in business. As an alternative to conventional methods of providing for depreciation he proposes to revalue his assets annually and to charge in the profit and loss account the loss in value between the beginning of each year and its end. He claims that this will lead to a more accurate balance sheet. What undesirable consequences are likely to follow from this policy?

5. "As depreciation is such an arbitrarily determined amount it should either be omitted from the profit and loss account altogether or else the full cost of all assets should be charged in the year in which they are bought." Discuss the merits of these ideas.

CHAPTER 8

Partnership I

OBJECTIVES

In this chapter we shall deal with the following important topics:

(*a*) the nature of partnership;
(*b*) legal principles;
(*c*) the division of profits;
(*d*) the appropriation account and current accounts.

1. INTRODUCTION

In Chapter 1 we referred briefly to three main forms of organisation of business enterprise. These were the sole trader, the partnership and the limited company. Many of their accounting features are common for the reason that they encounter the same sorts of situations in the commercial world and have similar sets of objectives. For example, the objective of making a profit by buying wholesale and selling retail is an activity which might be carried on by any of the forms of enterprise mentioned. There are, however, important organisational and legal differences which have implications needing to find expression in the accounting process and these we shall look at specifically now. We shall start by a review of the accounting procedures relating to a partnership.

2. THE NATURE OF PARTNERSHIPS

The main thing which distinguishes a partnership from a sole trader is that more than one proprietor is involved. Several reasons exist leading people to associate together in order to operate a business. Some of the more obvious are listed below.

(*a*) *Capital*. It is easier to raise the amount of money required to finance the business if the contributions of several individuals are pooled rather than having to rely on the resources of one person.

(*b*) *Skills*. Different people possess different skills. A management "team" of several people will often, for this reason, be more effective than management by a single individual and a partnership is one way of bringing this about.

(*c*) *Succession*. A one-man business cannot continue beyond the death or retirement of its proprietor. By bringing in younger partners at an appropriate stage the continued life of a business can be provided for. A man might, for example, take his son into partnership.

(*d*) *Desire for companionship*. To be the only decision maker, responsible for the success or failure of the business, can be a lonely position. One motive for entering into partnership, then, is to obtain the opportunity of discussing problems with others who are similarly involved.

(*e*) *To reward and retain employees*. In a small business it is not uncommon for individuals to become, by virtue of their expertise and long experience, very important to its continued success. Where such a person is an employee the proprietor might decide to take him into partnership in order to guarantee his services on a long-term basis.

Legal implications

Although it is a relatively simple matter to enter into partnership there are certain legal implications of so doing which need to be understood. First of all the law will uphold the partnership agreement as it will any other form of contract. A partner aggrieved by the conduct of another partner may pursue that grievance through the court. The partnership agreement will set out such matters as the capital contributions of the partners, the profits to which each is entitled and the contribution which each will make to the running of the business. Ideally it will be in writing and drawn up by a solicitor as this will make misunderstandings less likely. It may, however, be a verbal agreement or may be inferred from the conduct over a period of the parties to it. Partnership is one of the small group of contracts regarded in law as being *iuberrimae fidei*, i.e. of the utmost good faith. This means that there is a responsibility on the parties to it to reveal all facts of which they are aware which might influence the decision of the other parties on the terms of the contract or on whether they will enter into it at all.

The law places a restriction on the number of partners. Normally there must not be more than twenty although this restriction is lifted for partnerships of solicitors, accountants and members of the Stock Exchange. For a banking business (rare for a partnership) the upper limit is ten partners.

Once the partnership has been formed the partners are jointly liable on the debts of the business up to the full extent of their private wealth. Each partner is regarded as being, within the field in which the business operates, agent of the others and may bind them in contracts with outsiders even when they did not know that the contract was being made. Each partner is entitled to a full say in the management of the business and no new partner may be admitted without the agreement of all existing partners. A partnership is automatically dissolved on the death of any one partner. The survivors may continue in business but if they do this will be regarded as the creation of a new partnership.

The law protects two sets of rights. One is the right of outsiders in their dealings with the business. They are covered by ordinary commercial law and the fact that partners have unlimited liability for all the debts of the business. The other is the rights of partners amongst themselves. These the law protects by upholding the partnership agreement and by providing in the Partnership Act 1890 certain general rules as well as guidance on how to deal with matters not covered in the partnership agreement.

3. DIVISION OF PROFIT

The first accounting problem we shall need to consider in the case of partnership is the matter of the division of profits. The problem is in two parts. The first is the matter of how the shares of profit are calculated. The second is the matter of how they are recorded in the accounts. The method used to determine the shares of profits is entirely up to the partners themselves and will (presumably) reflect their relative bargaining strengths and their ideas of what is fair in the circumstances. Where we have partners who have contributed equal amounts of capital to an enterprise, work equally hard in its management and bring to bear equal amounts of skill, we might expect that they will share profits equally. On the other hand if one of the partners has established the business himself originally as a sole trader and has a greater proportion of the total investment of capital he might well be regarded as a senior partner and allowed a higher share of the profits. Whatever is agreed concerning the sharing of profits will normally also apply to any losses which might be made.

Because of this freedom which partners have to decide how profits shall be shared amongst them we cannot, of course, lay down how it ought to be done. We can, however, look at a few examples of typical profit sharing agreements and the thinking which underlies them.

The simplest and probably the most common method is to divide profits in some simple proportion, not necessarily equal. A, B and C, for example, are in partnership sharing profits A, 1/2; B, 1/3; and C, 1/6. A profit of £12,000 would thus be shared as follows.

A	£6,000	(1/2 of £12,000)
B	4,000	(1/3 of £12,000)
C	2,000	(1/6 of £12,000)

£12,000

Here is another example. D, E, F and G share profits equally. A profit of £20,000 would be shared:

D	£5,000
E	5,000
F	5,000
G	5,000

£20,000

As can be seen, this simple method has sufficient flexibility to accommodate differences between the partners in terms of their inputs to a fairly considerable extent. There are, however, situations in which a rather more complex formula is needed to ensure fairness. Suppose that H, I and J are in partnership and H has provided the major part of the capital, as follows.

CAPITAL SUPPLIED:

H	£20,000
I	5,000
J	5,000

£30,000

On the other hand, I and J bring considerable experience and ability to the business and make, with H, an equal contribution to its commercial success. H might argue that he should receive two-thirds of the profit because he has put up two-thirds of the capital. I and J might argue that each should receive one-third because they make equal contributions to the managerial effort. A way round this is to recognise the different nature of the two inputs and to share out different segments of the profit in different ways.

Interest on capital
Let us suppose that 10 per cent per annum is regarded as a reasonable rate of return on capital (i.e. the interest which it might be expected to earn). The first portion of profit, equal to 10 per cent of the capital invested, could then be shared in proportion to

capital and then whatever is left, being attributable to management effort, could be shared equally. This might be worded in the partnership agreement as follows. "Partners shall be entitled to receive out of profits 10 per cent per annum interest on their capitals and then the balance shall be divided equally". A very important point needs to be made here. The agreement is using the word "interest" as a convenient term to describe remuneration attributable to the capital investment. It is, however, of quite different nature from true interest as, for example, that paid to a bank. Interest then is a contractual payment given in return for the loan of funds. It is a business expense and will be shown as such in the profit and loss account. Since a business exists to earn profits on behalf of its proprietors any amounts which go to them are portions of the profit and not expenses to be charged in calculating it.

We will now see how H, I and J would share a profit of £9,000.

	H	I	J	Total
Interest				
(10 per cent of capital)	£2,000	£500	£500	£3,000
Balance of profit	2,000	2,000	2,000	6,000
	£4,000	£2,500	£2,500	£9,000

It will be obvious that there is no single simple ratio for profit sharing which would, at all levels of profit, give the same result as this formula.

Salaries

Sometimes, in seeking fairness, partners will adopt a formula which attempts to distinguish three separate inputs (which may each be in a different proportion). These are capital and managerial effort as before and then actual labour supplied to the business, i.e. work not of a managerial nature which could equally well have been done by a paid employee. Here is a case to illustrate this. K and L are in partnership operating a retail greengrocers. K has put up £20,000 in capital and L £10,000. Each contributes equally to the management of the business in the sense of taking joint decisions on policy and long-term operations. L works full time in the shop working behind the counter with employed assistants. K works only half time spending the afternoons only in delivering customers' orders. The partners' work, if done by paid employees, would cost the business £2,000 for K's work and £6,000 for L's work in each year. This can be allowed for by sharing one part of the profit as if it were salary. This part may, again, be described as salary in the partnership agreement but, as in the case of interest, it is not an expense of the business but an application of some of the profit. Thus the partnership agreement might read: "Partners shall receive salaries of K £2,000 and L £6,000 per annum; interest shall be allowed on capital at the rate of 10 per cent per annum and the balance shall then be divided equally." Under this agreement a profit of £20,000 would be shared as follows.

	K	L	Total
Salaries	£2,000	£6,000	£8,000
Interest	2,000	1,000	3,000
Balance of profit	4,500	4,500	9,000
	£8,500	£11,500	£20,000

It should be noted that exactly the same result could have been achieved if, in the agreement, L had been allowed a "salary" of only £4,000 and K none. Partnership agreements will therefore sometimes provide for differential salaries in this fashion, some partners getting no salary and some apparently rather small ones.

Division in the absence of agreement
Having considered the ways in which profits might typically be shared, there is one more case we need to look at. Although free to agree to share profits however they like, partners may sometimes omit to agree on this matter. This might occur if the business was started off in enthusiastic haste and no underlying written agreement was drawn up. If agreement cannot subsequently be reached the Partnership Act 1890 provides an answer. It states that in the absence of any agreement between the partners on this matter then the profits of a partnership are to be shared equally. No interest is to be allowed on capital but interest at the rate of five per cent per annum is to be allowed on any advances made by individual partners to the business over and above their capital contribution. Thus, had K and L in our example above, omitted or failed to agree on the matter of how they wanted to share their profits they would have received £10,000 each.

4. THE APPROPRIATION ACCOUNT

In the final accounts of the business the sharing of profits by the partners may conveniently be shown in the form of an appropriation account. This is a section attached to the profit and loss account to show how the net profit, once ascertained, is disposed of. Thus, for K and L:

APPROPRIATION ACCOUNT FOR THE YEAR ENDED . . .

Net profit			£20,000
Divided between partners:			
Salaries:			
K	£6,000		
L	2,000		
		£8,000	
Interest:			
K	2,000		
L	1,000		
		3,000	
Balance of profit:			
K	4,500		
L	4,500		
		9,000	
			£20,000

5. THE PARTNERSHIP BALANCE SHEET

The sharing of profit is one problem for partnerships and we have now considered this in some detail. Another is how the partners' interest in the business should be shown on the balance sheet. This, as one might expect, requires a little more detail than would be required for a sole trader. In that case the proprietor's interest is usually shown by a single capital account which contains both the original amount subscribed and any profits subsequently earned to the extent that he has not withdrawn them. In the case of a partnership certain developments from this simple principle are desirable.

Firstly, a distinction is made between one partner and another so that their separate interests can be represented. Secondly, a distinction is made between the capital originally subscribed by the partners and the amounts attributable to them as their shares of the profits. The total proprietorship interest is thus represented by two accounts for each partner. His capital account shows the amount of his permanent investment in the business and his current account shows any profit allocated to him which has not yet been withdrawn. The reason for this distinction between capital and profit is that a partner is not normally permitted under the terms of the partnership agreement to withdraw capital without the approval of the other partners. If he did so this might prejudice the operations of the business to the detriment of the others as well as himself. Income, on the other hand, is normally regarded as freely available for withdrawal.

Current accounts

Examples of the sole trader and partnership forms of organisation close together will make this point clear. A certain business has an originally subscribed capital of £50,000. In the first year of trading it made a profit of £15,000 and drawings (by the proprietor(s)) were £10,000. If the business were operated by a sole trader the following would appear in his balance sheet at the year end.

Capital		£55,000*
*Opening capital	£50,000	
Add profit	15,000	
	65,000	
Less drawings	10,000	
Closing capital	£55,000	

Suppose now that the business is operated by Y and Z in partnership. They share profits equally and Y's drawings totalled £6,000, whilst Z's were £4,000. The current account balances are calculated as follows.

	X	Y
Share of profit	£7,500	£7,500
Less drawings	6,000	4,000
	£1,500	£3,500

In the balance sheet the following would appear.

Capital accounts		
Y	£25,000	
Z	25,000	
		£50,000
Current accounts		
Y	1,500	
Z	3,500	
		5,000
		£55,000

It is, of course, possible that occasionally a partner will be in a position of having drawn more out of the business than his share of the profits will support. Our system of current accounts allows for that. The partner's current account will, in these circumstances, show a debit balance—a clear signal of what has happened. The partner concerned will be expected to restore the position either by repaying the overdrawn amount or, more probably, by moderating future drawings and allowing profits to build up. On the balance sheet an overdrawn (debit balance) current account will normally be shown deducted from the partner's capital account thus signifying that there has, in effect, been a partial withdrawal of capital.

6. EXAMPLE

Here, now, is an example illustrating some of the points made so far. K, L and M are in partnership having subscribed capitals as follows: K £25,000; L £50,000; and M £25,000. Their agreement provides for 15 per cent interest to be allowed on capital before any balance of profit is shared equally. Current account balances on 1st January in the financial year were: K £250 CR; L Nil; and M £500 DR. A profit and loss account for the year ended 31st December, drawn up by the partners, reported a profit of £15,000 but this was after charging as an expense £500 per month drawn by each partner and described in the accounts as "salaries". In addition to these amounts there have been further drawings debited to partners' current accounts as follows: K £3,200; L £6,800; and M £3,200. Show the appropriation account and the partners' current accounts to record these matters.

The first point to be dealt with is the calculation of the profit. A total of £18,000 (£500 × 3 × 12) has been charged as an expense to the profit and loss account which should have been treated as drawings. The correct net profit is therefore £15,000 + £18,000 = £33,000. The appropriation account is thus as follows.

K, L AND M

APPROPRIATION ACCOUNT FOR THE YEAR ENDED 31ST DECEMBER . . .

Net profit		£33,000
Interest on capital		
K	£3,750	
L	7,500	
M	3,750	
	———	£15,000

Share of balance of profit

K		6,000
L		6,000
M		6,000
		———
	18,000	
	———	
	£33,000	

The current accounts appear in columnar form below.

	K	L	M		K	L	M
Balance			£500	Interest	£3,750	£7,500	£3,750
Drawings	£9,200	£12,800	9,200	Profit	6,000	6,000	6,000
Balance	800	700	50	Balance	250		
	———	———	———		———	———	———
	£10,000	£13,500	£9,750		£10,000	£13,500	£9,750
					———	———	———
				Balance	£800	£700	£50

SUMMARY

1. The partnership is a common form of business enterprise. The motives which lead business people to go into partnership are various but the most important are probably:

(*a*) capital—it enables the resources of more than one individual to be pooled;

(*b*) skills—it enables a number of different skills to be brought together, to mutual benefit;

(*c*) succession—it makes possible an extension of the life of the business beyond the death or retirement of its original proprietor;

(*d*) desire for companionship—it gives the opportunity to discuss problems with people who are as greatly involved with them; and

(*e*) to reward and retain employees—it is a useful way of giving key people a personal stake in the business.

2. Every partnership is founded on a partnership agreement even if this is merely an agreement evidenced by the conduct of the parties to it. Ideally, such an important agreement should be a written document drafted in legal form. Partnership is a contract *iuberrimae fidei*, i.e. of the utmost good faith. This means that the parties to it must disclose all material facts.

3. The main statute relating to partnerships is the Partnership Act 1890. Important legal matters are the restrictions, in most cases, on the number of partners, the partners' rights with respect to other partners and the rights of outsiders with respect to the partnership.

4. Partners may divide profits in any way they choose. Most agreements encountered in practice allow for a division of profits

on the basis of some ratio. An agreement may allow for "interest" on capital and/or partners' "salaries" to give recognition to differences between partners before the ratio is applied to the residue.

5. An appropriation account is used to show how the net profit, determined by the profit and loss account, is divided amongst the partners. A partner's share of the profit is then credited to a current account in his name thus maintaining a separation between this and the amount which he has subscribed as capital. Drawings are debited to current accounts.

6. The proprietorship section of a partnership balance sheet will show partners' interests separately. The amounts originally subscribed as capital will be shown in capital accounts and any undrawn profits will be shown as balances on current accounts. An occasional debit balance on a partner's current account (which should be only temporary) should be deducted from his capital account indicating that some capital has been withdrawn.

QUESTIONS

1. Finger, Thumb and Toe are in partnership. Their agreement provides that Finger and Thumb should receive salaries of £3,000 and £2,000 respectively and that residual profit should then be divided equally. In 19— the business earned a profit of £18,000 after charging partners' salaries, which had been paid in monthly instalments. Partners' drawings, not charged in the profit and loss account, were: Finger £5,800; Thumb £5,500; and Toe £5,750. At the beginning of the year current account balances had been: Finger £250 DR; Thumb £300 DR; and Toe £100 CR. Show the appropriation account and the partners' Current Accounts for 19—.

2. Left and Right, who share profits equally, have produced a balance sheet as shown below.

Capital			*Fixed assets*		
Left		£20,000	Building		£10,000
Right		20,000	Fixtures and		
Current			fittings		18,290
Left	£152				———
Right	289				28,290
	———	441			
		———			
		40,441			
Current liabilities			*Current assets*		
Creditors	£14,221		Stock	£12,168	
Bank overdraft	2,217		Debtors	16,421	
	———	16,438		———	28,589
		———			———
		£56,879			£56,879
		═══			═══

An audit reveals the following.

(a) The building had been professionally revalued at £20,000. The partners wish to incorporate this value in the balance sheet but have not yet done so.

(b) No depreciation had been provided in respect of fixtures and fittings. The amount should be £3,658.

(c) Partners' drawings of £8,200 for Left and £7,600 for Right had been charged (as "wages") in the profit and loss account.

(d) The bank had charged interest on the overdraft of £264 but this had not been recorded in the books.

(e) Stock worth £4,000 had been omitted from the year end valuation.

(f) Left had received a fee of £800 for work done on behalf of the partnership. He had inadvertently paid this into his personal bank account and it had not been recorded in the books of the partnership.

Show how each of these errors should be correct and draw up a revised balance sheet to show the position when this has been done.

3. Jekyll and Hyde have set up in business as greengrocers and have learnt that the following legal principles apply to them. They believe them to be unreasonable and you are asked to provide a justification in each case.

(a) As the business expands they plan to bring in new partners. The total number may not, however, exceed twenty.

(b) If the business gets into financial difficulties and loses all of its capital the partners may have to produce extra funds from their private resources to meet its debts.

(c) If one partner enters into an unwise contract on behalf of the business the other partner is equally bound by it even though he was not consulted and knows nothing of it.

(d) If the partners omit to agree on a profit sharing formula they will have to share profits equally.

4. Mr Lonewolf wants to expand his business and requires extra capital. He is considering the alternatives of taking a partner and of borrowing from the bank. Set out the respective advantages and disadvantages in a way which will help him to decide what to do.

5. Having operated as a sole trader for many years, Head has recently entered into partnership with Shoulders. In order to simplify record keeping he has decided to maintain a single capital account as he has done in the past. To this will be credited all contributions to capital made by the partners and the total profits of the business. All partners' drawings will be debited to the account. Why is this degree of simplification unwise?

CHAPTER 9

Parternership II

OBJECTIVES

In this chapter we shall deal with the following important topics:

(*a*) goodwill;
(*b*) admission of new partner;
(*c*) change in profit sharing ratio;
(*d*) dissolution of partnership.

1. INTRODUCTION

We have learnt enough about accounting valuation and its limitations to appreciate that a balance sheet is not a particularly good
guide to the overall value of a business. This derives from a
number of factors. One is the concept of conservatism which
ensures that we shall tend, if anything, to undervalue assets (and,
perhaps, to overstate liabilities). Another is the cost principle
which has the effect not only that assets will be valued at cost but
also that assets acquired otherwise than by purchase will not be
recorded at all. Finally, the value of a business, like that of
anything else, depends in the last resort on the market in which it is
traded and on the bargaining strengths of the parties to the
transaction.

2. GOODWILL

A very important element in business valuation, which creates a
special kind of accounting problem, is that known as goodwill. As
it has particular relevance to some important matters relating to
partnership, this is a convenient point at which to discuss it. It
should be noted, however, that the concept has a more general
importance than that.

When a business person collects together a set of assets and uses
management skill in order to blend them together into a profitable
business, he thereby creates an entity which is more valuable than
the sum of its parts. This is not a phenomenon peculiar to a
business. An artist can create a painting which is more than just a
collection of paint, canvas and a frame and a craftsman can

construct furniture which is not just wood, varnish and glue. In the case of a business this factor which makes it, as a going concern, more valuable than the collection of assets making it up is known as goodwill. Broadly speaking goodwill can be equated with the reputation and momentum which a business acquires from successful operations. It is valuable in that its existence obviously leads to higher profits than would otherwise be earned.

In many respects, therfore, goodwill can be regarded as a business asset and a case can be made for including it in the balance sheet. There are, however, considerable objections to this. One is that goodwill is not a separable, physically identifiable, asset like a building or a motor vehicle and it cannot, therefore, usually be sold except along with a substantial part of the other business assets. Another is that it is not normally purchased (an exception to this will be referred to presently) but is generated spontaneously as the business develops. This rules out a valuation at cost. A third is that the value of goodwill is a volatile quality. It can be lost by a single mistake, or, on the other hand, boosted by a single piece of good fortune. To be meaningful in a balance sheet it would thus need to be revalued frequently. Finally no satisfactory technique exists whereby goodwill can be valued in any objective way and so any valuation which was used would amount to no more than an expression of opinion.

There are no particular disadvantages arising from omitting goodwill from a balance sheet and so this is what is generally done. All that needs to be remembered is that, should the business be sold, the purchaser would be expected to make some payment for goodwill and this amount would be based on agreement after negotiations between himself and the seller. When goodwill is realised in this way conventional accounting can deal with it. It results in a profit on the sale of the business and accrues to the proprietor as do all profits.

One exception to the general practice that goodwill is omitted from the balance sheet is the case of purchased goodwill. This has a cost and may be recorded at that cost. Here is an example. A wishes to purchase an existing business currently operated by B. B's balance sheet appears below.

Capital	£30,000	Fixed assets	£20,000
		Net current assets	10,000
	£30,000		£30,000

A agrees to pay £50,000 for the business which consists of the balance sheet values for the tangible assets (i.e. those appearing in

B's balance sheet) plus £20,000 for goodwill. A has invested
£50,000 in his new (for him) enterprise and might draw up his
balance sheet as follows

Capital	£50,000	Fixed assets	£20,000
		Net current assets	10,000
		Goodwill	20,000
	£50,000		£50,000

The figure for goodwill may remain indefinitely on A's balance
sheet. Many would take the view, however, that it is better
removed and it is quite common for purchased goodwill to be
written off against profits (like depreciation) over a period of time.

3. ADMISSION OF A NEW PARTNER

Below there appears the balance sheet of Cat and Dog, who have
been in partnership for many years, sharing profits equally.

Capitals:			
Cat	£10,000	Fixed assets	£14,000
Dog	10,000	Net current assets	6,000
	£20,000		£20,000

Capital is required for expansion and it is proposed to bring into
the partnership Fish who will thereafter share in profits equally
with the existing partners, i.e. each will receive one third.

The admission of Fish amounts to a sale to him of part of the
business and it will therefore be necessary to agree a valuation, as
it would be for any sale. We will suppose that it is agreed amongst
the parties that the business as a whole is worth £29,000, the
difference between this figure and its book value (£9,000) being
attributed to goodwill. The goodwill has not previously been
recorded in the books and it is not intended to record it in the
future.

This goodwill may be seen as an unrealised and therefore
unrecorded profit in which Fish will be entitled to a one third share
should it be realised in the future. In order to be fair to the existing
partners he must therefore compensate them by making a payment
into the business equal to his share in the undisclosed goodwill.
This amount is £3,000 (£9,000 ÷ 3) and may be described as a
premium paid by Fish for goodwill. It will be credited in equal
shares to Cat and Dog. In addition to this amount Fish will pay in
an amount for his own capital. This amount will depend on the

business's need for cash and on the agreement reached by the parties but we will suppose it to be £11,500, which places Fish on the same basis as Cat and Dog. The total amount paid in by Fish will be £14,500 of which £11,500 will be credited to his own capital account and £1,500 each to the capital accounts of Cat and Dog.

The balance sheet after Fish's admission is:

Capitals			
Cat	£11,500	Fixed assets	£14,000
Dog	11,500	Net current assets[1]	20,500
Fish	11,500		
	£34,500		£34,500

(1) This includes the cash paid in by Fish

Here is another example using a more realistically detailed balance sheet. Line, Square and Circle are in partnership sharing equally in profits. They require £100,000 of extra capital for expansion and propose to obtain this from Triangle, who will be admitted to the partnership. The balance sheet of the existing business is as shown below.

Capital accounts			Fixed assets		
Line		£52,000	Building		£90,000
Square		48,000	Equipment		65,248
Circle		45,000			
					155,248
		145,000			
Current accounts			Current assets		
Line	£200		Stock	£31,483	
Square	300		Debtors	15,446	
	——	500	Cash	5,123	
		145,500			52,052
Current liabilities		61,800			
		£207,300			£207,300

It is agreed that Triangle will be admitted to the partnership on the following terms.

(a) The building will be revalued at £150,000 and this value incorporated in the balance sheet.

(b) Goodwill will be valued at £120,000 but this will not appear in the balance sheet.

(c) Triangle will pay £100,000, inclusive of the premium for goodwill and his capital contribution, and will participate in profits to the extent of one quarter (as will each of the existing partners).

The premium for goodwill is £120,000 ÷ 4 = £30,000.

The following entries are required in the books.

To revalue the building:

DR Building	£60,000	CR	Line	£20,000
			Square	20,000
			Circle	20,000

To record the cash paid in by Triangle:

DR Cash	£100,000	CR	Line[1]	£10,000
			Square[1]	10,000
			Circle[1]	10,000
			Triangle	70,000

(1) Each gets one third of the premium.

Two important points should be noted. One is that the £60,000 increase in the value of the building does not enter into the calculation of premium because it is recorded on the balance sheet. If unrecorded it would be treated exactly like goodwill. The other is that the existence of current account balances for Line and Square presents no problems and these remain undisturbed. The adjustment made on the admission of Triangle is dealt with through the capital accounts.

The balance sheet after Triangle's admission appears as follows.

Capital accounts			Fixed assets		
Line			Building		£150,000
Square		£82,000	Equipment		65,248
Circle		78,000			
Triangle		75,000			215,248
		70,000			
		———			
		305,000			
Current accounts			Current assets		
Line	£200		Stock	£31,483	
Square	300		Debtors	15,446	
	———	500	Cash	105,123	
		———		———	152,052
		305,500			
Current liabilities		61,800			
		———			———
		£367,300			£367,300
		══════			══════

4. CHANGES IN THE PROFIT SHARING RATIO

Sometimes partners will decide to make a change in the way in which they share profits. This may follow some change in their circumstances. One of the partners might, for example, be approaching retirement and decide to give less time to the business. It might, therefore, be appropriate for him to take a reduced share of the profits in the future.

A change in the profit sharing ratio is really a special case of the admission of a new partner. It is effectively a sale of part of the business by partner(s) taking a reduced share of the profit in the future to partner(s) taking an increased share. A valuation of goodwill must be agreed for the purpose and a calculation made of the amounts involved for each partner. No cash payment will normally be made, the whole matter being effected by transfers between capital accounts.

Here is an example. A, B, C and D have always shared profits equally. They have now agreed that henceforth the shares will be: A 0.4; B 0.3; C 0.2; and D 0.1. Goodwill is to be valued for the purpose of the change at £30,000 but is not to appear in the balance sheet. The proportions acquired or given up by partners can be calculated in a simple table.

	Old share	New share	Change (+ acquired, − given up)	Entry in capital account
A	¼ (= 5/20)	0.4 (= 8/20)	+ 3/20	DR £4,500
B	¼ (= 5/20)	0.3 (= 6/20)	+ 1/20	DR £1,500
C	¼ (= 5/20)	0.2 (= 4/20)	− 1/20	CR £1,500
D	¼ (= 5/20)	0.1 (= 2/20)	− 3/20	CR £4,500
			Net nil	Balanced

A partner giving up a share is compensated by a credit to his capital account. A partner gaining a share is charged by a debit to his capital account. The fractions are applied to the total figure for goodwill.

5. DISSOLUTION OF A PARTNERSHIP

Partners may sometimes decide that they wish to bring their business association to an end and sell off the partnership business. From an accounting point of view this is a straightforward procedure. After all assets have been sold and all liabilities settled the available cash will be used to pay out the partners. In the unlikely event that all balance sheet values represent market values the residual cash will exactly equal the combined total of the capital accounts. Otherwise there will be either a profit or a loss on dissolution which will be divided amongst partners in their normal profit sharing proportions (disregarding any "salary" or "interest", which would already have been dealt with in apportioning trading profit).

On a dissolution assets are often sold in lots which do not relate to balance sheet headings. Thus the buildings together with goodwill and some of the equipment might be sold to one purchaser, more equipment and some stock might be sold to another and yet more stock might be sold to a third. For this reason it is convenient to open a Realisation Account and transfer to it all assets except for cash and debtors. These are omitted because they require detailed attention during the realisation. Debtors will be collected individually and the cash account will be required to record the progress of the dissolution.

An example will make the process clear. After some years of trading Cat, Dog and Fish (referred to above) decided to dissolve their partnership and dispose of the business. At that date their detailed balance sheet was as follows.

Capital			*Fixed assets*		
Cat		£11,500	Building		£20,000
Dog		11,500	Fixtures and fittings		10,399
Fish		11,500			
					30,399
		34,500			
			Current assets		
Creditors		12,620	Stock	£8,293	
			Debtors	6,848	
			Cash	1,580	
					16,721
		£47,120			£47,120

The following transactions took place in connection with the dissolution.

(*a*) Some of the fixtures and fittings were sold for £2,800.

(*b*) £3,600 was paid to creditors.

(*c*) £2,932 was received from debtors.

(*d*) Some more fixtures and fittings, some stock and the goodwill were sold for £16,250.

(*e*) £4,500 was paid to creditors.

(*f*) £1,769 was received from debtors.

(*g*) £4,520 was paid to creditors.

(*h*) £2,091 was received from debtors. All other debts were bad.

(*i*) The building was sold for £25,000.

(*j*) The rest of the stock was sold for £1,201.

(*k*) The expenses of the dissolution were £500.

The accounts recording these matters appear below.

REALISATION ACCOUNT

Building		£20,000	Cash	£2,800
Fixtures and fittings		10,399	Cash	16,250
Stock		8,293	Cash	25,000
Bad debts		56	Cash	1,201
Expenses of dissolution		500		
Profit on realisation				
Cat	£2,001			
Digs	2,001			
Fish	2,001			
		6,003		
		£45,251		£45,251

CAPITALS

	Cat	Dog	Fish		Cat	Dog	Fish
Cash	£13,501	£13,501	£13,501	Balances	£11,500	£11,500	£11,500
				Profit on realisation	2,001	2,001	2,001
	£13,501	£13,501	£13,501		£13,501	£13,501	£13,501

CASH

Balance	£1,580	Creditors	£3,600
Fixtures and fittings	2,800	Creditors	4,500
Debtors	2,932	Creditors	4,520
Fixtures, goodwill, etc.	16,250	Expenses	500
Debtors	1,769	Cat	13,501
Debtors	2,091	Dog	13,501
Building	25,000	Fish	13,501
Stock	1,201		
	£53,623		£53,623

The rule in Garner *v.* Murray

In the example in the previous section, largely because of the existence of goodwill, the partnership business was sold at a profit and the partners were able to draw out more than the original balances on their capital accounts. Occasionally, however, a partnership business will be dissolved in less happy circumstances, perhaps after it has been trading at a loss. There may then be a further loss on realisation particularly if this had to take place in a hurry to satisfy pressing creditors.

Ordinarily this circumstance presents no particular accounting problem. The loss on realisation is determined by means of a realisation account and is debited to the partners' capital accounts in their profit sharing ratio. They are then paid out at this reduced level. If the loss is so great that the capital accounts go into debit then the partners must pay in these amounts so that the cash available becomes enough to meet the claims of creditors. If they lack the resources to meet this obligation then they become personally bankrupt and the normal legal processes of that condition follow.

There is one special case which must be referred to where a special rule applies. The case is that where one (or more) partner(s) has a debit balance on his capital account following a dissolution which he (or they) is unable to meet because of personal insolvency. Other partners are solvent and, therefore, they have to meet not only their share of the loss on realisation but also a share of the loss due to the default of the partner(s) in debit. The rule is known as the rule in Garner *v*. Murray as it arises from the judgment following a celebrated case of that name. It is that a loss occasioned by a partner's inability to repay a debit balance on his capital account shall be borne by the remaining partners in proportion to their original *capital* balances and *not* in the normal profit sharing ratio.

Here is an example. X, Y and Z have been in partnership for some time sharing profits equally. There capital account balances are: X £20,000; Y £30,000; and Z £10,000. The business is in financial difficulty and the bank is pressing for repayment of a substantial loan. Accordingly the partnership is dissolved and the assets realised. There is a loss on realisation of £45,000.

The first step is to share this in the profit sharing ratio, i.e. equally. Thus:

	X	Y	Z
Capital balance	£20,000	£30,000	£10,000
Less Loss on realisation	15,000	15,000	15,000
New balance	£5,000	£15,000	(£5,000)

The figure in brackets is a debit balance. If he is able to do so, Z must now pay in £5,000 which will leave cash in the business sufficient to pay the bank and other creditors. If Z is unable to pay, and only in this case, his debit balance must be borne by the remaining partners following the rule in Garner *v*. Murray, i.e. in proportion to their original capital balances. This proportion is X 2/5 and Y 3/5. Thus:

	X	Y	Z
Balances as above	£5,000	£15,000	(£5,000)
Allocation of Z's debit balance	(2,000)	(3,000)	5,000
Amount receivable on closure of books	£3,000	£12,000	Nil

Piecemeal realisation

The realisation of a business may be a fairly lengthy process and hardship may be caused to the partners if the distribution of the proceeds is held up until all is complete. In the case of a piecemeal realisation, i.e. where assets are sold a few at a time, interim distributions are usual. Two points need to be observed in this connection. One is that all creditors of the business must be paid in full before any amounts at all can be paid to the partners. The other is that when payments are made to the partners care must be taken to ensure that no partner receives any amount which, in future, he might be required to repay. If he does, and later proves insolvent, this will unnecessarily increase the burden of his default on the remaining partners.

It is generally not correct to distribute available cash either in the partners' profit sharing ratio or in proportion to the balances on their capital accounts. On each occasion of a distribution partners' entitlement must be calculated on the most pessimistic possible assumptions. These are that no further cash will be forthcoming from the realisation and that no partner will be able to meet a debit balance arising on his capital account. The example below illustrates the procedure.

Hook, Line and Sinker, who share profits $2:1:1$, have decided to end their partnership and realise the assets of the business. The balance sheet immediately before this occurred appeared as follows.

Capital accounts		Fixed assets		
Hook	£20,000	Building		£50,000
Line	20,000	Plant and machinery		18,770
Sinker	40,000			
	80,000			68,770
		Current assets		
Bank loan	28,616	Stock	£26,948	
Creditors	12,448	Debtors	25,246	
		Cash	100	
				52,294
	£121,064			£121,064

The amounts received, in chronological order, were:
 (a) £10,100 received from debtors;
 (b) £12,300 received from sales of stock;
 (c) £15,000 received for some of the plant and machinery;
 (d) £62,000 received from the sale of the building;
 (e) £14,932 received from debtors, the rest being bad;
 (f) £6,000 received from the sale of the rest of the stock; and
 (g) £5,100 received from the sale of the rest of the plant and machinery.
Note that:
 (a) the bank loan was secured on the building and was repaid out of the proceeds of the sale of the building;
 (b) apart from a retention of £1,000 to cover the expenses of the dissolution, all available cash was distributed to the partners as soon as possible; and
 (c) the expenses actually amounted to £772 and were paid when all other transactions had been completed.
 The cash received may be analysed in a tabulation as below.

	Cash received	Creditors	Bank	Retained expenses	Partners
Balance	£100	£100			
(a)	10,100	10,100			
(b)	12,300	2,248		£1,000	£9,052
(c)	15,000				15,000
(d)	62,000		£28,616		33,384
(e)	14,932				14,932
(f)	6,000				6,000
(g)	5,100				5,100
Expenses				(228)	228
	£125,532	£12,448	£28,616	£772	£83,696

We can now calculate the distribution of each amount of cash due to the partners.

1st distribution	Hook	Line	Sinker
Capital	£20,000	£20,000	£40,000
"Loss" at time of 1st distribution (£80,000 − £9,052)	35,474	17,737	17,737
New balance	(15,474)	2,263	22,263
G. v. M (but Line's share restricted to his present balance)	15,474	(2.263)	13,211
Amount payable	Nil	Nil	£9,052

2nd distribution	Hook	Line	Sinker
Capital	£20,000	£20,000	£40,000
"Loss" at time of 2nd distribution (£80,000 − £24,052)	27,974	13,987	13,987
New balance	(7,974)	6,013	26,013
G. v. M	7,974	(2,658)	(5,316)
Amounts payable	Nil	3,355	20,697
Already paid	Nil	Nil	9,052
Payable now	Nil	£3,355	£11,645

3rd distribution	Hook	Line	Sinker
Capital	£20,000	£20,000	£40,000
"Loss" at time of 3rd distribution (£80,000 − £57,436)	11,282	5,641	5,641
New balance (amounts payable)	8,718	14,359	34,359
Already paid	Nil	3,355	20,697
Payable now	£8,718	£11,004	£13,662

4th distribution	Hook	Line	Sinker
Capital	£20,000	£20,000	£40,000
"Loss" at time of 4th distribution (£80,000 − £72,368)	3,816	1,908	1,908
New balance (amounts payable)	16,184	18,092	38,092
Already paid	8,718	14,359	34,359
Payable now	£7,466	£3,733	£3,733

Note that this last distribution is in the profit sharing ratio. When this occurs all subsequent payments will be in the same ratio so that further calculations are unnecessary.

	Hook	Line	Sinker
5th distribution	£3,000	£1,500	£1,500
6th distribution	£2,550	£1,275	£1,275
7th distribution	£114	£57	£57

The book-keeping records appear as follows.

REALISATION ACCOUNT

Building		£50,000	Cash	£12,300
Plant and machinery		18,770	Cash	15,000
Stock		26,948	Cash	62,000
Bad debts		214	Cash	6,000
Expenses		772	Cash	5,100
Profit and realisation:				
Hook	£1,848			
Line	924			
Sinker	924			
	—	3,696		
		£100,400		£100,400

CASH

Balance	£100	Creditors	£100
Debtors	10,100	Creditors	10,100
Realisation:		Creditors	2,248
Stock	12,300	Sinker	9,052
Plant	15,000	Line	3,355
Building	62,000	Sinker	11,645
Debtors	14,932	Bank	28,616
Realisation:		Hook	8,718
Stock	6,000	Line	11,004
Plant	5,100	Sinker	13,662
		Hook	7,466
		Line	3,733
		Sinker	3,733
		Hook	3,000
		Line	1,500
		Sinker	1,500
		Hook	2,550
		Line	1,275
		Sinker	1,275
		Expenses	772
		Hook	114
		Line	57
		Sinker	57
	£125,532		£125,532

CAPITAL

	Hook	Line	Sinker		Hook	Line	Sinker
Cash			£9,052	Balance	£20,000	£20,000	£40,000
Cash		£3,355	11,645	Profit on			
Cash	£8,718	11,004	13,662	realisation	1,848	924	924
Cash	7,466	3,733	3,733				
Cash	3,000	1,500	1,500				
Cash	2,550	1,275	1,275				
Cash	114	57	57				
	£21,848	£20,924	£40,924		£21,848	£20,924	£40,924

SUMMARY

1. All successful businesses generate goodwill which both arises from and maintains that success. It is rarely valued on a balance sheet unless actually purchased. Even then the cost will usually be written off as soon as possible.

2. It is necessary to value goodwill when a business, or a part of it, changes hands. This includes, in the case of a partnership, the admission of a new partner and a change in the profit sharing ratio of partners, as well as a complete disposal of the business.

3. Even when valued for such a purpose goodwill is normally omitted from the balance sheet. Compensating entries are made in their capital accounts to preserve equity amongst the partners.

4. When a partnership is dissolved there may be a profit or loss arising from the realisation of the assets. This profit or loss will be shared amongst partners in their normal profit sharing ratio. "Salaries" or "interest on capital" are ignored in this process as they will have been dealt with in dividing trading profits.

5. Any loss occasioned by the default of an insolvent partner who has a debit balance on his capital account is borne by the remaining partners in proportion to their original capital balances. This is known as the rule in Garner v. Murray.

6. Where it is desired to make interim payments to partners during a piecemeal realisation of assets care must be taken to ensure that no partner is paid an amount which he may subsequently have to refund.

QUESTIONS

1. Tom and Dick have been in business as partners for some years, sharing profits equally. At 31st December 19–1 their balance sheet appeared as below.

Capital accounts			Fixed assets		
Tom		£50,000	Building		£50,000
Dick		50,000	Plant and Machinery		34,864
			Furniture		14,630
		100,000			99,494
Current accounts			Current assets		
Tom	£180		Stock	£31,842	
Dick	220		Debtors	22,196	
	——	400	Cash	12,289	
				——	66,327
		100,400			
Bank loan		50,000			
Current liabilities					
Creditors		15,421			
		£165,821			£165,821

More capital is required and it is agreed that Harry will be admitted to the partnership as from 1st January 19–2. He will pay into the business £100,000 and will be entitled to share in the profits equally with Tom and Dick. It was agreed that:

(*a*) the building was now worth £75,000;

(*b*) the plant and machinery was worth £40,000; and

(*c*) the furniture was worth £10,000.

These new valuations were to be incorporated into the balance sheet. It was further agreed that goodwill was worth £75,000 but that this should not appear in the balance sheet.

After Harry's admission his money was used to pay off the bank loan and to purchase new plant and machinery for £25,000 and new furniture for £10,000. A further £25,000 was spent on extending the building and Tom and Dick withdrew the balances on their current accounts. Draw up the balance sheet of the partnership as it would appear after all these transactions had been carried out.

2. In the circumstances of the previous question an alternative plan, previously discussed, was that Dick should introduce an extra £50,000 in cash into the business. Had this plan been put into effect there would have been no revaluations of fixed assets, nor would the bank loan have been paid off. The further investments in fixed assets would, however, have taken place. In recognition of his increased contribution the profit sharing ratio would have been adjusted so that Dick took two thirds of the profits. The two had agreed a figure of £60,000 for goodwill and an adjustment, based on this figure, would have been made in the capital accounts. Show the balance sheet as it would have appeared had this plan been put into effect.

3. Immediately before dissolving their partnership Lion, Tiger and Panther each had a balance of £25,000 to the credit of his

capital account. Under the partnership agreement Lion took half of all profits, Tiger took one third and Panther took one sixth. The proceeds of the realisation of the assets amounted to only £20,000 after creditors had been paid in full and expenses met. Show how this amount would be shared amongst the partners on the alternative assumptions that (*a*) all are personally solvent and (*b*) all are insolvent.

4. Thrush, Sparrow, Starling and Finch are in partnership sharing profits equally. Their balance sheet at 31st December 19–, when they ceased trading, was as follows.

Capital accounts			Fixed assets		
Thrush		£200,000	Building		£150,000
Sparrow		150,000	Equipment		98,264
Starling		50,000	Vehicles		64,222
Finch		50,000			——
		——			312,486
		450,000			
Current accounts			Current assets		
Thrush	£5,463		Stock	£114,289	
Sparrow	8,218		Debtors	89,927	
Starling	4,687		Cash	7,519	
Finch	3,990			——	211,735
	——	22,358			
Creditors		51,863			
		——			——
		£524,221			£524,221

The assets of the business were realised and the following amounts, given in chronological order, received.

(*a*) Debtors paid £22,168.
(*b*) Some of the stock was sold for £50,000.
(*c*) Some of the vehicles were sold for £25,800.
(*d*) Debtors paid £25,663.
(*e*) The rest of the vehicles were sold for £12,690.
(*f*) Debtors paid £22,500.
(*g*) The building, equipment and goodwill were sold for £300,000.
(*h*) Debtors paid £18,960. The rest of the debts were bad.
(*i*) The rest of the stock was sold for £50,000.

Apart from a retention for expenses, estimated at £2,000, all cash was paid to the partners as available. The expenses, paid when the realisation, was complete, actually amounted to £1,999. Record these events appropriately in the books.

5. Discuss the nature of goodwill and the problems involved in valuing it. Explain why it rarely appears on a balance sheet.

CHAPTER 10

Limited Companies

OBJECTIVES

In this chapter we shall deal with the following important topics:

(*a*) limited companies and their nature;
(*b*) legal principles;
(*c*) formation of companies and the issue of shares;
(*d*) distribution of profits;
(*e*) reserves;
(*f*) share premium;
(*g*) rights and bonus issues.

1. INTRODUCTION

In this chapter we turn our attention to a third main form of business enterprise—the limited company. It is a particularly important form for a number of reasons. One is that most big businesses in the private sector are organised in this way. Another is that a high proportion of people engaged in preparing financial information do so within the framework of the limited liability form of enterprise. Finally, companies provide, through the Stock Exchange, a very important outlet for investment funds and the financial information they produce is an important factor in guiding the decisions taken to direct that investment.

As in the case of partnership there are large areas of company activity which are common to all forms of business enterprise and we need to concern ourselves specially only with the areas of difference which again are generally those parts of accounting concerned with proprietorship. Our point of departure must be to establish what a limited company is. Two elements are important and they will be explained separately. The first is that it is an incorporated body and the other is that its proprietors have limited liability.

2. INCORPORATION

Incorporation means that legal reality is given to our entity concept. We have seen that a contract with Mr Smith's business is legally the same thing as a contract directly with Mr Smith who thus incurs full personal obligations under it. A contract with Smith plc, however, is not a contract with the proprietor in any sense but purely a contract with the company. The law, in short, recognises the company as a person distinct from the living persons who own it. This legal recognition in the case of a trading company normally follows simple registration with the Registrar of Companies under a procedure governed by various Companies Acts. Other methods of incorporation, used only in special cases, are by Royal Charter and by special Act of Parliament. The Institute of Chartered Accountants in England and Wales is an example of a body incorporated by Royal Charter and the National Coal Board is an example of one established by special Act of Parliament.

3. LIMITED LIABILITY

The privilege of limited liability usually, but not necessarily, attaches to an incorporated body. This privilege is given legal status and means that the proprietors' obligations towards the company are limited to the amount of capital which they have agreed to place at risk. Thus, if Mr Smith's unincorporated business fails leaving behind it debts totalling, say, £10,000 then Mr Smith will be personally liable even though he might be ruined thereby. If Smith plc fails with the same amount of outstanding debt the loss will fall on its creditors who are barred from looking to Mr Smith personally for satisfaction, however wealthy and able to afford it he might be. The privilege of limited liability is given under strict safeguards to prevent its abuse and these will be considered later.

4. ADVANTAGES OF A LIMITED COMPANY

Let us now look at some of the advantages of the company form of organisation.

(a) *Access to capital*. A large business requires considerable finance and in many cases this will be beyond the resources of a single individual or of a small group of individuals. A company may invite subscriptions to its capital fund (i.e. by the issue of shares) to as many people as desired and thus may have many hundreds or even thousands of proprietors (shareholders). This would be an impossibility under the partnership form of organisation. Quite apart from the legal restriction on the number of partners which applies to most businesses the close liaison necessary amongst the members would be quite impossible to achieve and, without it, few would be willing to invest money with the risk that further substantial liability might accrue in the case of the failure of the business. A limited company thus allows the capital of a very large number of participants to be successfully mobilised.

(*b*) *Perpetual succession.* Although it has full legal recognition as a person a company is not mortal as is a natural person. This means that it can last for ever and no special steps are needed to ensure its physical survival. Continuity is permanently a problem with sole traders and partnerships but is no problem with a limited company. This is not to say that a company will never terminate. This can happen if the purpose for which it was formed has ceased to exist or if it becomes unable to survive commercially.

(*c*) *Separation of management and capital provision.* Because companies have their own separate existence they are not committed to obtaining their management services from the same sources as they do their capital. The management of a company is in the hands of its directors who, despite their importance and power, are paid employees of the business just as are any of its other workers. They may, therefore, be recruited purely on the strength of their management skills. Directors may sometimes also be shareholders (the company may even require that its directors hold a minimum number of shares to qualify for appointment) but this should be regarded as a quite separate relationship with the company.

5. COMPANY LAW

The activities of registered limited companies are closely circumscribed by law. This is contained in a series of Companies Acts and other legislation of which the founding statute is the Companies Act 1948. This legislation is very voluminous and has many detailed provisions. We shall not need to concern ourselves with all of these as many of them do not have any specific implications for accounting. The main results which will concern us, however, are as follows.

(*a*) Every company must maintain "proper books of account". These must be adequate to describe and record the transactions of the company.

(*b*) A company must preserve a distinction between its capital and revenue funds. In broad terms capital funds derive from the original subscription of capital by the members and certain other defined sources and may not normally be redistributed to the shareholders. This fund is maintained to support the obligations which the company has to third parties. The source of revenue funds is profit earned by the company in its trading activities and this may legally be distributed to members. The distribution will be in the form of what is known as a dividend.

(c) A company must produce an annual profit and loss account and balance sheet containing, as a minimum, the information specified by law (to be described later). Copies of the accounts must be sent to each member and also deposited, for public consultation, with the Registrar of Companies.

(d) The annual accounts referred to in the previous paragraph must be subjected to independent audit by qualified accountants who must report that the accounts do (or do not) give a "true and fair view" of the company's profit for the year and its state of affairs at the end of the year and that the accounts comply in all respects with the law. They must also satisfy themselves (and report accordingly if they cannot) that proper books of account have been kept and that the accounts are in accordance with those books.

The aim of these rules is simple and apparent, i.e. that every company should conduct its financial affairs in an orderly and responsible manner, that the rights of creditors and shareholders should be safeguarded and that these things are demonstrably seen to be done.

6. FORMATION OF A COMPANY

Let us now look at a few stages in the life of a company so as to illustrate its nature and the ways in which the accounting process will bend to this. We shall use as an example a company starting from scratch with a public issue of shares. It ought to be mentioned that, although this will conveniently illustrate the points which we need to make, it is nowadays an unusual occurrence. Most companies are formed after established businesses have been created perhaps as sole traders or partnerships.

Mr A wishes to form a company, to be known as Warmhome plc, for the purpose of manufacturing and selling "Warmhome" a new material which he has developed for insulating buildings. He hopes that the company will grow to a considerable size quite quickly and so decides that he will form a public company and invite public subscription for its shares. His first step is to locate six other people who will join with him as promoters of the company because the law requires that a public company shall have at least seven members. There need not be any intention for the promoters to provide any major part of the capital of the business themselves. It is sufficient for them to lend their names to the project and to agree to make a subscription of some small portion of the capital required.

The promoters will apply to the Registrar of Companies for registration of the company. They must submit the following documents which we have both listed and described in outline.

(*a*) *The Memorandum of Association*. This sets out the company's proposed name, the country (England or Scotland) where its registered office will be situated, its objects (in this case the manufacture and distribution of a particular type of product), a statement that liability is to be limited, the amount of share capital with which it is to be registered and a declaration by the promoters that they wish to form the company and that they agree to subscribe for a stated number of shares. The objects clause of the Memorandum is important because it defines the company's powers. It will be *ultra vires*, that is beyond the power of the company and therefore illegal, for it to do anything not permitted by the objects clause. It is usual, for this reason, to make this clause fairly wide ranging so as to cover any activity which in future might seem to be desirable as well as those which are currently contemplated. The statement of initial capital (on which an *ad valorem* duty will be payable) sets what is known as the authorised capital of the company. This may not be exceeded without amending the registration.

(*b*) *The Articles of Association*. These set out how the company will be conducted so far as its internal affairs are concerned. It deals with such matters as the rights and duties of directors, the calling and conduct of meeting and the classes and rights of various classes of shares. Articles tend to be very highly standardised as between different companies. A model set of articles is reproduced as Table A to the 1st Schedule of The Companies Act 1948 and a company may, if it chooses, adopt Table A as its articles without amendment.

(*c*) *A formal statement of nominal capital*. This must agree with the figure given in the Memorandum.

(*d*) *A statutory declaration* to the effect that all legal requirements relating to registration have been complied with.

(*e*) *A notice of the situation of the registered office*. This is not always the company's place of business but is often the address of its accountant or solicitor who may provide a registered office address for a number of companies. It is the official address for receiving formal notices having legal effect, e.g. from the Registrar of Companies.

If satisfied that all requirements have been complied with the Registrar of Companies will issue a certificate of incorporation and the company will come formally into being. It may not, however, commence trading until its capital has been raised and a certificate of entitlement to commence business obtained.

7. ISSUE OF SHARES

We will suppose that our company has been formed with an authorised share capital of £1,000,000 and that this is to be raised by public subscription. It has to be offered in the form of shares of a specified denomination which is selected by the promoters of the company. This may be any amount but an obviously convenient, and therefore very common, denomination is that of £1. One million shares of £1 each would raise the required amount of capital. £1 would be described as the nominal value of the share. The offer is advertised and interested persons are issued with a prospectus. This is a legal document whose precise content need not concern us here but basically it sets out information on what the company is to do and what are the expected outcomes which will enable an informed decision to be made on whether or not to invest. Shares may be offered on the basis that applicants send a deposit against those applied for, the balance to be paid when the shares are allotted or in instalments thereafter. Alternatively, payment in full may be required with each application. The number of shares which can be issued is limited to the amount of the offer (here one million), and there can, therefore, be no guarantee that an applicant for shares will actually be allotted any.

In our example we will suppose that the shares are offered on the basis that 40p per share is payable on application and the balance of 60p per share on allotment. The offer is an attractive one (there would be no point in proceeding if it were not) and the total number of shares applied for is 1,6000,000. The applications are accompanied by cash totalling £640,000 (i.e. 40p per share applied for). This money cannot as yet be regarded as capital nor the applicants as shareholders. Until allotment has taken place the applicants are a special kind of creditor. Transactions with them will be recorded in an account known as an Applications and Allotments account.

CASH

Application for shares   £640,000

APPLICATIONS AND ALLOTMENTS

Cash   £640,000

A decision now has to be taken as to the basis of allotment. Different companies have different views on this matter depending partly on their views of what is fair and partly on whether they think it desirable to have a wide spread of share ownership or whether they prefer the shares to be concentrated in relatively few hands. Thus, some companies might allot to small applicants in full and scale down or reject the larger applications. Others would reject the small applications and allot to the larger ones. Yet others might draw lots and allow chance to decide which applicants are to be successful. In this case our company decides that it will allot in full to those who applied for up to 500 shares. This will use up 500,000 shares. These applicants will have paid £200,000 already and will now be expected to pay a further £300,000. Half the number applied for will be allotted to applicants for 501 up to 1,500 shares. Applications in this category totalled 600,000 so that they will receive 300,000 shares. They will already have paid £240,000 (600,000 × 40p) and there will now be due from them a further £60,000 (making up the total of £300,000). Finally, the remaining 200,000 shares will be allotted to the remaining applicants (for 1,501 shares and upwards) on the basis that they will receive two shares for every five applied for. They have already paid £200,000 so that there will be, for them, no more to pay.

The entries in the books are shown in the accounts below.

CASH

Application for shares	£640,000
Received after allotment	
Group 1–500	300,000
Group 501–1,500	60,000

APPLICATIONS AND ALLOTMENTS

Share capital	£1,000,000	Cash	£640,000
		Cash	300,000
		Cash	60,000
	£1,000,000		£1,000,000

SHARE CAPITAL
Ordinary Shares

Applications and allotments	£1,000,000

Note carefully how the entries in the accounts derive from the nature of the transactions concerned. The eventual effect has been a debit in the cash account for the total amount of the money subscribed and a corresponding credit in the share capital account for the nominal value of the shares issued. The Applications and Allotments account has had a temporary significance in maintaining a record of transactions with applicants before they became shareholders. The fact that it is closed off signifies that all money receivable and due has now been paid.

The company has now been formed and its capital raised. It will have appointed a Board of Directors (no doubt A and some of his colleagues). It is ready to commence trading. As it manufactures and sells its product this will give rise to the ordinary trading transactions of which we have already seen many examples and they will all be recorded by the methods we have discussed. Eventually a trading and profit and loss account can be prepared and the gross and net profits determined. The only special features of these accounts which might be noted are that there are certain items of expense, peculiar to the limited company form of organisation, which may appear. Examples are directors' remuneration, auditors' remuneration and debenture interest (to be explained later).

8. DISTRIBUTION OF PROFIT

In its first year our imaginary company has made a profit of £400,000. Of this about one-half will be claimed by the Government in the form of taxation and thus about £200,000 will be left as an amount legally distributable to the shareholders. In the case of unincorporated businesses we have been accustomed to seeing the proprietors draw on their business profits at will. Presumably they have had an eye on the adequacy of the profit when deciding what to draw but there has been no absolute bar to withdrawing even more than the amount of the profit so that there is an encroachment on the subscribed capital. A shareholder is in a quite different position. It is illegal for him to withdraw capital, so that the profit for a year places a ceiling on the amount available for withdrawal. In the present instance the shareholders collectively are limited to the withdrawal of £200,000. Even this, however, cannot be withdrawn by them at will. They must wait for the directors to declare or recommend a dividend. The distinction between these two is somewhat technical but it is usual for directors to declare and pay an interim dividend (i.e. a dividend part way through the year on account of the year's total) and to recommend a final dividend, subject to approval by the shareholders at the Annual General Meeting, to be paid after the results for the full year are known. Since the total dividend for the year must not exceed the total profit any interim dividend will normally be declared on a very conservative basis to avoid any possibility that it will subsequently turn out to have been excessive.

We will suppose that during the first year A and his colleagues have not paid any interim dividend and that they therefore now have to decide what dividend, if any, should be paid in respect of the full year. The directors may decide on any level of dividend between nil and £200,000. Either extreme would be unusual. If it is decided to pay no dividend at all their shareholders will be disappointed and may lose confidence in their investment. Apart from being unfair to them this might cause difficulty should it be desired to raise extra capital by means of a further issue of shares in the future. On the other hand it will be useful to retain some of the profit in order to finance expansion by ploughing it back or in order to provide a buffer against future reductions of dividends should profits in later years prove to be less good.

On this occasion we will suppose that the directors decide to pay out £100,000. This will be stated as being a dividend of 10 per cent (i.e. relative to the nominal value of the capital) or 10p per share. Subject to the approval of shareholders at the Annual General Meeting this amount will be paid some time after the end of the year to which it relates.

Like partnerships, companies prepare an appropriation account to record the disposition of their profits although, obviously, it takes a slightly different form since not all of the profit is necessarily being allocated to the proprietors. The appropriation account for Warmhome plc is shown below displaying all the information already given.

WARMHOME PLC

APPROPRIATION ACCOUNT FOR THE YEAR ENDED . . .

Net profit (from profit and loss account)	£400,000
Deduct Taxation on the profit of the year	200,000
Profit after taxation, available for distribution	200,000
Less Proposed dividend (10%)	100,000
Retained profit	£100,000

The final amount on this account, described there as retained profit, is the residue of profit which is not to be distributed. This will not be added to capital as it would be for an unincorporated business but will be shown as a separate balance on the balance sheet described simply as the profit and loss account. This separation is necessary if we are to ensure that the rigid distinction between capital and revenue required by company law is preserved. A summarised form of the year end balance sheet appears below.

WARMHOME PLC

BALANCE SHEET AT . . .

Share capital				
1,000,000 ordinary shares of £1 each		£1,000,000	Net assets[1]	£1,400,000
Profit and loss account		100,000		
		1,100,000		
Current liabilities[2]				
Taxation	£200,000			
Proposed div.	100,000	300,000		
		£1,400,000		£1,400,000

(1) We do not know how the net assets are made up.

(2) It has been assumed that at the time of the balance sheet neither the taxation liability nor the proposed dividend have been paid.

9. PREFERENCE SHARES

So far we have considered the case of a company entirely financed by ordinary share capital. Ordinary shareholders are the financial risk-bearers of the business and are its ultimate proprietors. One important advantage of a limited company, however, is that it can have different kinds of proprietor who bear different degrees of risk. This means that the company can appeal to a wider market when seeking its capital funds. This facility has led at various times to the invention of many ingenious forms of shares. Of these, by far the most important are preference shares and we shall limit our discussion here to those.

Preference shareholders have a preferential relationship with their company. It follows, therefore, that there must exist another group of shareholders over which they hold a preference. Every company must have ordinary shareholders and may in addition have preference shareholders. A wholly preference-financed company is not a possibility.

The preference given is in two areas. Firstly, and most importantly, there is a preference as regards the payment of dividends. Although all dividends are subject both to the availability of profits and to the director's willingness to pay, where any dividend is paid the first distribution must be to the preference shareholders. The amount they receive is subject to a maximum which is normally incorporated into the full title of the shares. As an example, eight per cent preference shares will be entitled to be first in the queue for dividends and to receive up to eight per cent (calculated on their nominal value) before any amount may be paid to the ordinary shareholders. In no circumstances will they receive more than this maximum.

The second area of preference is that of capital but this will only apply in the event of winding up (i.e. terminating) of the company. In such cases the preference shareholders must receive back the full nominal value of their investment (but again no more) before the residue, if any, is paid out to the ordinary shareholders. It will be clear that preference shares represent a very safe investment—full payment of the stated maximum dividend is usually virtually guanteed—but they are not a very exciting one. Even if the company fares extremely well they will be restricted in the amount of benefit which they can receive from this. An issue of preference shares is recorded in the books of the company in an exactly similar fashion to that already described for an issue of ordinary shares. They will be recorded, of course, in a separate share capital account. As with ordinary shares the capital value of the shares may not normally be repaid during the life of the company. In order to preserve the safety of the investment (on which its special attraction rests) it is normal for preference shares to represent a very small part of the company's total capital.

It will be instructive to see how ordinary and preference shareholders fare relatively in conditions of differing levels of profit. This is illustrated below.

A certain company has a total capital of £12,000,000 of which £10,000,000 is in ordinary shares and £2,000,000 in 10 per cent preference shares. The table below shows what happens at different levels of profit.

	Normal profit	Very good profit	Very poor profit
Profit	£1,200,000	£2,400,000	£600,000
Preference dividend	200,000	200,000	200,000
Available for ordinary dividend	£1,000,000	£2,200,000	£400,000
	10%	22%	4%

Note that in all cases the preference dividend has a fair degree of security. Even when the profit is very poor it is covered three times over by the profit. Note, too, the sensitivity of the rate of dividend available to ordinary shareholders to change in the level of profit. This effect is known as gearing.

10. LOAN CAPITAL

Both ordinary shareholders and preference shareholders are proprietors of the business. Their status differs but they both rely on the success of the business in the earning of profit to provide their income and the security of their capital investment. An alternative way in which a company might obtain finance is to borrow it. Borrowed funds are of quite a different nature from risk capital and they can only supplement it, not replace it. The terms of any loan are a matter between the lender and the borrower but they will include provision for interest to be paid and, usually, for eventual repayment of the principal. Any interest paid by a company is a normal business expense and appears in the profit and loss account. It does not depend on the availability or otherwise of revenues to meet it. Repayment of the principal must take place as agreed even if this requires further borrowing or other capital raising operations.

Like any other business a company may borrow from a single lender such as a bank but it may also borrow from the public by issuing debentures. These are merely small portions of the total borrowing. They are negotiable through the Stock Exchange and are treated superficially like ordinary and preference shares. The fundamentally different status of their holders, however, as lenders and not as proprietors, is important and must not be overlooked. It is important both in assessing the investment potential of the debentures and in analysing the situation of a company which relies on them for part of its finance.

Having looked at some of the capital raising possibilities open to it we need now to return to the story of Warmhome plc. At the end of its first year's trading we drew up a balance sheet and in this its capital still stood at one million pounds divided into shares of £1 each. This £1 nominal value will normally remain unchanged indefinitely. A share in a limited company is, however, a marketable investment. Provided that a fair price can be agreed and a willing buyer found (the Stock Exchange is the main mechanism for achieving this), a shareholder can dispose of his interest in the company to another who thereby stands in his place as a part-proprietor. This does not mean, however, that he will sell his share for the value attached to it when it was issued. In the year which has elapsed in our example a number of things have happened. One year's experience, for example, will have helped to give a clearer picture of the business's potential which might either be better or not so good as originally expected. Another factor is that, regardless of future potential, each holder of a £1 share has become ultimately entitled to a portion of the retained profit which did not exist when the shares were issued. Market conditions generally may have changed during the year making the whole idea of investing in business either more or less attractive than it was before. A share of nominal value £1, therefore, may be traded in the market at, say, £2 or, just as easily, at 70p. This cannot be deduced except by reference to actual market conditions. None of this matters directly to the company, however, who will take no notice of it in drawing up its balance sheet.

11. RESERVES

A company's reserves are amounts attributable to its shareholders over and above the nominal amount of the capital. They are thus portions of what can usefully be thought of as the capital account, segregated in the balance sheet because of the law relating to companies. Reserves are of two kinds. A revenue reserve is a reserve representing amounts which may legally be distributed to shareholders by way of dividend. A capital reserve (of which we shall see an example in due course) represents an amount which may not legally be distributed to the shareholders. The most common example of a revenue reserve is the undistributed balance on the profit and loss account and Warmhome plc has such a revenue reserve on its recent balance sheet. Other revenue reserves have the profit and loss account as their source and are in effect merely a method of applying labels to relevant parts of the retained profit to indicate in some way the intention behind that retention. Some would argue that this device is of no value and would not make any use of it. The profit and loss account balance would then be the only revenue reserve on the balancing sheet. Others believe that the use of reserves makes a balance sheet more informative by revealing the explanation of why certain amounts of profit have been retained.

Revenue reserves

Let us look at an example of the creation of a new revenue reserve. A and the other directors had particular motives in deciding to retain £100,000 of the profit. The Board was aware that, in a period of inflation, fixed assets which fall due for replacement are likely to cost substantially more on each successive occasion. This means that, for this reason alone, progressively more finance will be required and rather than raise this extra capital on the market they have decided to try to obtain it internally. In the long run the amount needed for this purpose is expected to average £20,000 per annum and so, in order to ensure that this amount is withheld from distribution the directors decide to make a transfer from profit and loss account to another revenue reserve which will be described as a plant replacement reserve. They also think it prudent to retain a further £30,000 each year for unforeseen circumstances and decide to transfer this to a reserve which will be called a general reserve.

The residue of the retention is an amount for which no special use is intended.

Here are the appropriation account and balance sheet redrafted to give effect to the directors' wishes.

WARMHOME PLC

APPROPRIATION ACCOUNT FOR THE YEAR ENDED . . .

Net profit (from profit and loss account)			£400,000
Deduct Taxation on the profit of the year			200,000
Profit after taxation, available for distribution			200,000
Less Proposed dividend (10%)		£100,000	
Transfers to reserves			
Plant replacement reserve	£20,000		
General reserve	30,000		
		50,000	
			150,000
Retained profit			£50,000

BALANCE SHEET AT . . .

Share capital				
1,000,000 ordinary shares of £1 each		£1,000,000	Net assets	£1,400,000
Plant replacement reserve		20,000		
General reserve		30,000		
Profit and loss account		50,000		
		1,100,000[1]		
Current liabilities				
Taxation	£200,000			
Proposed dividend	100,000			
		300,000		
		£1,400,000		£1,400,000

(1) It should be noted that this figure, total shareholders' interest in the company, is unaffected by the creation of reserves. The effect is merely to label certain portions of the complete capital account in a particular way.

Since, by definition, all revenue reserves are distributable the entries just made are all reversible. If in a future year, for example, the plant replacement reserve proved, in the light of experience, to be excessive, part or all of the balance could be transferred back to the profit and loss account in order to support the payment of a dividend. It should be noted that since all entries relating to reserves pass through the appropriation account they have no effect whatsoever on the reported profit of the year. There is no possibility, therefore, that unscrupulous directors will manipulate reserves in order to conceal poor results.

12. SUBSEQUENT ISSUES OF SHARES

We will suppose that our company has been running now for some years and that it has accumulated some revenue reserves (for the sake of simplicity we will take it that all lie under the balance sheet heading of profit and loss account). These have assisted in the finance of a gentle expansion but now the opening of new markets means a major investment in premises and equipment which cannot be paid for out of current resources. The directors decide that the developments should be financed by a new issue of ordinary shares to augment those already in existence. There are two ways in which this can be done and we shall, by turns, consider both of them. The first method is by a further offer to the general public and the second is by means of a rights issue. A rights issue is an offer of new shares restricted to the existing shareholders.

The amount of money required for the expansion is £250,000. The balance sheet currently appears as below:

WARMHOME PLC

BALANCE SHEET AS AT . . .

Share capital		Net assets	£1,500,000
1,000,000 ordinary			
shares of £1 each	£1,000,000		
Profit and loss account	500,000		
	£1,500,000		£1,500,000

It may be seen that each of the one million shares currently in issue has an underlying claim on the assets of the company worth £1.50 at balance sheet values. The market price must be expected to reflect this as well as any expectations which might be held about the company's future. Let us suppose that the shares are currently on offer in the market at £1.80 each. This creates a slight difficulty concerning the pricing of the new issue. If new shares are offered to the general public at their nominal value of £1 then those who subscribe to them will obtain a very good bargain. Their gain, however, will be at the expense of the existing shareholders who, although having been with the company during its formative period will now give up part of their reward for this to others.

The way in which this might happen can very clearly be demonstrated making simple and plausible assumptions as shown below:

Total value of shares now $1,000,000 \times £1.80 = £1,800,000$.
Total value after issuing 250,000 shares at £1 each $= £2,050,000$.

This assumes that the value of the company increases by exactly the amount of the cash subscribed. Each share would then have a market value of £1.64. New shareholders would thus receive an instant unearned gain of 64p per share bought. Old shareholders would lose 16p per share held. The difference between the two figures is because the transfer of benefit is received and shared amongst fewer shares than it is drawn from.

The way in which the company should deal with this situation is to issue the new shares at a premium, i.e. at a price exceeding their nominal value. Theoretically, they could be offered at a price of £1.80 each, level with the market value of the existing shares. Normally, however, in order to make the offer attractive and thus to guarantee its success a price slightly less than this would be fixed. Thus the new shares might be offered at a price of £1.70 each. Note that if this is done it will no longer be necessary to issue as many as 250,000 shares in order to raise the money required. The number of shares needed is $250,000 \div 1.70$, which is 147,059. This may conveniently be rounded off to 150,000.

It has now been decided that an offer of 150,000 shares will be made at a price of £1.70 per share, i.e. they are £1 shares sold at a premium of 70p per share. Entries recording the process of application and allotment will be exactly the same as with our original issue of shares right up to the stage of actual allotment. We then come up against a requirement of company law that any premium on shares is shown separately in the accounts. This will be recorded, therefore, as DR Application and Allotment £255,000: CR Share Capital: Ordinary shares £150,000, CR Share Premium £105,000. The balance sheet after these events is shown below. It should be noted that a share premium account is an example of a capital reserve. It represents a fund held by the company on behalf of its shareholders but it may not legally be distributed to them as a dividend.

WARMHOME PLC

BALANCE SHEET AFTER NEW ISSUE OF SHARES

Share capital			
1,150,000 ordinary shares of £1 each	£1,150,000	Net assets[1]	£1,755,000
Share premium account	105,000		
Profit and loss account	500,000		
	£1,755,000		£1,755,000

(1) This includes cash raised by new issue.

Although a share premium account may not be distributed it may be used to meet the costs of issue, or discounts on, shares or debentures or the preliminary expenses of forming the company.

Rights issue

The second method of raising additional finance by means of a new share issue, which we referred to earlier, is the rights issue. This has the advantage of being less expensive than a public issue. Fixing the price of the issue is also easier as it can be pitched fairly low in order to ensure success. Because the new shareholders are the same people as the old a transfer of benefit from one group to another which occurs if the premium is inadequate does not matter. The existing body of shareholders, however, usually provides a limited source of finance and a rights issue is normally used only where relatively small amounts of capital are required.

Let us suppose that the company is to make a rights issue of shares at a price of £1.50 each. The number of shares to be offered is 170,000 thus again yielding £255,000. The offer would be made on what would be called a "17 for 100" basis, i.e. each existing shareholder would be given the right to subscribe for 17 new shares for every 100 which he currently holds. The rights would be offered in the form of a provisional allotment letter. This is a negotiable document and any shareholder not wishing to take up his rights may sell his entitlement in the market. The price he will receive depends on what advantage over the current market price is conferred by the rights.

The book-keeping record of a rights issue is exactly as for any other issue of shares. It is made more simple by the fact that an oversubscription is impossible since only the exact number of shares required to be issued is made available in the rights.

Bonus issue

The share issues we have looked at so far have been for the purpose of raising additional finance for the company's operations. One type of issue, however, known as a bonus issue, does not have this function. Bonus issues are made only to existing ordinary shareholders pro rata to their existing shareholdings and are an issue of shares free of charge. This apparently pointlessly generous action is, in fact, a device for rationalising the balance sheet. It occurs, typically, when revenue reserves have accumulated to a level where it is no longer realistic commercially (as opposed to legally) to regard them as being available for the payment of dividends although capital reserves may also be used in bonus issues.

The balance sheet below shows the situation of a longstanding company which has pursued a policy of expansion by the steady retention of profits.

BALANCE SHEET AT . . .

Share capital		Fixed assets	£2,300,000
1,000,000 ordinary shares			
of £1 each	£1,000,000	Current assets	200,000
Profit and loss account	1,500,000		
	£2,500,000		£2,500,000

Although the company could quite legally pay a dividend totalling £1,500,000, i.e. 150 per cent on its nominal share capital, it is clear that this could only be done in practice by selling substantial parts of the fixed assets which would inevitably undermine the future operation of the company. There is thus a divergence between the legal availability of the profit and loss account balance and its physical availability since it is now permanently invested in the business. The actuality could be better expressed by transferring a substantial amount from the profit and loss account to the share capital account. This is precisely the effect of a bonus issue.

Let us suppose that the company's directors decide to make a bonus issue on a 1 for 1 basis. Each existing shareholder would receive a new £1 share free of charge to add to each £1 share he already held. This would actually be paid for out of his profit and loss account entitlement. Here are the book-keeping entries relating to the bonus issue and the balance sheet after they have taken place. The Bonus Share account takes the place of the application and allotment account in the case of issues for cash.

SHARE CAPITAL

ORDINARY SHARES

Balance	£2,000,000	Balance	£1,000,000
		Bonus shares	1,000,000
	£2,000,000		£2,000,000
		Balance	£2,000,000

PROFIT AND LOSS ACCOUNT

Bonus shares	£1,000,000	Balance	£1,500,000
Balance	500,000		
	£1,500,000		£1,500,000
		Balance	£500,000

BONUS SHARES

Share capital	£1,000,000	Profit and loss account	£1,000,000

Other things being equal, a bonus issue of shares does not make any difference to a shareholder's wealth. If he held 100 shares having a value of, say, £2.50 each before the bonus issue, he would hold 200 shares having a value of £1.25 each after it. Shareholders, however, normally like a bonus issue. It is usually believed to signify that the directors have great confidence in the future of the company and may herald the payment of increased dividends.

SUMMARY

1. The limited company is a very important form of organisation as most large businesses are organised in this way. Its two essential features are:

(a) incorporation, which means that the company is an entity recognised in law to be separate from the people operating or financing it; and

(b) limited liability, which means that the financial liability of its proprietors is limited to the amount of capital which they have chosen to subscribe.

2. Most trading companies are incorporated by registration with the Registrar of Companies. Alternative methods of incorporation, used in special cases, are by Royal Charter and by special Act of Parliament.

3. The advantages of the company form of organisation are as follows.

(a) *Access to capital.* There is no limit to the number of members and, since the liability of each is limited, the resources of large numbers of investors may be tapped.

(b) *Perpetual succession.* The life of a company is indefinite. It may be terminated if this is thought desirable but otherwise will exist in perpetuity.

(c) *Separation of management and capital provision.* Management ability can be hired and need not reside in those providing the capital. A company's management is in the hands of its directors.

4. Important legal rules applying to limited companies are that:

(*a*) they must keep proper books of account;

(*b*) they must preserve a distinction between capital funds, which may not normally be distributed, and revenue funds which may;

(*c*) a company must publish annual accounts in prescribed form; and

(*d*) the accounts must be audited by an independent, suitably qualified, person.

5. On registration, a company must submit to the Registrar of Companies:

(*a*) the Memorandum of Association, which will contain the important objects clause;

(*b*) the Articles of Association, although Table A of the Companies Act 1948 may be adopted;

(*c*) a formal statement of nominal capital;

(*d*) a statutory declaration to the effect that all legal requirements relating to registration have been complied with; and

(*e*) a notice of the situation of the registered office.

6. A company comes into being when the Registrar issues its certificate of incorporation. It may not commence business until its capital has been raised and a certificate of entitlement to commence business obtained.

7. Capital is raised by the issue of shares in appropriate numbers and in a convenient denomination. This denomination is known as the share's nominal value. Accounting for an issue of shares makes use of an Application and Allotment Account.

8. Distributions of company profits are by means of the payment of dividends. Effectively, the directors have complete power to determine what the dividend will be within the limit imposed by the level of total profit. Dividends appear in a company's appropriation account the balance on which is carried forward in the balance sheet as retained profit or, simply, profit and loss account.

9. There are several different investment opportunities which may be offered by a company in order to attract capital. The most important are listed below.

(*a*) Ordinary shares—the basic risk capital of the business.

(*b*) Preference shares—risk capital with the benefit of substantial preferential rights over ordinary shares. This reduces the risk, often to negligible proportions, but also curtails the potential benefits.

(*c*) Debentures—these represent borrowing by the business. Debenture holders are entitled to a rate of interest on their money and to repayment, in most cases, on an agreed date. Except under disastrous circumstances neither entitlement depends on the fortunes of the company.

10. A company's reserves are amounts attributable to ordinary shareholders over and above the nominal amount of their capital. Revenue reserves, derived from the profit and loss account, are legally distributable. Capital reserves are not.

11. Shares issued subsequently to the initial issue may be issued at a price higher than their nominal value. This excess is described as a premium and the profit to the company which this represents must, by law, be credited to a Share Premium Account. This is an example of a statutory capital reserve and its use is restricted.

12. A rights issue of shares is an issue made *pro rata* to existing shareholders. It is useful where the amount of extra capital required is relatively small. It has the benefit of economy and the advantage that the calculation of a fair premium is a less important matter.

13. A bonus issue of shares is a free issue of shares *pro rata* to existing shareholders. It is a method whereby reserves, whether capital or revenue, may be permanently converted to share capital.

QUESTIONS

1. In its first five years of life the following events occur to Silverfoil plc.

(a) It issued its original capital of two million ordinary shares of £1 each at par.

(b) It issued one million 8 per cent preference shares of 50p each also at par.

(c) It issued £500,000 15 per cent debentures.

(d) Profits and dividends were:

Year	Profit after tax and debenture interest	Ordinary dividends	Preference dividends
1	£250,000	£200,000	—
2	300,000	200,000	£20,000
3	400,000	300,000	40,000
4	500,000	400,000	40,000
5	600,000	500,000	40,000

(e) It made a rights issue at £1.10 per share to its ordinary shareholders on a 1 for 4 basis.

(f) It made a bonus issue on a 1 for 10 basis.

Trace these events carefully and draw up a summarised balance sheet at the end of the five years.

2. Why is it necessary for the operations of companies to be so carefully controlled by law?

3. A shareholder is puzzled by certain items on his company's accounts. Explain each of the following to him.

(*a*) The balance sheet shows very substantial reserves yet the chairman says that the company is short of cash. Why can we not use the reserves?

(*b*) The profit and loss account says that we have made a profit of £1,200,000 this year. On the balance sheet I read, however, "Profit and Loss Account £5,800,000". Is this an error?

(*c*) The dividend on the preference shares was only 8 per cent whereas 20 per cent was paid on the ordinary shares. What is meant by "preference" if the holders of those shares do so much less well?

(*d*) I paid £1,000 for my ordinary shares which I bought through the Stock Exchange. I therefore expected a dividend of 20 per cent of this, i.e. £200. I actually received only £100. Why is this?

(*e*) The directors say that they plan to make a free issue of shares to us. Would it not be better to conserve resources in these difficult times?

4. Rhubarb plc made a public offer of five million £1 shares at £1.20 each. Under the terms of the offer, 50p of this was payable on application and 70p on allotment. Ten million shares were actually applied for and applications were therefore designated as small, medium and large. Small applications were met in full, medium applications received half the number applied for and large applications one quarter of the number applied for. Details appear below.

Category	Total number applied for	Total number allotted
Small	2,000,000	2,000,000
Medium	4,000,000	2,000,000
Large	4,000,000	1,000,000

Write up the accounts to record this and comment on the basis of allotment.

5. Compare and contrast the limited company form of organisation with the partnership.

CHAPTER 11

Taxation in Company Accounts

OBJECTIVES

In this chapter we shall deal with the following important topics:

(a) tax collected by a company as agent for the government;
(b) indirect taxation borne by a company;
(c) direct taxation borne by a company:
(d) the deferred tax account.

1. INTRODUCTION

Taxation is a big and important factor in the business world and we need to consider a number of aspects of the accounting for it. Because generally it is the proprietors of unincorporated businesses who are taxed, rather than their businesses, we shall consider the matter of accounting for taxation purely in the context of the limited company. We shall not be concerned with the detail of the law relating to taxation and its computation but only with the method of accounting for tax once it has been calculated. This will simplify our task considerably as we shall need to concern ourselves only with those points of tax law which have a direct bearing on accounting matters.

It will be as well first of all to map out the ground we are to cover. This falls into four distinct areas. The first of these relates to the duty which is placed on companies to act as agent for the Inland Revenue in the collection of certain taxes, the burden of which they do not themselves bear. The examples we shall look at are value added tax and pay as you earn (PAYE) income tax. The second area concerns the indirect taxes borne by a company. Indirect taxes are those which are not aimed specifically at an individual company and which do not arise directly from its ability to pay as evidenced by its earnings. Thirdly, we shall look at direct taxes borne by the company. This is the company's corporation tax on its profits. Finally, we shall consider the matter of the provision for deferred taxation, a specific problem of the reporting of results which is an offshoot of the matter of accounting for taxation itself. All four of these areas represent fundamentally different matters of principle and are grouped together in this chapter only as a convenience of classification.

2. THE COMPANY AS AGENT FOR THE COLLECTION OF TAX

It is a feature of our system of taxation in the UK that much of the administration and collection of taxes is delegated by law to individuals and businesses. Thus, when a person buys a bottle of whisky the price which he pays will include a large element of tax and it is the responsibility of the seller to see that this ultimately finds its way to the Revenue. Similarly, if someone is employed, income tax will be deducted from his wage before it is paid to him and again it is the responsibility of the employer to pay this to the appropriate authority. Where a company acts as agent for the government in this way it is important to keep a careful record of the amounts concerned in order to ensure that the correct payments are made. It is also important to note that such an activity does not give rise to either revenues or expenses to appear in the company's profit and loss account.

Here is an example. A plc employed X for one week at a wage of £100. X was liable to income tax of £20 calculated according to PAYE rules. These are fairly complicated but we do not need to understand them in order to appreciate the accounting procedure involved. In A's profit and loss account there will appear, under wages, the item of £100 representing the cost to the company of employing X. This is quite independent of and unaffected by the amount of the tax to be borne by X. A pays to X the net amount of his wages, i.e. £80, and pays to the Collector of Taxes on behalf of X the amount of the tax deduction, i.e. £20. The tax thus affects to whom A pays the money but not in any way the total amount paid. The entries in the books are shown below.

WAGES

Cash	£80
PAYE	20

The balance on this account will ultimately be transferred to the profit and loss account as an expense.

PAYE

Wages	£20

This is the current account with the Inland Revenue. It is a liability which will be settled in cash.

CASH

Wages	£80

Another case where a company acts as agent in collecting a tax which it does not bear is that of value added tax (VAT). This is a little more complicated than PAYE. VAT is chargeable on a wide range of goods and services and will initially be invoiced to any company which makes purchases of such items from other businesses. Similarly, the company will charge VAT on its output to its own customers. Since VAT is a tax which is to be borne by the final consumer the company is allowed to set off against the tax which it has collected, the tax it has itself paid. A simple illustration will make this clear.

In a certain month A plc bought taxable goods and services at a net cost of £10,000. VAT was charged on this at the rate of 15 per cent so that the amount payable to the suppliers was £11,500. In this same month A sold taxable goods for £15,000 charging 15 per cent tax on this and thus receiving a total of £17,250. Only the net values of sales and purchases are to go in the company's profit and loss account. The tax element is dealt with entirely separately through the medium of a VAT account. Thus:

CASH

Sales including VAT	£17,250	Purchases including VAT	£11,500

PURCHASES

Cash	£10,000		

SALES

		Cash	£15,000

VAT

Tax on purchases	£1,500	Tax on sales	£2,250

The credit balance on the VAT account represents the amount due to Customs and Excise who will thus collect ultimately, from various sources, the full amount of 15 per cent on the output.

It should be noted that there are occasional circumstances in which a company will actually bear VAT. This can occur when it is charged VAT by another business but is unable, for some reason, to set this off against VAT it has itself collected. Possible reasons are that it is a very small business not registered for VAT or that it supplies goods and services which are exempt from the tax. In such a case the tax borne should appear as an expense in the profit and loss account. It is not usual to show it as a separate item but it is included as an additional cost of the taxed goods or services.

3. INDIRECT TAXES BORNE BY A COMPANY

This is a very simple matter. Indirect taxes, such as employer's national insurance contributions and vehicle licences, are treated exactly as any other expense of the business and are included as such in the profit and loss account. The normal principle of matching applies and care needs to be taken to see that this is accurately done.

4. DIRECT TAXATION BORNE BY A COMPANY

The first essential difference between direct and indirect taxation is that the former is seen as an appropriation of profit rather than as an expense. This means that profits are first of all computed in the conventional manner without regard to direct taxation and then a share of those profits is allocated to the state. The state is seen, in effect, as a special kind of proprietor of the business entitled, as such, to a share in its profits. This is not an analogy which can be carried too far, of course, as the state has no risk capital invested in the business and nor will it take any share of losses should these occur. Apart from this distinction, appropriation rather than expense, direct taxation is considerably more complex than indirect and we shall have to devote some careful attention to it.

Corporation tax

The direct tax to which companies are subject is known as corporation tax. It is charged on profits at a rate which is varied from time to time but which is around 50 per cent. This is the rate which we shall assume for most of our examples. The tax is charged on the profit of each year and is payable at a date following the end of the year which is determined by certain rules. For a company formed since 1st April, 1965 the tax is payable normally nine months after the end of the accounting period to which it relates. For companies older than this the tax is payable on the anniversary of the date on which they used to pay income tax. This is always a 1st January and may be anything from nine to twenty-one months after the termination of the accounting period in which the profit was earned. The precise interval until payment depends on the date of the company's own year end.

An important consequence of what we have learnt so far is that, for any company, there will be in its balance sheet, as a liability, at least the corporation tax payable in respect of the year just ended and frequently also the corporation tax in respect of the year previous to that. The amount which appears in respect of the year just ended will be an estimated figure. The figure finally agreed with the Inland Revenue is likely to be a little different from this. There are two reasons for this. One is that the determination of taxable, as opposed to reported, profit is to a limited extent dependent upon the outcome of negotiations with the Inland Revenue as to which expenses are allowable for tax purposes. The other is that the rate of corporation tax is set retrospectively in each year's Budget so that a change may occur after the company has made its estimate on the basis of the current rate.

Example of balance sheet treatment of taxation

Here is an example which will illustrate these points. The summarised balance sheet of Snow plc at 31st December, year 5, appears below.

SNOW PLC

BALANCE SHEET AT 31ST DECEMBER, YEAR 5

Share capital and reserves	£1,000,000	Fixed assets	£800,000
Corporation tax year 5[1]	120,000	Current assets	430,000
Current liabilities			
Corporation tax year 4[2]	110,000		
	£1,230,000		£1,230,000

(1) This tax is payable on 1st January, year 7. It is shown as a non-current liability, below share capital and reserves and below loan capital (if any).

(2) This tax is payable on 1st January, year 6, the day after the balance sheet date, and is therefore shown as a current liability.

During the year subsequent to this balance sheet, the year ended 31st December, year 6 the following occurred.

(*a*) On 1st January the tax in respect of year 4 was paid.

(*b*) The tax in respect of year 5 was agreed at £115,000, a little less than the estimate made.

(*c*) A reported profit of £280,000 was earned in the year ended 31st December, year 6.

One problem we shall need to tackle is that of estimating Snow's liability to corporation tax in respect of the year ended 31st December, year 6. Unfortunately, this is not just a matter of applying the tax rate to the reported profit. This is because taxable profit has to be calculated according to special rules which are not always followed in drawing up the conventional profit and loss account. One example of this difference is that some of the expenses of the business, such as charitable donations, will not be allowed in the calculation of taxable profit and will have to be added back to the reported profit. The major source of difference, however, is in the area of depreciation. In determining the amount of profit earned by a business for tax purposes fairness obviously demands that this should be done on as consistent a basis as possible. The biggest potential for diversity lies probably in depreciation. Tax law has therefore, for a very long time, required that businesses substitute, for their own depreciation, amounts known as capital allowances which, in effect, are government prescribed rates of depreciation. Capital allowances are varied from time to time and are thus an important instrument of government policy which can be used either to encourage or discourage capital investment. This can be done overall or selectively by region or by type of investment. Currently and for a few years into the past, government has wished to give the maximum encouragement to investment and capital allowances have been given equal to 100 per cent of the capital expenditure of the year. Thus, the tax benefit of the expenditure is received immediately with consequently favourable effect on the company's cash flow. Most businesses would regard the provision of depreciation on this scale as being over conservative and will continue to use more prolonged depreciation in their accounts. This may create a substantial difference between reported and taxable profit.

Let us suppose that, for Snow, depreciation already charged in its profit and loss account amounted to £40,000 and that capital expenditure in the year totalled £70,000. There were certain expenses charged in the profit and loss account but not allowable for tax purposes and these totalled £10,000. The calculation of the corporation tax liability is as follows.

Profit per accounts	£280,000
Add Disallowed expenses	10,000
Depreciation	40,000
	330,000
Less Capital allowances	70,000
Taxable profit	£260,000
Corporation tax @ 50%	£130,000

Thus the estimated tax liability for year 6 is £130,000 and this will be payable on 1st January, year 8.

We are now ready to write up accounts to record these transactions and to show the balance sheet at 31st December, year 6.

CORPORATION TAX, YEAR 4

Cash	£110,000	Balance	£110,000

CORPORATION TAX, YEAR 5

Profit and loss account:		Balance	£120,000
adjustment	£5,000		
Balance	115,000		
	£120,000		£120,000
		Balance	£115,000

CORPORATION TAX, YEAR 6

Profit and loss account:	
estimate	£130,000

In the balance sheet at 31st December, year 6, corporation tax year 5 will appear as a current liability and corporation tax year 6 as a non-current liability.

Payment of dividends

There is another problem connected with corporation tax to which we now have to give attention. This arises from the payment of dividends to the company's shareholders. The recipient of any dividend is likely to be a taxpayer. If an individual or an unincorporated body the relevant tax will be income tax and if a body corporate, corporation tax. The source of dividends, however, is an already taxed fund of profit. In order to provide for this situation the law requires that all dividends paid should have imputed to them a certain amount of tax which is noted as a tax credit. This, however, is not to be calculated at the current rate of corporation tax but at the current basic rate of income tax. If we take this to be 30 per cent (of gross income) then the tax credit is 3/7 of the payment (which is the net amount). This method of dealing with dividends is known as the imputation system.

Where the recipient of a dividend is itself a company such income, described as franked investment income, is subject to no further tax charge. Where the recipient is an individual the income is regarded as tax paid at the basic rate of income tax. If the recipient has an income so low that he is not subject to income tax he may reclaim from the Inland Revenue the amount of the tax credit (but no more even though the corporation tax actually paid exceeds this). If he is a taxpayer at a rate higher than the basic rate then he will be called upon to pay more tax to make this up from the basic rate deemed to have been paid up to the actual rate to which he is subject.

A simple example, using the figures already introduced, will explain this. The directors of Snow plc decide to pay a dividend of £105,000 out of the company's profit after taxation. The appropriation section of the profit and loss account will appear as follows.

Profit before taxation		£280,000
Less Corporation tax based		
on profit of year	£130,000	
Adjustment in respect		
of previous year	5,000	
	———	125,000
Profit after taxation		155,000
Less dividend		105,000
Retained profit		40,000

Note that the net dividend paid is recorded in the profit and loss account and that there is no further reference to taxation in connection with it. In remitting the dividend to the shareholder, however, it must be described as a net dividend of £105,000 bearing an attached tax credit of £45,000 (3/7 of £105,000). To the recipient the dividend looks like and is treated like income of £150,000 from which tax has been deducted at source of £45,000.

Advance corporation tax
Revenue law now imposes an additional complication. This is that, when a company pays a dividend, it must immediately make an advance payment of a part of its corporation tax liability. This payment is equal to the tax credit attached to the dividend. Thus, in the example, Snow has a corporation tax liability of £130,000 in respect of the year. £45,000 of that would be payable as advance corporation tax (ACT) at the time of the payment of the dividend. The rest, i.e. £85,000, known as the mainstream corporation tax, would be paid at the normal time. Notice that the ACT rule, which is devised to improve the government's cash flow, does not normally impose any additional tax burden on the company. It merely affects the timing of the payment of its tax. The payment of the dividend and the related ACT is shown in account form on the following page.

CORPORATION TAX YEAR 6

Cash (ACT)	£45,000	Balance	£130,000
Balance	85,000		
	£130,000		£130,000
		Balance	£85,000

CASH

Dividend (to shareholders)	£105,000
ACT	45,000

Franked investment income

We need, finally in this section, to review the process of accounting for franked investment income. As already explained this is tax free in the hands of the receiving company and the simplest way of dealing with it would be to bring it to the credit of the profit and loss account at its net amount. This, however, would involve mixing untaxed trading income with taxed investment income and might mislead. The recommended method, therefore, is to show as investment income the net franked investment income plus the tax credit, i.e. the notional gross amount, and then to add the amount of the tax credit to the company's tax charge for the year. Since this amount has, in effect, already been paid the procedure does not affect the liability for corporation tax appearing on the balance sheet. Let us suppose that Snow now receives franked investment income of £14,000 net on top of its trading income. The profit and loss account will be amended as follows.

Trading profit		£280,000
Add Investment income		20,000
Profit before taxation		300,000
Less Corporation tax based on the profit of the year	£130,000	
Adjustment in respect of previous year	(5,000)	
Tax credit on franked investment income	6,000	
		131,000
Profit after taxation		169,000
Less Dividend		105,000
Retained profit		£64,000

There is one further point to be made about franked investment income. This is that the tax credit attached to it also serves to relieve the company of some of its obligation to pay ACT in respect of its own dividend payments. Thus in this case the receipt of the franked investment income means that ACT payable on Snow's own dividend is now £39,000 calculated as follows.

ACT on dividend paid	£45,000
Less Tax credit on FII	6,000
ACT payable	£39,000

5. DEFERRED TAXATION

Deferred taxation is not of itself anything to do with the company's relationship with the taxing authorities. It is purely an accounting device used to match tax charges against the revenues which appear to have given rise to them. This needs a word or two of explanation.

We have frequently seen exemplified the basic profit and loss account concept of matching. This says that expenses are to be matched on some acceptable basis against the revenues to which they relate. Appropriations, of which proprietors' drawings in the case of unincorporated businesses and dividends in the case of limited companies are good examples, are not subject to this concept as they are not regarded as being in any sense expenses. They do not arise directly from the earning of revenues but are the result of decisions concerning the disposal of profit after that profit has been earned.

Direct taxation we have presented as an appropriation, i.e. as just another aspect of the sharing of profits. Nevertheless taxation does have some features which give it some of the characteristics of an expense. One of these is that it is involuntary so far as the business is concerned. It does not make any decision as to how much tax it should pay as it does make decisions about other appropriations. Another is that tax does indisputably arise directly out of the earning of revenues. If there is no revenue then there is no tax. Pragmatically we must also recognise that great significance is attached by accounts users to the figure for profit after taxation. This is the basis for the calculation of the important figure for Earnings per Share (*see* Chapter 14) and it also represents the fund which ultimately supports dividend payments. The matching of taxation charges to the revenues which give rise to them is therefore desirable both theoretically and from a practical point of view.

We have already seen that a tax rate of, say, 50 per cent does not automatically mean that the corporation tax charge is that proportion of reported profit. One reason is the items in the profit and loss account (e.g. disallowable expenses) which are excluded in the tax computation. These give rise to permanent differences between taxable and reported profits. Another reason is the items charged in the profit and loss account which are allowable for tax purposes but not necessarily in the same year. (The best example of this is depreciation.) This is a timing difference between taxable and reported profit. The deferred tax account concerns itself only with timing differences.

Here is an example to demonstrate the principle. B plc purchased an asset for £30,000. This was to be depreciated on the straight line basis over three years in each of which it will produce profits before depreciation or taxation of £40,000. For accounting purposes depreciation will be £10,000 in each year. For tax purposes the capital allowances will be £30,000 in year 1 but nothing for each of the other two years. Note that depreciation in total and capital allowances in total must be equal. It is their allocation to accounting periods which is different. The table below shows the effects of this.

	Year 1	Year 2	Year 3
Profit before depreciation or tax	£40,000	£40,000	£40,000
Less Depreciation	10,000	10,000	10,000
	30,000	30,000	30,000
Less Taxation	5,000	20,000	20,000
Profit after tax	£25,000	£10,000	£10,000
Apparent rate of tax	16.7%	66.7%	66.7%

It is easy to observe the distortion caused to profit after tax by this mismatching of taxation to profit. A deferred tax account will remedy this. It should particularly be noted that this account is a kind of revenue reserve and its creation does not affect in any way at all the company's actual liability to tax either in total or in its incidence from one year to another. The argument it follows is that the consequence of the light taxation in year 1 (caused by the 100 per cent capital allowance given then) is the heavier tax of years 2 and 3. Foreseeing this the company ought to set aside a reserve in year 1 which can be used to support the profit and loss account in each of the other two years.

The amount of transfer to or from the deferred tax account is calculated as the tax rate applied to the difference between depreciation and capital allowances.

Year	Depreciation	Capital allowances	Transfer
1	£10,000	£30,000	£10,000 to reserve
2	£10,000	Nil	£5,000 from reserve
3	£10,000	Nil	£5,000 from reserve

The amended profit and loss accounts will appear as follows:

		Year 1		Year 2		Year 3
Profit after depreciation		£30,000		£30,000		£30,000
Less Taxation	£5,000		£20,000		£20,000	
Deferred tax	10,000		(5,000)		(5,000)	
		15,000		15,000		15,000
Profit after tax		£15,000		£15,000		£15,000

It can be seen that, by this device, the three similar years are once again made to appear similar and the distorting effects of timing differences have been removed.

Varying tax rates

So far we have assumed a constant tax rate. Over a period of time, of course, the rate of corporation tax may vary and this is a problem which must be dealt with so far as the deferred tax account is concerned. It may happen that amounts are put to reserve when one rate prevails and withdrawn when there is a different rate. There are two ways of dealing with this. The first is known as the deferral method. Under this method amounts are withdrawn from the account at the same rate as they were first transferred into it regardless of the then current rate of tax. Unless the tax rate fluctuations are very wide, which is unlikely, this will give a reasonable matching of tax to revenues. The second method, known as the liability method, involves adjusting the whole account to the new tax rate whenever this changes. This adjustment requires an additional entry in the profit and loss account. It is a matter of opinion as to which of these two methods gives the more "accurate" result. They are both illustrated below. The figures are the same as before except that the tax rate for year 1 is 50 per cent and that for years 2 and 3 is 55 per cent.

Deferral method

		Year 1		Year 2		Year 3
Profit before depreciation		£30,000		£30,000		£30,000
Less Taxation	£5,000		£22,000		£22,000	
Deferred tax	10,000		(5,000)		(5,000)	
		15,000		17,000		17,000
		£15,000		£13,000		£13,000

Liability method

		Year 1		Year 2		Year 3
Profit after depreciation		£30,000		£30,000		£30,000
Less Taxation	£5,000		£22,000		£22,000	
Deferred tax	10,000		(5,500)		(5,500)	
Adjustment	–		1,000		Nil	
		15,000		17,500		16,000
Profit after tax		£15,000		£12,500		£13,500

As presented above the deferred tax account is used whenever a timing difference occurs and all credit balances are exhausted as each timing difference is reversed. In the long run, therefore, we would expect the deferred tax account balance to tend to return to nil. Under conditions of inflation, however, it can be argued that the account will tend to grow over time and that since it bears no relation to any likely or foreseeable future tax liability it is misleading to maintain it. It was controversy over this point which led to the withdrawal of the original standard on deferred tax, SSAP 11, and its substitution by the present standard, SSAP 15.

The argument is as follows. When a company pursues a policy of phased asset replacement one might expect that a steady state will be reached where the annual depreciation charge and the annual expenditure would be approximately equal. There would thus be nil net timing differences and the deferred tax account would remain approximately constant. Under conditions of inflation the replacement costs of fixed assets (which give rise to capital allowances) would in that same steady state exceed depreciation which is based on historic cost. Thus the deferred tax account would grow without limit. This would lead to a growing apparent long-term liability to tax which would never actually crystallise.

Some would use this argument to support the total abandonment of the deferred tax account. SSAP 15 steers a compromise course saying that deferred tax should generally be provided for but allowing companies discretion not to do so if they can demonstrate a reasonable assurance that the reversal of timing differences will not take place.

SUMMARY

1. Taxation concerns companies in several ways and gives rise to a number of important accounting problems. Four areas can be distinguished.

2. The company acts as agent for the collection of taxes in some cases. Value added tax (VAT) and pay-as-you-earn income tax (PAYE) are the most frequently encountered examples. The accounting procedures used must ensure that money due to the government is correctly accounted for. They must also reflect that the company's own revenues and expenditures are unaffected by the tax.

3. A company may bear indirect taxation through, for example, the prices it pays for certain goods. Excise duty on petrol is an example of this. In accounting for this the tax is treated as part of the cost of the items purchased. It will, therefore, be charged in the profit and loss account or shown on the balance sheet as part of the cost of an asset as is appropriate.

4. Most of the taxation borne by a company is charged to it directly as corporation tax on its profits. This is treated as an appropriation of profits after they have been determined. Special rules relate to dividends paid to shareholders and to dividends received from other companies. These arise from the imputation system of dealing with taxation on these dividends.

5. A deferred tax account, prescribed in SSAP 15, is an accounting device for matching the corporation tax borne by a company against the profits which are deemed to give rise to it. The account does not affect the total amount of tax borne nor the timing of its payment. It controls, however, its impact on distributable profits.

QUESTIONS

1. Pile Driver plc is involved in the following tax matters during a certain financial year.

(a) It deducted a total of £152,000 from employees' wages under the PAYE rules.

(b) It paid £25,200 in car tax on vehicles which it had purchased.

(c) It received £346,000 from VAT charged on its sales and paid £98,400 on VAT charged on goods and services which it had bought.

(d) It estimated that £521,000 would be payable in corporation tax on its current year's profit.

(e) It paid £489,000 in corporation tax on its previous year's profit. Discuss the accounting implications of each of these.

2. Sledge Hammer plc, which has an issued capital of £1 million in £1 ordinary shares, reported a profit before taxation of £825,000 for the year ended 31st December 19—.

It was assessed for corporation tax as follows.

Profit per accounts	£825,000
Add Depreciation	35,000
Disallowed expenses	12,000
	872,000
Less Capital allowances	80,000
Taxable profit	£792,000

During the year the company had paid an interim dividend of 10p (gross) per share and the directors now propose a final dividend of 20p (gross) per share. Taking corporation tax to be at the rate of 50 per cent and income tax to be at the basic rate of 30 per cent show the appropriation section of the profit and loss account. Entries for current taxation, deferred taxation and dividends should be clearly shown and explained.

3. What is the difference between an appropriation and an expense? Under which of these categories does corporation tax, in your opinion, fall?

4. Define the following terms: (*a*) imputation system; (*b*) advance corporation tax; (*c*) franked investment income; and (*d*) capital allowances.

5. The following items appear, amongst others, on the balance sheet of Hitman plc: deferred taxation £448,273; future taxation £217,664; and current taxation £223,891.

Describe the nature of each of these balances, indicating clearly how they arose and the manner of their ultimate disposal.

CHAPTER 12

The Statement of Source and Application of Funds

OBJECTIVES

In this chapter we shall deal with the following important topics:

(a) the importance of cash flow;
(b) the requirements of SSAP 10;
(c) the preparation of a statement of source and application of funds.

1. INTRODUCTION

A great many of the techniques of financial accounting have the effect of moving us away from the naïve view that wealth can be equated with a cash balance and that profit or loss is equal to an increase or decrease in that balance. Thus on a balance sheet we recognise valuable assets other than cash and we record offsetting liabilities. On a profit and loss account we identify revenues and expenses with periods of time which may be different from those in which the related cash is actually received or paid. We have seen why such techniques are necessary and how they improve the quality of the information which emerges from the accounting system. There is a danger, however, that we shall move too far from our appreciation of cash flows.

Cash is important. Ultimately the long run excess of cash inflow over cash outflow is the test of business success. Without cash important opportunities may have to be foregone so that profits are held in check. In recognition of this all well-managed businesses prepare cash budgets as part of their internal decision informing processes and cash is as carefully managed as any other resource.

2. STATEMENT OF SOURCE AND APPLICATION OF FUNDS

The statement of source and application of funds ·is the financial accounting counterpart of the cash budget. It reports factually on how funds have moved within a company during the period of time covered by the related profit and loss account. Since 1976 this statement has been included as a routine in the published annual reports of limited companies as it has been required by a Standard, SSAP 10, published in the previous year.

The Statement is required to show:

(*a*) the funds generated by operations;

(*b*) dividends paid;

(*c*) funds arising from or absorbed by the disposal or acquisition of fixed assets; and

(*d*) change in net working capital subdivided into its components and movements in net liquid funds.

Although not required it is usual to show, as a separate item, payments of tax.

Example of preparation

Below is a balance sheet for Loganberry, plc at 31st December, year 2, together with comparative figures for the previous year and some explanatory notes on the figures. From this we can prepare a statement of source and application of funds for the year ended 31st December, year 2 along the lines prescribed in SSAP 10.

LOGANBERRY PLC

BALANCE SHEET AS AT 31ST DECEMBER

	Year 1 (£000s)	Year 2 (£000s)
Fixed assets		
Freehold land and buildings[1]	1,000	2,000
Plant and equipment[3]	2,380	3,950
	3,380	5,950
Goodwill less amounts written off	100	80
Net current assets[4]	2,520	3,100
	6,000	9,130
Less Future taxation	740	620
	5,260	8,510
Financed by:		
Share capital		
£1 ordinary shares fully paid[1,2]	2,000	3,500
Reserves		
Share premium		500
General reserve	500	1,000
Profit and loss account[5]	1,260	2,010
Loan capital	1,500	1,500
	5,260	8,510

(1) The freehold land and buildings, which had cost £1 million, were revalued during the year at £1.5 million. A further £500,000 was then spent on improvements and extensions. The surplus arising from the revaluation was applied in paying up a bonus issue of 500,000 ordinary shares.

(2) During the year there was a rights issue of £1 million ordinary shares at a price of £1.50 each.

(3) Changes on the plant and equipment account were:

	(£000s)
Balance at 1st January, year 2	2,380
Add Purchases	2,090
	4,470
Less Net book value of sales	120
	4,350
Less Depreciation for the year	400
	3,950

(4) An analysis of net current assets is:

	Year 1 (£000s)		Year 2 (£000s)	
Stock	4,240		4,680	
Debtors	1,200		2,800	
Bank	220		Nil	
		5,660		7,480
Creditors	2,240		2,560	
Bank overdraft	Nil		580	
Proposed dividend	300		500	
Current taxation	600		740	
		3,140		4,380
		2,520		3,100

(5) A summary of the profit and loss account shows:

			(£000s)
Trading profit after charging depreciation and amount written off goodwill			2,550
Add Surplus on sales of plant and equipment			70
			2,620
Less Taxation		620	
Dividend: Paid	250		
Proposed	500	750	
Transfer to General Reserve	—	500	1,870
Retained profit for the year			750

The figures required for the statement may now be calculated using the information given in the balance sheets and notes, combined with a knowledge of the accounting procedures used in compiling those figures.

Sources of funds

(*a*) Cash generated by operations. The basis for this figure is the profit before tax, dividends or other appropriations. This must be adjusted by any non-cash items in the account. Depreciation is a universal example of this and in the present example we also have the amount written off goodwill.

		(£000s)
Trading profit per account		2,550
Add Depreciation[1]	400	
Amount written off goodwill[2]	20	420
Amount generated from operations		2,970

(1) Given in note on changes in plant and machinery.
(2) This is the decline in the balance sheet value of goodwill between year 1 and year 2.

(*b*) Proceeds of sales of plant and machinery. The plant and machinery account contains only the book value of sales. This must be adjusted by adding or deducting respectively any surplus or deficit on the sales. This is given here in the profit and loss account.

	(£000s)
Net book value of sales	120
Add Surplus arising on sale	70
Proceeds of sale	190

(*c*) Proceeds of share issue. The issue was at a premium and the proceeds must include that. Thus:

	(£000s)
Nominal value of issue	1,000
Add Share premium	500
Proceeds of issue	1,500

Note that the bonus issue of shares is excluded from the calculation because no movement of funds was involved in that.

Applications of funds
    (*a*) Purchases of plant and equipment.

	(£000s)
This figure is given in the account	2,090

(*b*) Payment of dividends.

	(£000s)
Proposed dividend at 31st December year 1 (paid during year 2)	300
Interim dividend in respect of year 2	250
	550

Note that the proposed dividend at 31st December year 2 has not been paid during the period covered by the statement.
    (*c*) Taxation. The amount paid out is that classified as current taxation in the balance sheet at 31st December year 1. Thus:

	(£000s)
Tax paid	600

Future taxation in the balance sheet at 31st December year 1 is still unpaid at the end of year 2 but is now classifed as current taxation.

(*d*) Improvement and extensions to freehold land and buildings.

	(£000s)
This figure is given	500

We are now in a position to set out our statement. The changes in the elements of funds are appended to it.

Completed statement

LOGANBERRY PLC
STATEMENT OF SOURCE AND APPLICATION OF FUNDS
FOR THE YEAR ENDED 31ST DECEMBER, YEAR 2

		£000s
Source of funds		
Profit before tax		2,550
Adjustments for items not involving the movement of funds:		
Depreciation	400	
Written off goodwill	20	
	——	420
Total generated from operations		2,970
Funds from other sources		
Issue of shares for cash		1,500
Sales of plant and equipment		190
		4,660
Application of funds		
Dividends paid		550
Taxation paid		600
Improvement to freehold land and buildings		500
Purchases of plant and equipment		2,090
		3,740
		920
Increase/Decrease in working capital		
Increase in stocks	440	
Increase in debtors	1,600	
Increase in creditors (excluding taxation and proposed dividends)	(320)	
Movement in net liquid funds		
Decrease in cash balance	(800)	920

SUMMARY

1. Important though the determination of profit is, the significance of cash flows within a business should not be overlooked.

2. A source and application of funds statement is required by SSAP 10 as part of the package making up the annual accounts of a company. It describes what have been the main sources of funds during the year and how those funds have been applied. Items featured are:

(*a*) the funds generated by operations;

(*b*) dividends paid;

(*c*) funds arising from or absorbed by the disposal or acquisition of fixed assets; and

(*d*) taxation paid (this last item is not required by the Standard).

The changes in net working capital and in liquid funds are analysed.

QUESTIONS

1. "The statement of source and application of funds is at least as informative of a company's health as is the profit and loss account". Explain the essential differences between these two reports and say whether you agree with the quotation.

2. Both the statement of source and application of funds and the cash account may be said to be descriptive of the movement of funds. In what sense, if at all, are they alternatives to one another and where do the essential differences lie?

3. From the following information prepare the source and application of funds statement for Medlar, plc for the year ended 31st December, 19–2.

MEDLAR PLC
BALANCE SHEETS AT 31ST DECEMBER

	19–1	19–2
Fixed assets		
Leasehold buildings[1]	£80,000	£70,000
Furniture and fittings[2]	31,846	37,168
	111,846	107,168
Investments at market value[3]	51,889	46,335
Net current assets[4]	65,227	70,168
	228,962	223,671
Less Future taxation	27,294	26,199
	£201,668	£197,472

Financed by:
Share capital

Ordinary shares of £1 each fully paid[6]	£80,000	£100,000
Preference shares of 50p each fully paid[7]	20,000	30,000
Share premium account		4,000
Profit and loss account[5]	21,668	23,472
Loan capital	80,000	40,000
	£201,668	£197,472

(1) The leasehold buildings originally cost £100,000. They are being written off over the ten year life of the lease.

(2) An analysis of furniture and fittings is:

	Cost	Deprecia-tion	Book value
Balance at 31st December 19–1	£64,873	£33,027	£31,846
Add Purchases	18,779	Nil	18,779
	83,652	33,027	50,625
Less Sales	18,162	8,922	9,240
	65,490	24,105	41,385
Less Depreciation	Nil	4,217	4,217
Balance at 31st December 19–2	£65,490	£28,322	£37,168

(3) Investments at market value:

Value at 31st December, 19–1	£50,221
Add Purchases	13,987
	64,208
Less Book value of disposals	24,681
	39,527
Less Amount required to reduce to market value	2,359
Value at 31st December, 19–2	£37,168

(4) Net current assets:

	31st December 19–1		31st December 19–2	
Stock	£83,481		£91,442	
Debtors	63,986		59,825	
Cash	6,753		8,065	
		£154,220		£159,332
Creditors	£42,168		£41,870	
Proposed dividend	15,000		20,000	
Current taxation	31,825		27,294	
		88,993		89,164
		£65,227		£70,168

(5) Profit and loss account:

Trading profit after depreciation and amount written off leasehold property		£58,053
Add Profit on sale of furniture and fittings		2,460
		60,513
Less Net loss on sales and revaluation of investments		1,415
		59,098
Less Taxation	£27,294	
Dividends: paid	10,000	
proposed	20,000	
		57,294
Retained profit		£1,804

(6) The company made a rights issue of ordinary shares, at a price of £1.25 per share, on a 1 for 4 basis.

(7) The company also issued 20,000 preference shares of 50p each at par.

4. There appear below the balance sheets of Gooseberry plc as at 31st January year 1 and year 2. From these and the information given below them you are required to construct a source and application of funds statement for the year ended 31st January, year 2.

	31st January year 1 (£000s)	31st January year 2 (£000s)
Fixed assets		
Freehold land and buildings[1]	1,000	1,400
Plant and equipment[2]	2,420	2,680
Investments (current market value)[3]	540	490
Net current assets[4]	3,160	3,310
	7,120	7,880
Financed by:		
Share capital		
£1 ordinary shares fully paid[5]	4,000	5,000
Reserves		
Share premium account		100
Plant replacement reserve	1,800	2,000
Profit and loss account[6]	1,320	780
	7,120	7,880

(1) There has been expenditure of £400,000 on improvements to the buildings during the year.

(2) The plant and machinery account is summarised as follows.

	Cost (£000s)	Deprecia-tion (£000s)	Net book value (£000s)
Balance at 31st January year 1	5,300	2,880	2,420
Add Purchases	1,090	–	1,090
	6,390	2,880	3,510
Less Sales (book value)	710	420	290
	5,680	2,460	3,220
Less Depreciation	–	540	540
Balance at 31st January year 2	5,680	3,000	2,680

(3) Investments:

	(£000s)
Market value at 31st January year 1	540
Less Sales (market value at 31st January year 1)	30
	510
Add Purchases	62
	572
Less Amount to reduce to market value at 31st January year 2	82
Market value at 31st January year 2	490

(4) Net current assets are made up as follows.

	31st January year 1 (£000s)		31st January year 2 (£000s)	
Stock	3,900		4,200	
Debtors	2,300		2,250	
Cash	200		40	
		6,400		6,490
Less Creditors	1,890		2,010	
Proposed dividend	400		500	
Taxation	950		670	
		3,240		3,180
		3,160		3,310

(5) One million ordinary shares were issued during the year at a price of £1.10 each.

(6) Profit and loss account:

	(£000s)
Balance at 31st January year 1	1,320
Add Trading profit for year	1,063
Profit on sale of plant and machinery	60
	2,443

Less Net loss on sales and
      revaluation of investments   93
  Taxation   670

Less Net loss on sales and revaluation of investments		93
Taxation		670
Dividends: paid	200	
proposed	500	
		700
Transfer to plant replacement reserve	200	
		1,663
Balance at 31st January year 2		780

5. Fig plc has been trading at a loss for some years and hopes to rectify this by a capital raising and reorganisation programme which took place during the year ended 31st March 19–8. The company's balance sheets at the beginning and end of this year appear below and from these, and the other information given, you are asked to prepare a source and application of funds statement for the company for the year.

	31st March 19–73	31st March 19–8
Fixed assets		
Building[1]	£300,000	£500,000
Plant and machinery[2]	191,592	481,678
	491,592	981,678
Net current assets[3]	476,218	823,462
Goodwill	25,000	Nil
	£992,810	£1,805,140
Financed by		
Share capital		
Fully paid ordinary shares[4,5]	£1,000,000	£1,000,000
Building revaluation reserve	Nil	200,000
Profit and loss account[6]	(507,190)	(144,860)
Loan capital[7]	500,000	750,000
	£992,810	£1,805,140

(1) The building was professionally revalued during the year. The surplus thereby arising was transferred to a building revaluation reserve.

(2) Old plant and machinery was sold for £67,166 and purchases of new plant and machinery were made to the value of £485,020. The depreciation charge for the year was £102,468.

(3) Net current assets

	31st March 19–7		31st March 19–8	
Stock	£406,231		£593,670	
Debtors	411,740		348,260	
Cash	Nil		13,411	
		£817,971		£955,341
Less Bank overdraft	£241,890		Nil	
Creditors	99,863		£131,879	
		341,753		131,879
		£476,218		£823,462

(4) Under a scheme of capital reduction, approved by the court, the £1 ordinary shares were reduced in nominal value to 50p each. This was effected by writing off £500,000 of past losses against share capital.

(5) A rights issue of 50p ordinary shares was made at par on a 1 for 1 basis. This was fully subscribed.

(6) Profit and loss account:

Trading loss (inclusive of depreciation)	£87,370
Add Losses on sales of plant and machinery	25,300
Amount written off goodwill	25,000
Carried forward	£137,670

(7) Additional loan capital of £250,000 was raised by an issue of debentures at par.

CHAPTER 13

Consolidated Accounts

OBJECTIVES

In this chapter we shall deal with the following important topics:

(*a*) the need for consolidated accounts;
(*b*) the consolidated balance sheet;
(*c*) the consolidated profit and loss account;
(*d*) the merger method of consolidation.

1. INTRODUCTION

The entity concept in accounting requires us to select an appropriate reporting focus for our profit and loss account and balance sheet. This is usually fairly easily determined as the business itself is a natural entity whether it be a limited company or some other form of organisation. In this chapter we consider the case where the appropriate reporting entity consists of a group of legal entities related in such a way that separate reports would be misleading. For the sake of simplicity each group exemplified here will consist of two companies but the principles can easily be extended to apply to groups of whatever size. For companies registered under the Companies Acts, group accounts are a legal requirement wherever a group exists.

It is very common for one company to acquire shares in another company. The implication of this depends upon the degree of involvement and on the intention behind the acquisition. At one end of the scale there might be a small investment intended as a temporary profitable home for surplus cash. At the other end a company may purchase all the shares in another as part of a policy of expanding its own business interests by integration. The critical point on this scale so far as our present purposes are concerned is that at which one company becomes the subsidiary of another which would then be termed the parent company.

An investing company becomes a parent when it obtains control over the activities of the acquired company. This is normally achieved when it owns in excess of 50 per cent of the ordinary shares. Two points should, however, be made here briefly. One is that control may in some cases be achieved by means other than a majority shareholding, e.g. by the directors of the investing company being also directors of the acquired company. The other is that there is an intermediate status of associated company where the acquired company is not controlled but is substantially influenced by the investing company's voting power. The former case is dealt with in exactly the same way as any other subsidiary but will not be directly referred to again. The latter is covered by a special Standard, SSAP 1, referred to in Chapter 18.

We will look now at the preparation of accounts for groups of companies. This is done by a process known as consolidation whereby the individual balance sheets and profit and loss accounts are combined in a particular way. We shall look first at the balance sheet and shall consider a number of cases of increasing complexity until we have considered all the points which may arise.

2. A WHOLLY OWNED SUBSIDIARY

Where the shares were subscribed for at par by the parent when they were originally issued

This is the simplest possible case and is useful because it illustrates clearly the need for consolidated accounts. Here are the summarised balance sheets of two companies at 31st December 19— superimposed so as to save space. S is the subsidiary of P.

	P	S		P	S
Ordinary shares	£1,000	£1,000	Investment in S	£1,000	Nil
Current liabilities	500	200	Fixed assets	300	£700
			Current assets	200	500
	£1,500	£1,200		£1,500	£1,200

Note first of all that if P reports to its shareholders as a single and independent entity (presenting the balance sheet shown above) they will gain very restricted information about the business which is operated on their behalf. They have information on the business assets held by P and (in the profit and loss account) information on the profitability of their use. They have, however, no information, beyond the original cost of the investment, on assets just as certainly under their company's control but legally owned by S. As this amounts to two-thirds of the value of the total assets this is a big omission. Furthermore, no information will appear in P's profit and loss account about S's activities except the income from such dividends as S chooses, or is directed, to pay. This is a very unreliable indicator of the outcome of its activities.

The solution to the problem is to treat P and S as one entity (the group). In such an exercise those items relating to the relationship between the companies disappear and other headings are amalgamated. Thus:

P PLC AND ITS SUBSIDIARY

CONSOLIDATED BALANCE SHEET AT 31ST DECEMBER 19—

Share capital[1]	£1,000	Fixed assets[2]	£1,000
Current liabilities[2]	700	Current assets[2]	700
	£1,700		£1,700

(1) Share capital for the group is always the figure for the share capital of the parent company.

(2) Current liabilities and fixed and current assets for the group are the summation of the corresponding figures in the individual balance sheets. Note that the item share capital of S and Investment in S exactly cancel out and do not appear in the consolidated balance sheet.

Where the shares were bought from the original holders at a premium

Where S was already a going concern at the time P bought its shares, it is likely that P would have to pay more than the apparent balance sheet value of the shares in order to gain control. Such a situation is represented in the balance sheet below.

	P	S		P	S
Share capital	£1,000	£1,000	Investment in S	£1,100	
Current liabilities	500	200	Fixed assets	300	£700
			Current assets	100	500
	£1,500	£1,200		£1,500	£1,200

In such cases the amounts representing the linkage between the companies do not cancel. The difference (in this case £100) must appear on the consolidated balance sheet if this is to balance. Since this difference on consolidation arose because P has paid more for the share than their apparent book value it can conveniently be regarded as a payment for goodwill and is normally so described. Thus:

P PLC AND ITS SUBSIDIARY

CONSOLIDATED BALANCE SHEET AS AT 31ST DECEMBER 19—

Share capital	£1,000	Fixed assets	£1,000
Current liabilities	700	Current assets	600
		Goodwill arising on consolidation	100
	£1,700		£1,700

Where the difference arising on consolidation is a credit balance, i.e. where the amount paid for the shares is *less* than their apparent value, this may conveniently be regarded as a non-distributable profit to the shareholder of the parent company and thus described as capital reserve.

3. A PARTLY OWNED SUBSIDIARY

A partly owned subsidiary is one where the parent company owns sufficient shares to obtain control (i.e. over 50 per cent) but the rest are held by other shareholders who are described as having a minority interest in the subsidiary. We should note that although holding less than 100 per cent of the shares, the parent company nevertheless has complete control, because of its decisive voting power, over the activities of the subsidiary. This includes control over the disposal or deployment of its assets. These should therefore appear in full in the consolidated balance sheet even though, in one sense, only partly owned by the group. There will also be shown, as a liability of the group, the total value of the minority interest in the subsidiary. Here is an example.

BALANCE SHEET AT 31ST DECEMBER 19—

	P	S		P	S
Share Capital	£1,000	£800	Investment in S (60% equity)	£500	
Current liabilities	350	300	Fixed assets	450	£600
			Current assets	400	500
	£1,350	£1,100		£1,350	£1,100

The consolidated balance sheet appears as follows.

Share capital	£1,000	Fixed assets	£1,050
Minority interest[1]	320	Current assets	900
		Goodwill arising on consolidation[2]	20
	£1,320		£1,320

(1) Total equity of subsidiary × 40% = £800 × 40%.
(2)

Assets acquired (60% of total)	£480
Amount paid	500
Goodwill	£20

4. A PARTLY OWNED SUBSIDIARY HAVING REVENUE RESERVES

A very important issue in consolidations is the treatment of revenue reserves in the balance sheets of subsidiaries. This is a matter that we have avoided so far by ensuring that none existed. In practice, however, they are common.

A useful way of looking at the problem is as follows. The amounts shown for share capital and reserves in any balance sheet are in effect a labelling of the fund of net assets which the business commands. The revenue reserves label part of the fund as legally distributable and share capital and capital reserves label the rest as not distributable. This labelling is not a function of the nature of the assets but arises from the history of the way in which they were assembled. It is thus unique to the company to which they relate. It follows that, since the legality of distribution or otherwise depends on this history, it must not be open to another company aquiring those assets by takeover also to acquire this history. If it were then "capital" cash of the parent company could acquire "revenue" assets of a subsidiary enabling, by this device, an illegal distribution of assets. here is an example. At 31st December 19— A acquired 100 per cent of the shares of B. The balance sheets of the two companies at that date appear below.

	A	B		A	B
Share capital	£2,000	£1,500	Investment in B	£1,600	
Profit and loss account	500	250	Net other assets	900	£1,750
	£2,500	£1,750		£2,500	£1,750

B's balance sheet contains a balance of £250 legally distributable to its own shareholders (now A only!). As it was entirely earned before A came on the scene, however, it cannot be regarded as profit earned on A's behalf and thus distributable to A's shareholders. Such retained profit balances (i.e. existing at the date of the acquisition of the shares) are known as the pre-acquisition profits of the subsidiary. They must be treated as part of the value of the assets acquired and thus contribute to the calculation of goodwill or capital reserve. The correct consolidation is shown below.

A PLC AND ITS SUBSIDIARY

CONSOLIDATED BALANCE SHEET AT 31ST DECEMBER 19—

Share capital	£2,000	Net other assets	£2,650
Capital reserve	150		
Profit and loss account	500		
	£2,650		£2,650

Here is another example. It relates to a consolidation occurring several years after the controlling interest was acquired.

	X	Y		X	Y
Share capital	£5,000	£4,000	Investment in Y (80% equity)	£4,500	
Profit and loss account	1,500	2,000	Fixed assets	1,900	£4,000
Current liabilities	700	500	Current assets	800	2,500
	£7,200	£6,500		£7,200	£6,500

X purchased its holding in Y when Y's profit and loss account balance stood at £1,200.

From this note to the balance sheet Y's profit and loss account balance can be analysed as follows.

Pre-acquisition profit	£1,200	(the balance on acquisition)
Post-acquisition profit	800	(the amount credited subsequently)
	£2,000	(the present balance)

Consolidation calculations are:

Profit and loss account

Profit and loss account of X	£1,500
80% of post-acquisition profit of Y	640
	£2,140

Minority interest

20% of share capital of Y	£800
20% of profit and loss account of Y	400
	£1,200

Goodwill

Assets acquired—80% of share capital and 80% of reserves at date of acquisition (£4,000 + £1,200)	£4,160
Amount paid	4,500
Goodwill	£340

X PLC AND ITS SUBSIDIARY

CONSOLIDATED BALANCE SHEET AT . . .

Share capital	£5,000	Fixed assets	£5,900
Profit and loss account	2,140	Current assets	3,300
Minority interest	1,200	Goodwill	340
Current liabilities	1,200		
	£9,540		£9,540

5. OTHER CONSOLIDATION MATTERS

The only financial connection between companies in a group so far referred to is that of a shareholding. There are, however, other possibilities which we need to consider.

Intercompany loans

It is common for the cash shortages of one member of a group to be met by loans from other members of the group having cash surpluses. This is an obviously economical source of finance.

Where such loans occur they will appear as a liability on the balance sheet of the borrowing company and as an asset on the balance sheet of the lending company. On consolidation such balances are cancelled against one another and do not appear.

Intercompany trading debts

It is quite likely that companies in a group will trade with one another. Where they do so ordinary trading debts will appear on the balance sheets of the two companies. Unlike intercompany loans they will not normally appear separately but will be part of the debtors and creditors as appropriate. Theoretically these will be identical in amount and can be cancelled out against one another. In practice, precise cancellation may not be possible because of uncompleted transactions at the year end. Here is an example. P sells goods to its subsidiary S. At the year end S appears in P's books as a debtor for £1,000 made up as follows.

Goods supplied 15th December		£2,000
Goods supplied 31st December		500
		£2,500
Less Cash received 20th December		1,500
Amount owed		£1,000

In S's books P appears as a creditor for £250. This is made up as follows.

Goods received 15th December		£2000
Less Cash paid 20th December	£1,500	
Cash paid 31st December	250	
		1,750
Amount owing		£250

The discrepancy between the two figures can be seen to be made up of two items. These are £500 worth of goods sent by P but not received by S until after the year end and £250 of cash sent by S but not received by P.

On consolidation the balance should be cancelled so far as possible. This leaves a debit balance uncancelled of £750 (£1,000 − £250). This should be split into its components and added to stock (£500) and cash (£250).

Profit on intercompany trading

When intercompany trading occurs it will normally be at a profit to the selling company. Provided that the goods have passed outside the group by the date of the consolidation this has no implications for the procedure. Where they are retained in stock by the purchasing company, however, an adjustment is required. If this is not made stock within the group will be valued at a figure in excess of cost to the group, allowing to be reported a profit which, from the group point of view, has not been realised. Here is an example. P sells goods to its subsidiary, S, at cost plus 25 per cent. At the year end S retains a stock of such goods valued at cost to itself of £1,000. P holds 60 per cent of the equity of S. The total profit loading on the stock is £200 (cost £800). If S were wholly owned the adjustment required would reduce stock and group profit by this £200. For a partly owned subsidiary, as here, the group can be regarded as having earned part of its profit from the minority shareholders and the group proportion only of the profit loading is eliminated. Thus the adjustment will reduce stock and profit by £120 (60 per cent of £200).

Sometimes the subject of intercompany trading is a fixed asset to the buying company. In this case the treatment is still as described above, the net book value of the asset being regarded as "stock". Here is an example. Y is an 80 per cent owned subsidiary of X. The company is a motor dealer and sold a van to X some time ago for £8,000. This gave Y a profit of £2,000. The value of the van in X's balance sheet is currently £4,000. The profit loading on the full £8,000 cost of the van was £2,000. On the £4,000 remaining it is therefore £1,000 (the profit loading reducing *pro rata* as the van is depreciated). The adjustment required is the group proportion of the profit, i.e. £800 (80 per cent of £1,000). Note that for the purposes of this adjustment it makes no difference whether it is the parent company selling to the subsidiary or the subsidiary selling to the parent. It should not be overlooked that stocks in transit between companies (discussed in the last section) may bear a profit loading which will require adjustment.

Proposed dividends

Dividends paid during a year should have been correctly recorded by the paying and receiving companies and require no special treatment on consolidation. It should be noted, however, that any dividend paid out of *pre*-acquisition profit should not be credited to the parent's profit and loss account but to the account Investment in Subsidiary. As a transfer of part of the assets acquired when the shares were bought it is in effect a part reimbursement of the purchase price. This circumstance is unlikely to arise except in the early days immediately after the acquisition.

So far as proposed dividends are concerned it should be realised that these are a part of the profit and loss account earmarked for payment and for this reason transferred to current liabilities. On consolidation the minority shareholders entitlement should be added to the figure for minority interest and the group portion added to the group profit and loss account.

6. EXAMPLE OF CONSOLIDATION PROCEDURES

Here now is a full example of a consolidated balance sheet incorporating all of the points made so far. Cat plc holds 75 per cent of the equity of Mouse plc which it acquired when that company had a credit balance on its profit and loss account of £220,000. At 31st March 19— the two companies' balance sheets were as follows.

	Cat £000s	Mouse £000s		Cat £000s	Mouse £000s
Share capital			Fixed assets		
Ordinary	2,000	1,000	Buildings	1,100	800
Preference	500	300	Equipment	986	762
Profit and loss	648	480	Motor vehicles	428	516
	3,148	1,780		2,514	2,078
Loan capital			Current assets		
5% debentures		2,000	Stock	927	777
Loan from Mouse	950		Debtor's	629	648
Current liabilities			Cash	337	223
Creditors	340	271		1,893	1,648
Taxation	669	525	Investment		
Proposed dividend	500	100	Shares in Mouse	1,200	
	1,509	896	Loan to Cat		950
	5,607	4,676		5,607	4,676

(*a*) Mouse sells its products to Cat at cost plus $33\frac{1}{3}$ per cent. At the balance sheet date Cat held in stock such goods to the value of £112,000.

(*b*) In Mouse's Sales Ledger Cat appeared as a debtor for £25,000. In Cat's Purchase Ledger Mouse appeared as a creditor for £28,000. A cheque for £3,000 was in transit from Mouse to Cat.

(*c*) Cat has not taken credit for its share of the proposed dividend from Mouse.

(*d*) Mouse owns equipment having a written down value of £30,000. It had been purchased from Cat for £60,000 several years ago at a profit to that company of £16,000.

The consolidation calculations are as follows (all figures are in £000s).

Profit and loss account

Cat	648	
Mouse—group proportion of post-acquisition	195	(75% of 480–220)
Mouse's proposed dividend—group proportion	75	
	918	
Less Intercompany profit on stock	21	
Intercompany profit on equipment	6	
	— 27	
Group balance	891	

Minority interest

25% of share capital and reserves of Mouse	370
Preference shares of Mouse	300
Minority portion of Mouse's proposed dividend	25
	695

Creditors

Cat	340
Mouse	271
	611
Less Intercompany balance	25
	586

Fixed assets

	Buildings	Equipment	Motor vehicles
Cat	1,100	986	428
Mouse	800	762	516
	1,900	1,748	944
Less intercompany profit		6	
		1,742	

Current assets

	Stock	Debtors	Cash
Cat	927	629	337
Mouse	777	648	223
	1,704	1,277	560
Less intercompany	21	25	Nil
	1,683	1,252	560
Transfer		(3)	3
		1,249	563

Goodwill

Assets acquired	915	(75% of 1,220)
Amount paid	1,200	
	285	

CAT PLC AND ITS SUBSIDIARY
CONSOLIDATED BALANCE SHEET AT 31ST MARCH 19—

	£000s		£000s
Share capital		*Fixed assets*	
Ordinary shares	2,000	Buildings	1,900
Preference shares	500	Equipment	1,742
Profit and loss account	891	Motor vehicles	944
	3,391		4,586
Minority interest	695	*Current assets*	
Loan capital	2,000	Stock	1,683
		Debtors	1,249
Current liabilities		Cash	563
Creditors	586		3,495
Taxation	1,194	Goodwill arising on consolidation	285
Proposed dividend	500 2,280		
	8,366		8,366

7. CONSOLIDATED PROFIT AND LOSS ACCOUNT

This can best be explained by means of an example related to the balance sheet just considered. Below there appear Cat and Mouse's separate profit and loss accounts for the year ended 31st March 19—.

		Cat (£000s)		*Mouse* (£000s)
Sales		15,897		12,166
Less Cost of sales		10,645		8,955
Gross profit		5,252		3,211
Less Distribution costs	1,689		744	
Administrative expenses	2,113	3,802	1,562	2,306
		1,450		905
Add Income from shares in group company[1]		75		
		1,525		905
Less Interest payable				100
Profit before taxation		1,525		805
Less Taxation		669		525
Profit after taxation		856		280
Less Dividends		800		200
Retained profit		56		80

(1) The tax credit on this franked investment income has been ignored in order not to introduce an unnecessary complication.

Note that included in the amounts charged in arriving at profit are:

	(£000s)	(£000s)
Directors' emoluments	80	60
Auditors' remuneration	100	50
Depreciation	192	186

You are informed that:

(a) of Cat's sales a total of £420,000 was to Mouse;

(b) one of Cat's directors was also a director of Mouse and he received £10,000 from the latter company; and

(c) depreciation on the equipment which Mouse bought from Cat was £10,000.

The figures for the consolidation are calculated as follows.

		(£000s)
(a) Sales		
Cat		15,897
Mouse		12,166
		28,063
Less Intercompany		420
		27,643
(b) Cost of sales		
Cat		10,645
Mouse		8,955
		19,600
Less Intercompany sales	420	
Intercompany profit on equipment released by depreciation	3	423
		19,177
Add Intercompany profit on stock		21
		19,198
(c) Directors' emoluments		
Cat		80
Mouse (amount paid to director of Cat)		10
		90

(*d*) *Depreciation*

Cat	192
Mouse	186
	378
Less Intercompany profit element	3
	375

CAT PLC AND ITS SUBSIDIARY

CONSOLIDATED PROFIT AND LOSS ACCOUNT FOR THE YEAR ENDED 31ST MARCH 19—

	(*£000s*)	(*£000s*)
Sales		27,643
Less Cost of sales		19,198
Gross profit		8,445
Less Distribution costs	2,433	
Administrative expenses	3,675	
	——	6,108
		2,337
Less Interest payable		100
Profit before taxation		2,237
Less Taxation		1,194
Profit after taxation		1,043
Minority interest in subsidiary		70
Profit attributable to group		973
Dividends		800
Retained profit		173

Note that included in the amounts charged in arriving at profit are:

Directors' emoluments	90
Auditors' remuneration	150
Depreciation	375

8. MERGER ACCOUNTING

The method of consolidation of balance sheets and profit and loss accounts so far described is known as the acquisition method of consolidation and may be regarded as the one which is normally to be used. There is an alternative method, however, known as the merger method which may be used in carefully defined circumstances. This has the immediate merit of being a great deal simpler to understand and to apply but more importantly it has the implication that the pre-acquisition profit of a subsidiary company is not "frozen" but remains distributable to the shareholders of the parent company. This is why it can be allowed only in certain circumstances.

Historical background

Merger accounting has an interesting history in the United Kingdom and before we look at the method it will be instructive to consider the issues and the way in which they have developed. We shall consider an example. P and S are two independent companies having separate bodies of shareholders but P is on the point of making a bid to obtain S as its subsidiary. It may do so either by acquiring the shares of S for cash or, alternatively, by offering the shareholders of S new shares in P in exchange for their existing holdings. In the former case the present shareholders of S will depart from the scene and the acquisition method of consolidation will be used so that shareholders in P are barred from distributing to themselves any of the existing revenue reserves of S. For reasons already explained this is clearly correct. In the latter case, however, the shareholders of P after the takeover include those who were previously shareholders of S. Application of the acquisition method, therefore, bars the distribution of profits to those to whom they could legally have been distributed only a short time previously. It may be argued that this is to protect the rights of creditors to an absurd extent and that the integrity of that principle is preserved in these circumstances where all revenue reserves of both companies are amalgamated without regard to the date when they were earned. This is the underlying principle of the merger method of consolidation.

For many years doubt existed as to whether this method was legal in this country. At the heart of the doubt lay Section 56 of the Companies Act 1948 which requires a company to create a share premium account when it issues shares for a consideration valued in excess of the nominal value of those shares. When that consideration consisted of shares in another company, was the question, were they to be valued at their nominal value or at their market value?

In 1971 the Accounting Standards Steering Committee (now Accounting Standards Committee) issued ED 3 "Accounting for Acquisitions and Mergers". This proposed Standard allowed for merger accounting in appropriate circumstances. Owing to the many doubts expressed about this ED 3 was never translated into a Standard although it lay on the programme of unfinished business for many years. Meanwhile a number of companies did adopt merger accounts, where they felt that this could be justified, and risked that this might be challeneged in the Courts.

In the event the challenge came from a quite unexpected quarter and in an unexpected way. The case was not a company law case but a tax case and it did not challenge the legality of merger accounting but sought to establish this. The facts in Shearer *v.* Bercain Ltd, in summary form, were as follows. B acquired the whole of the share capitals of L and A in return for an issue of its own shares to the existing shareholders of each of those companies. L was valued at £84,000 and 3,500 £1 shares in B were issued for it. A was worth £12,000 and acquired by the issue of 600 shares in B. B accounted for these transactions by increasing its share capital by £4,100 (£3,500 + £600) and by creating a share premium account of £91,900 (£84,000 + £12,000 − £4,100). L and A subsequently paid dividends out of pre-acquisition profits which B (as the acquisition method requires) credited against the cost of its investments in subsidiaries as undistributable to its own members.

B was a close company which means that, for tax purposes, the Inland Revenue is entitled to treat it as though it had distributed a substantial part of its profits even where this is not the case. Such a treatment gives rise to what is known as a shortfall assessment and it is made so that companies controlled by a small number of wealthy people cannot be used to prevent the inclusion of income into a higher personal income tax bracket by leaving it as retained profit. The Inspector of Taxes contended that, although B *had* treated its takeovers as acquisitions, it *could* have treated them as mergers. Had it done so the dividends from L and A would have been distributable to its members and thus eligible for a shortfall assessment. B won the case and this seemed to establish that merger accounting was, indeed, illegal. The case, however, led directly to a provision inserted into the Companies Act 1981 relieving companies from the need to create a share premium account when acquiring a major interest in another company which thereby becomes a virtually wholly-owned subsidiary.

Merger accounting may thus, apparently, be used where the following conditions apply.

(*a*) The subsidiary must have been acquired in return for an issue of shares by the parent.

(b) The parent must have acquired at least 90 per cent of the equity of the subsidiary.

These are the minimum legal requirements and it is likely that they will be added to by an Accounting Standard in due course. Under ED 3 there would have been two further requirements, namely:

(c) that the equity voting rights in the parent held by the former shareholders of any of the constituent companies of the group must not exceed three times the equity voting rights of any other such group of shareholders (i.e. there must be not too great a disparity of size in the merging businesses); and

(d) that the substance of the main business of each of the members of the merged group must remain the same as it was before.

Example

Here is an example of the merger method of consolidating balance sheets. A balance sheet drawn up on the acquisition basis is also given for the purpose of comparison. Alice acquired 95 per cent of the share capital of Christopher some years ago on the basis that the shareholders of Christopher received one new Alice share for every Christopher share then held. At that date Christopher had a balance on its profit and loss account of £250,000 (not relevant for the merger method). There are no intercompany balances and no intercompany trading (which, if there were, would be treated identically under either method). Alice's shares at the date the new shares were issued had a market value of £1.50 each (again, not relevant for the merger method). The balance sheets at 31st December 19— were:

	Alice (£000s)	Christopher (£000s)		Alice (£000s)	Christopher (£000s)
Share capital	1,760	800	Fixed assets	900	800
Profit and loss			Current assets	650	520
account	300	400	Investment in C[1]	760	
Current liabilities	250	120			
	2,310	1,320		2,310	1,320

(1) Valued at the nominal value of the shares in Alice issued— this would be incorrect for the acquisition method when they would be valued at the market value of the shares issued, i.e. £1,140,000. In that case these shares would also be shown to have been issued at a premium of 50p per share.

Merger method

ALICE PLC AND ITS SUBSIDIARY

CONSOLIDATED BALANCE SHEET AT 31ST DECEMBER 19—

	(£000s)		(£000s)
Share capital	1,760	Fixed assets	1,700
Profit and loss account[1]	680	Current assets	1,170
Minority interest[2]	60		
Current liabilities	370		
	2,870		2,870

(1)

Alice		300
Christopher	400	
Less Minority share, 5%	20	
	—	380
		680

(2) Five per cent of share capital and reserves of Christopher.

Acquisition method

ALICE PLC AND ITS SUBSIDIARY

CONSOLIDATED BALANCE SHEET AT 31ST DECEMBER 19—

	(£000s)		(£000s)
Share capital	1,760	Fixed assets	1,700
Share premium	380	Current assets	1,170
Profit and loss account[3]	442.5	Goodwill	142.5
Minority interest	60		
Current liabilities	370		
	3,012.5		3,012.5

(3)

Alice	300
Christopher (95% of post-acquisition)	142.5
	442.5

(4)

Assets acquired 95% of share capital and pre-acquisition profit	997.5
Amount "paid"	1,140
Goodwill	142.5

The consolidation of profit and loss accounts is identical whether acquisition or merger accounting is applied to the balance sheets.

SUMMARY

1. Where the appropriate accounting entity is a group rather than an individual company accounts may be amalgamated in the form of consolidated statements.

2. Group accounts, of which consolidated accounts are the most convenient form, are required under company law wherever one company controls another. This control is normally effected by the acquisition of over 50 per cent of the share capital. A company so controlled is termed a subsidiary company.

3. In the consolidation of a balance sheet the post-acquisition profits only of a subsidiary company may enter into the group revenue reserves. Pre-acquisition profits are regarded as part of the value of the assets acquired in the share purchase and are used in the calculation of goodwill or capital reserve arising on consolidation.

4. A subsidiary company may be either wholly owned or partly owned. In the latter case there will be an item in the consolidated balance sheet representing the minority interest in the subsidiary.

5. Items requiring special attention in a consolidation are:
(*a*) intercompany loans;
(*b*) intercompany trading debts;
(*c*) intercompany profits; and
(*d*) intercompany dividends.

6. A consolidated profit and loss account deals initially with the total profit of all members of the group. The minority's share of profit, where applicable, are then deducted from profit after taxation before the other appropriations.

7. In appropriate circumstances a simplified form of consolidation, known as the merger form, may be used. The circumstances required would seem to be:
(*a*) the subsidiary must have been acquired in return for an issue of shares by the parent;

(b) the parent must have acquired at least 90 per cent of the equity of the subsidiary;

(c) the equity voting rights in the parent held by the former shareholders of any of the constituent companies of the group must not exceed three times the equity voting rights of any other such group of shareholders; and

(d) the substance of the main business of each of the members of the merged group must remain the same as it was before.

QUESTIONS

1. The balance sheets of Start plc and Finish plc, at 31st December 19—, appear below in summary form.

	Start	Finish		Start	Finish
Share capital	£5,000	£2,000	Fixed assets	£3,940	£2,488
Profit and loss			Current assets	3,466	2,142
account	2,984	1,864			
			Investment in Finish		
Current liabilities	1,922	766	75% share capital	2,500	
	£9,906	£4,630		£9,906	£4,630

(a) When Start acquired its shares in Finish, the latter company had a balance on its profit and loss account of £984.

(b) Start sells goods to Finish. At the balance sheet date Finish included Start amongst its creditors at a figure of £136. Start included Finish amongst its debtors at a figure of £168. The difference between these figures was accounted for by cash in transit from Finish to Start of £32.

(c) Finish holds a stock of goods valued at £520 which it had purchased from Start. Start had paid £380 for them.

Prepare a consolidated balance sheet using the acquisition method.

2. Below appear the highly summarised balance sheets of Punch plc and Judy plc at 31st December 19—.

	Punch	Judy		Punch	Judy
Share capital			Net assets	£12,460	£12,280
(£1 shares)	£10,000	£8,000			
Profit and loss					
account	2,460	4,280			
	£12,460	£12,280		£12,460	£12,280

The market price for a Punch share is currently £2 and for a Judy share £2.50. Punch and Judy wish to merge and two possibilities are being considered. These are:

(a) Punch will issue 10,000 shares to the shareholders of Judy in exchange for their entire existing holdings; or

(b) Judy will issue 8,000 shares to the shareholders of Punch in exchange for their entire existing holdings.

Advise on the accounting and practical consequences of each alternative as reflected in the consolidated balance sheet of the group as prepared by either the acquisition or merger method.

3. Explain why the use of the merger method of consolidation must be very carefully controlled and, in particular, why it can be allowed only in certain circumstances.

4. Flea plc is a subsidiary of Gnat plc. From the separate profit and loss accounts given below and the notes appended to them, prepare a consolidated profit and loss account for the group.

		Flea		Gnat
Sales		£855,463		£801,460
Less Cost of sales		575,962		531,698
Gross profit		279,501		269,762
Less Distribution costs	£64,673		£75,263	
Administrative expenses	93,472		82,466	
		158,145		157,729
Net trading profit		121,356		112,033
Add Other income: Dividend from Gnat (gross)		7,500		–
Profit before taxation		128,856		112,033
Deduct Corporation tax		63,218		54,632
Profit after taxation		65,638		57,401
Add Balance brought forward		156,840		23,460
Profit available for distribution		222,478		80,861
Less Dividends: paid (net)	£20,000		£7,000	
proposed (net)	30,000		14,000	
		50,000		21,000
Balance brought forward		£172,478		£59,861

(a) Gnat's sales include £92,300 sold to Flea. All sales were at a profit of 30 per cent of cost.

(b) Flea's cost of sales included £90,350 purchased from Gnat.

(c) Flea invoices Gnat at cost for certain group administrative services. It credits the amount to its own administrative expenses.

(d) The dividend paid by Gnat to Flea was £7,500 gross, £5,250 net.

(e) When Flea purchased its shares in Gnat the balance on the latter's profit and loss account stood at £16,424.

5. B and C are subsidiary companies of A. Ninety per cent of B's capital was acquired in exchange for an issue of shares in A

some years ago. The circumstances make it appropriate for this to be treated on a merger basis. Sixty per cent of C's capital was acquired for cash when the balance on C's profit and loss account was £2,500. Prepare a consolidated balance sheet from the individual balance sheets given below.

BALANCE SHEETS AT 31ST DECEMBER 19—

	A		B		C	
Fixed assets		£22,111		£28,463		£17,690
Current assets	£17,600		£17,781		£12,662	
Less Current liabilities	7,249		6,348		5,882	
		10,351		11,433		6,780
Investment in subsidiaries:						
B		30,000				
C		15,000				
		£77,462		£39,896		£24,470
Financed by:						
Share capital		£70,000		£30,000		£20,000
Share premium account		2,000		5,000		1,000
Profit and loss account		5,462		4,896		3,470
		£77,462		£39,896		£24,470

(a) Amongst its current liabilities A shows B and C as creditors at amounts of £542 and £448 respectively.

(b) Amongst current assets B shows A as a debtor for £592 and C shows A as a debtor for £548.

(c) There is cash in transit from A to B of £50.

(d) There are goods in transit between C and A of £100 (invoiced price). Their cost was £80.

(e) A holds in stock goods bought from B for £820 (cost £600) and from C £630 (cost £400).

(f) Proposed dividends included in current liabilities are B £1,000 and C £500. Ignore taxation.

CHAPTER 14

Financial Ratios

OBJECTIVES

In this chapter we shall deal with the following important topics:

(a) the importance of financial ratios;
(b) the need for their careful interpretation;
(c) the most significant ratios calculated and discussed.

1. INTRODUCTION

Accounts are intended to communicate information about an economic entity and there must be two parties to any act of communication. Our discussions so far have centred on the provision of information. We have examined the concepts on which accounts are based and the techniques which have been developed to make those concepts operational. We turn our interest now to the consumer of the information. He will always have a particular point of view. His need for information may be very specific and clearly defined such as, for example, the requirement of the Inland Revenue to know taxable profit for a particular year. The need may, on the other hand, be fairly general, such as that of the potential investor seeking out a suitable home for his funds.

To make this chapter of as wide an interest as possible we shall consider many examples of requirements for information and it will be our intention to concentrate on reading between the lines of accounts rather than on the more obvious of the pieces of information given on the face of them. It is obvious, and needs no comment, how one determines the level of a business's debtors or what profit it has earned from an inspection of its final accounts. It is much more difficult, however, to judge such matters as its performance, its degree of vulnerability to risk, its capital structure, etc., without an informed analysis of the information available.

The key to this analysis is the examination of figures within a context. For a full analysis the context must include other figures within the same set of accounts, a knowledge of the conventions and limitations of the financial accounting process and an understanding of unrecorded but important facts about the environment in which the business operates.

A very simple example will make clear how important context is and how as it changes it will change the interpretation of the accounting information provided. Suppose that we are told that A and B each engage in a project under contract and that A receives a fee of £500 whilst B receives £5,000. On the face of it B has been more successful than A. Closer examination, however, shows that A was required to spend only one day on the work whereas B's project took a whole month. Clearly this changes our original interpretation. A is paid £500 per day and B £250 per day (assuming twenty working days in the month). Now it would appear that A is the more successful. Finally, however, we learn that A's work is difficult, unpleasant and dangerous. B's is easy and comfortable and there is no risk attached to it. Once again we might change our view and see B as the more successful income-earner.

All this serves to show that it is often meaningless to try to form a judgment based on a single figure drawn from a set of accounts. We cannot say whether a particular figure for profit is satisfactory without having regard to the effort or to the capital investment required to produce it. We cannot comment on the adequacy of cash resources without forming a view as to the demands which will be made on them.

One very important aid to the understanding of accounting information is the computation of ratios and relationships between one figure in the accounts and another. A judgment can then be made as to whether the relationship is, in the circumstances of the case, the right one. It should, however, be stressed, and we shall hope to make this very clear as we proceed, that such analysis is an aid only to judgment and does not replace it. Many factors, not least of which are the deficiencies in the accounting process itself, combine to make ratios dangerous tools if they are used carelessly or with reckless reliance on the story they seem to tell. It should also be stated that the ratios which are calculated by any particular user of accounts will depend both on his point of view and on his access to information. The shareholder in a company, for instance, will be interested in ratios having a bearing on the income or capital value of the investment and on its degree of security. He will, however, be restricted to calculations which can be based on the relatively limited number of figures appearing in the published accounts. The directors, on the other hand, will have a much broader interest in the workings of the business and will also have available far more detailed accounts together with much additional background information.

In our discussion of accounting ratios it will be useful to have before us a set of accounts to work on. The accounts of an imaginary company which we can use for this purpose are set out below.

SUN AND MOON PLC

TRADING AND PROFIT AND LOSS ACCOUNT FOR THE YEAR ENDED 31ST MARCH 19—

	(£000s)	
Sales		5,580
Less Cost of sales		3,172 ✓
Gross profit		2,408
Less Administrative and other expenses:		
Wages and salaries	982	
Electricity	41	
Telephone, postage and stationery	112	
Rates	200	
Insurances	58	
Maintenance	35	
Bank charges and interest	17	
Depreciation	180	
		1,625
Net profit before taxation		783
Less Corporation tax		385
Profit after taxation		398
Less Dividends: Paid—Preference	20	
Ordinary	100	
Proposed—Preference	20	
Ordinary	150	
		290
Retained profit		108

BALANCE SHEET AS AT 31ST MARCH 19—

	(£000s)			(£000s)
Share capital			*Fixed assets*	
Ordinary shares of £1		2,500	Building	1,500
8% Preference shares			Furniture and	
of £1		500	equipment	1,306
Profit and loss			Motor vehicles	522
account		942		
		3,942		3,328
Current liabilities			*Current assets*	
Taxation	285		Stock	732
Proposed dividends	170		Debtors	543
Creditors	265		Bank	59
		720		1,334
		4,662		4,662

2. CALCULATION OF RATIOS FROM THE PROFIT AND LOSS ACCOUNT

Gross profit rate

The gross profit rate is defined as the percentage which gross profit is of sales. It can be regarded as a useful measure of the effectiveness of the basic profit earning activity of the business. For Sun and Moon plc:

$$\text{Gross profit rate} = \frac{\text{Gross profit}}{\text{Sales}} \times 100\%$$
$$= \frac{2,408}{5,580}$$
$$= 43\%$$

Since sales turnover can be seen as a measure of effort put into the selling process, this rate shows how well that effort has been rewarded. In this case we are informed that every £1 worth of sales yields the company 43p in terms of gross profit.

It cannot be assumed that the company is necessarily seeking the maximum possible gross profit rate and that any decline in this quantity should be viewed with dismay. In comparisons between one business and another it should be noted that what should be seen as a satisfactory level of the gross profit rate depends on the nature of the business. A retailer of food whose turnover consists of a very large number of individually small transactions and who is dealing in a highly perishable product would need a higher gross profit rate to cover his other costs and still leave a satisfactory net profit. A manufacturer of heavy machinery selling against firm orders to relatively few customers may regard a much lower gross rate as satisfactory.

The overall gross profit rate also depends on the mix of products being sold. Here is an analysis of the sales and the cost of sales for Sun and Moon plc.

	PRODUCTS				
	A	B	C	D	Total
	(£000s)	(£000s)	(£000s)	(£000s)	(£000s)
Sales	1,206	1,598	947	1,829	5,580
Cost of sales	784	1,150	462	776	3,172
Gross profit	422	448	485	1,053	2,408
Gross profit rate	35%	28%	51%	58%	43%

It can be seen from this that the overall gross profit rate is a weighted average over the four products. A and B have relatively low rates of gross profit and C and D have relatively high ones. If, in a future year, the mix of turnover changed so that more of A and B were sold and less of C and D, then the gross profit rate would drop. It would not, however, be fair to judge this as representing a decline in performance.

Another point we ought to consider is that gross profit rate will be a function of pricing policy and that the ultimate objective is to maximise the absolute level of the net profit and not *per se* the gross profit rate. In a competitive situation one way of achieving this objective may be to reduce prices. This will inevitably have an adverse effect on the gross profit rate but not necessarily on overall profit.

We will suppose that the directors of the company plan to reduce all prices by 5 per cent for the forthcoming year and that they anticipate that this will result in an increase of 30 per cent in the volume of all goods sold. The proportions sold of each of the four products will be the same as in the year just past. The result of this decision can be predicted as follows.

	This year (£000s)	Volume increase 30% at constant prices (£000s)	Volume increase 30% at 5% reduced prices (£000s)
Sales	5,580	7,254	6,891
Cost of sales	3,172	4,124	4,124
Gross profit	2,408	3,130	2,767
Gross profit rate	43%		40%

It would be wrong for the directors to judge their proposed policy as being a failure because it will result in a decline in the gross profit rate from 43 per cent to 40 per cent. It should be judged a success because it increases total gross profit from £2,408,000 to £2,767,000.

Apart from aiding judgments as to the effectiveness of the profit earning process a calculation of the gross profit rate is a very good control procedure. A sharp drop in the gross profit rate which cannot be explained by a change in sales mix or in pricing policy should always be investigated. It may signify that cash or goods are being misappropriated or that errors are being made in record keeping. Inaccurate stocktaking might also have this effect.

Expenses to sales

The gross profit is a very important figure but represents only the first step towards the determination of the final net profit. From it have to be deducted all the administrative, selling and other expenses of the business. These represent the cost of running the services required to support the basic profit earning process. The main headings are administration (concerned with the organisation and operation of the business including the maintenance of its accounting records), product development (concerned with developing new products and keeping old ones technically up-to-date) and selling and distribution (concerned with market research, the promotion of products and their efficient transfer to sales outlets). It would be wrong to say, as is sometimes done, that these represent unproductive expenses because they do not directly contribute to the profit earned. Without them the productive process would collapse and therefore they are every bit as contributive to the ultimate profit as it is. Nevertheless it is difficult to measure the effectiveness of such ancillary services and therefore there is considerable scope for uncontrolled wastefulness if this area is not watched.

The relationship between the expenses and the level of sales gives an indication of the efficiency with which this function is working. If, for example, administrative and other expenses amount to 10 per cent of sales revenue then, other things being equal, efficiency is higher than when they amount to 20 per cent of sales revenue.

For Sun and Moon plc the relevant calculation is:

$$\text{Expenses to sales} = \frac{\text{Administrative and other expenses}}{\text{Sales}} \times 100\%$$
$$= \frac{1{,}625}{5{,}580} \times 100\%$$
$$= 29\%$$

Again, care is needed in interpreting this figure and two points in particular must be noted. Firstly, because it is, by definition, not possible to match these expenses directly against sales their correlation with the level of sales is rough and ready. Although in the long run a higher level of sales will probably require a higher level of administrative and other expenses, in the short run the latter will be relatively unresponsive to changes in the level of activity. Increasing sales, therefore, may mean that the proportion of expenses to sales falls. Such a change in the percentage may have relatively little meaning.

Secondly we must have regard to the quality of the service arising from the expenses. We cannot say that our objective will, in all circumstances, be to minimise administrative and other expenses. Pursued to the ultimate such a policy will lead to an inadequate service. Too little spent on administration may mean that the organisation breaks down. Too little spent on promotion may mean that valuable market opportunities are lost. Too little spent on development may mean that the future of the business is less bright than its potential should allow. A judgment has therefore to be made as to what proportion of resources should be diverted into these activities.

The calculation of the ratio of expenses to sales may be helpful in forming a judgment as, in a sense, this will show what can be afforded. The detail with which the percentages are determined will depend on the amount of information required. For example one business might calculate the percentage which all non-trading account expenses bear in relation to sales. Another might calculate separately the percentage for each of administrative, research and development, and selling and distribution expenses. Yet another might calculate the percentage for items of expense which for some reason had become of special interest.

Calculation of individual percentages for the various components of total expense will ensure that significant changes in individual elements are not concealed by being offset by other changes within the overall total. An analysis for Sun and Moon plc is given below

Administrative and other expenses	*(£000s)*	*(% sales)*
Wages and salaries	982	17.6
Electricity	41	0.7
Telephone, postage and stationery	112	2.0
Rates	200	3.6
Insurances	58	1.0
Maintenance	35	0.6
Bank charges and interest	17	0.3
Depreciation	180	3.2
	1,625	29.0

From this it can be seen, amongst other things, that wages and salaries are by far the most significant part of administrative and other expenses in terms of their size and should therefore be kept under close scrutiny.

The two ratios we have now looked at are both concerned with the profit and loss account and thus with the activity of the business. Ratios and relationships calculated from the balance sheet give indications concerning the immediate position of the business. We shall now look at some of the more important of these.

3. CALCULATION OF RATIOS FROM THE BALANCE SHEET

The current ratio and the liquidity ratio

One very important matter of concern is the short term solvency of a business—the extent to which it can pay its bills as they fall due. This can be critical to business success. It is quite possible for a business to be fully solvent in the absolute sense (i.e. its assets could be realised for a sum which would fully meet its liabilities) and to be making excellent profits but for it nevertheless not to be generating sufficient liquid funds in the short run to meet its regular bills. In the less severe cases this will mean adherence to an exhausting policy of paying all bills at the last possible moment and of running a series of short term overdrafts at the bank. In the more severe cases it might mean the curtailment of vital supplies as suppliers refuse to allow credit until they are paid.

The current ratio is one measure of the short term ability of a business to pay its way. It is the ratio between current assets and current liabilities. For Sun and Moon plc:

$$\text{Current ratio} = \frac{\text{Current assets}}{\text{Current liabilities}}$$
$$= \frac{1,334}{720}$$
$$= 1.85.$$

Usually a figure for this ratio in the region of 2 is regarded as a reasonable average level but it may vary quite a lot from this figure and depends to an extent on the nature of the business engaged in.

Because the current ratio conceals important structural features of current assets, e.g. the extent to which funds might be locked up in slow moving stocks, a more stringent ratio is sometimes used. This is known as the liquidity ratio and is calculated as liquid assets ÷ current liabilities. Liquid assets are defined as cash and balances which can readily be turned into cash. Both debtors and bank balances are usually regarded as coming under this heading. A liquidity ratio of about 1 is usually considered to be about right for most businesses.

For Sun and Moon plc:

$$\text{Liquidity ratio} = \frac{\text{Debtors} + \text{Bank}}{\text{Current liabilities}}$$
$$= \frac{543 + 59}{720}$$
$$= 0.84.$$

From this it can be seen that both the current ratio and the liquidity ratio for Sun and Moon, plc are somewhat on the low side and the company is likely to feel itself a little pressed for liquid funds.

Gearing

A very important fact about a business is what is known as its gearing, that is the relationship between loan finance and equity finance. For the purpose of calculating gearing preference capital is normally (technically incorrectly) classified as debt. This is because it is to all intents and purposes a fixed interest security.

Gearing has very important implications for what is known as financial risk. All businesses face commercial risk, i.e. the possibility of unforeseen fluctuations in income, and the degree of this will vary from one type of business to another. Financial risk is added to commercial risk and is imposed by the capital structure of the business. An example will very clearly show the difference between a geared and an ungeared company in this respect.

A and B have each invested resources of £1,000,000 and earn a fluctuating annual profit. Their financial structures are shown below.

	A	*B*
Ordinary share capital	£1,000,000	£750,000
12½% Loan and preference share capital	Nil	250,000
	£1,000,000	£1,000,000

In two consecutive years A and B each earn a profit of £250,000 in the first year and £100,000 in the second year. These figures are before interest or dividend. Calculations of the amounts available to ordinary shareholders are shown below.

| | Year 1 | | Year 2 | |
	A	B	A	B
Profit	£250,000	£250,000	£100,000	£100,000
Interest and preference dividends	Nil	31,250	Nil	31,250
Available to ordinary shareholders	£250,000	£218,750	£100,000	£68,750
% dividend possible	25%	29%	10%	9%

Because the company uses gearing the ordinary shareholders of B will do better in good times but worse in bad times than the shareholders in A. They will, that is, be subject to greater fluctuations in their income.

For Sun and Moon plc:

$$\text{Gearing} = \frac{\text{Preference share capital}}{\text{Ordinary capital}}$$

$$= \frac{500}{3,442^1}$$

$$= 0.15.$$

(1) Note that this figure includes all reserves attributable to shareholders and not merely the nominal value of the capital.

Gearing may also be important from the point of view of the cost of financing a business. Since debt and equity may require different levels of remuneration there is an argument which says that for every business there is an optimum, i.e. least cost combination of the two. This is, however, a controversial matter not yet fully resolved and, in any case, is beyond the scope of a text on financial accounting. We might merely note that management is likely to be interested in gearing and its implications.

4. CALCULATION OF RATIOS FROM THE BALANCE SHEET AND THE PROFIT AND LOSS ACCOUNT

Debtors to credit sales

As we have seen elsewhere, credit control is vitally important to any business. Slackness in the giving of credit and in the collection of amounts owed is likely to lead to an unnecessarily large volume of funds being tied up in debts and may lead to excessive losses from bad debts. An overall indication of the efficiency of credit control can be obtained by comparing debtors with that element of total sales representing sales to those debtors and thereby obtaining an estimate for the average age of debts.

We are informed, let us say, that all sales by Sun and Moon plc are on credit and that one month is allowed for payment. A simple formula will determine what period of credit is actually being taken by debtors.

$$\text{Period of credit (days)} = \frac{\text{Debtors at year end}}{\text{sales for year}} \times 365$$

$$= \frac{543}{5,580} \times 365$$

$$= 35\tfrac{1}{2} \text{ days}$$

This shows that the average age of debtors is a little higher than the period of credit officially allowed. Customers are, therefore, generally taking as much credit as they can and control over them needs careful attention. No bad debts are shown in the profit and loss account and so payment seems to be reliable even though a little late. Some "drift" is almost inevitable in practice but it is important that any large discrepancy (particularly if it is growing) between the official period of credit and the actual collection period be investigated.

It should be noted that there is one important case where the collection period calculated by the above method could be misleading. This is where there is any marked seasonal pattern to sales. One month's debtors at the end of a period of high seasonal activity will be higher relative to a full year's sales than will a month's debtors at the end of a period of low seasonal sales. It is possible, where the books allow for sufficient analysis, to adjust for this in the calculation (e.g. by relating debtors to the most recent quarter's sales).

Stock turnover
Stock turnover is a measure of the movement of stocks. Since the holding of stocks is costly in terms of storage charges and the cost of the capital tied up in them it is desirable to move stocks as quickly as possible. We should be seeking, therefore, the highest rate of stock turnover compatible with an adequate stock level. Stocks should never be allowed to fall to a level where delays in production or in meeting customers' requirements threaten the smooth running of the business or its goodwill.

For Sun and Moon plc:

$$\text{Stock turnover} = \frac{\text{Cost of sales}}{\text{Average stock}[1]}$$

$$= \frac{3,172}{732}$$

$$= 4.3$$

(1) Since we have no value for average stock we have here assumed that the closing stock gives a fair approximation to this.

What is to be regarded as a optimum level of stock turnover depends on the type of stock. An item which, when ordered, is delivered very quickly can be stocked at a lower level (giving a higher stock turnover) than can one where delivery is likely to be delayed. Again high stock turnover is more important with stocks of high value than it would be for items of small value. For the latter the costs of running out may be very high and this would justify the maintenance of large stocks.

We must not overlook that Sun and Moon has four lines of product and the stock turnover for each can be calculated separately if we are given an analysis of stock and cost of sales. This information appears below

	A	*B*	*C*	*D*	*Total*
			(£000s)		
Cost of sales	784	1,150	462	776	3,172
Stock	88	155	228	261	732
Stock turnover	8.9	7.4	2.0	3.0	4.3

This analysis of stock turnover reveals wide variations between one line and another. The overall value on its own, therefore, would have been of limited interest.

Asset turnover

A figure known as asset turnover is sometimes calculated. It expresses a relationship between sales and the value of the assets used in the business and is intended to be a measure of how hard those assets are being worked.

For Sun and Moon plc:

$$\text{Asset turnover} = \frac{\text{Turnover (Sales)}}{\text{Net assets}}$$

$$= \frac{5,580}{3,942}$$

$$= 1.42$$

Return on capital

Return on capital is often regarded as being the ultimate measure of the success or otherwise of a business. This derives from the proprietorship concept of accounting, as the return on his capital investment is a proprietor's main concern. A profit maximising business must be seeking to maximise the return on capital. The quantity is very simply calculated.

$$\text{Return on capital} = \frac{\text{Profit} \times 100\%}{\text{Capital}}$$

Some definitions of the components are required. Profit, for example, might be the profit before tax or that after tax has been deducted. Thus we may determine either before tax or after tax rate of return. Capital might be the total value of resources tied up in assets (i.e. the total of the right hand side of the balance sheet) or it may be the total invested capital (i.e. equity and preference capital and debt) or it might be purely equity capital. A director is probably most interested in before tax profit related to invested funds. A shareholder would be interested in after tax profit as a rate of return on equity. We will compute this latter for Sun and Moon plc.

$$\text{Return} = \frac{\text{After tax profit}}{\text{Ordinary share capital and reserves}} \times 100\%$$
$$= \frac{398}{3,442} \times 100\%$$
$$= 11.6\%$$

In interpreting this important quantity it is most important to remember that both profit and equity (the two components of the formula) are the outcome of less than perfect accounting techniques of measurement. It is therefore dangerous to compare rates of return between one business and another without ensuring that all computations are done on a strictly comparable basis.

We now come to a series of calculations which give figures of particular relevance to an actual or potential shareholder. They can all be derived from information which appears in the published accounts.

Earnings per share

This quantity is the subject of an Accounting Standard, SSAP 3. This standard requires all listed companies to compute and state earnings per share (EPS) in their annual accounts. It is there defined as: "The profit in pence attributable to each equity share, based on the consolidated profit of the period after tax and after deducting minority interests and preference dividends, but before taking into account extraordinary items, divided by the number of equity shares in issue and ranking for dividend in respect of the period". This rather long definition is necessary for formal precision but means basically total net profit divided by the number of shares entitled to participate in it. For Sun and Moon plc:

$$\text{EPS} = \frac{\text{Net profit after tax and preference dividends}}{\text{Number of ordinary shares}}$$

$$= \frac{358}{2,500}$$

$$= 14.32\text{p per share}$$

Dividend cover

This measure, which shows how many times the dividend of the year *could* have been paid out of the profit of the year, is a measure of how secure the dividend is. If a dividend is (say) twice covered by profit then profit could halve in future years before it became inadequate to maintain the dividend. Meanwhile reserves of retained profit are building up to provide even more underlying security for the dividend. The ordinary dividend cover for Sun and Moon plc is:

$$\frac{\text{EPS}}{\text{Dividend per share}} = \frac{14.32}{10}$$

$$= 1.432.$$

Asset cover

This measure is sometimes calculated by investors and is supposed to give a guide to the value of their shares. It must, however, be used with the greatest discretion. It is the total balance sheet value of assets attributable to the ordinary shareholders (i.e. ordinary share capital plus reserves divided by the number of shares in issue). The figure thus determined is often compared with the market price of the share. For Sun and Moon plc:

$$\text{Asset cover} = \frac{\text{Net assets}}{\text{Number of shares}}$$

$$= \frac{3,442}{2,500}$$

$$= £1.38.$$

The idea underlying this is that by buying an ordinary share the investor is obtaining a proportionate claim over the assets of the business which is worth £1.38. Let us say that the market price of such a share is £1.52. The share would then, by comparison with the value of the assets which it commands, seem slightly expensive. The important fallacies underlying the measure, however, must be borne in mind. Firstly, assets in a balance sheet are not valued at market value as is the share. The market value of asset cover may thus be either higher or lower than that calculated. Secondly, no element of goodwill is normally allowed in the balance sheet valuation but this may have substantial value. Thirdly, the purchase of a share does not in any case give direct access to the assets of the company. Only a substantial majority shareholder could enforce a realisation of the assets. In other cases a shareholding gives only an entitlement to a share in the outcome of the use of the assets by the management.

Price/earnings ratio

The price/earnings ratio is a ratio commonly calculated by investors and prospective investors seeking to evaluate a shareholding. It is simply the ratio between the market price of the share and the company's earnings per share. Thus for Sun and Moon plc:

$$\text{P/E ratio} = \frac{\text{market price of share}}{\text{EPS}}$$

$$= \frac{£1.52}{14.32\text{p}}$$

$$= 10.6.$$

A high P/E ratio means that a share is relatively expensive and a low one that it is relatively cheap. Unfortunately there is no ultimate standard of what an average P/E ratio should be. In any individual case, however, it is often useful to compare it to the value derived for other companies in the same type of business. If the P/E ratio for companies operating in same field as Sun and Moon is, say 8, then plainly Sun and Moon's shares are somewhat expensive and investment in them would need to be justified by some especially attractive features of that company.

Dividend and earnings yield

These quantities attempt to assess for the investor the rate of return he is earning on his present actual investment in the business, i.e. the market value of the holding. Dividend yield takes account only of the current dividend payment and earnings yield of the whole of the net profit attributable to shareholders, whether distributed or not.

For Sun and Moon plc:

$$\text{Dividend yield} = \frac{\text{Dividend per share}}{\text{Price of share}} \times 100\%$$

$$= \frac{10p}{£1.52}$$

$$= 6.6\% \text{ per annum}$$

$$\text{Earnings yield} = \frac{\text{Earnings per share}}{\text{Price per share}} \times 100\%$$

$$= \frac{14.3p}{£1.52} \times 100\%$$

$$= 9.4\% \text{ per annum}$$

SUMMARY

1. The calculation of ratios can considerably enhance the process of obtaining information from a set of accounts. The relationship between one figure and another is often more revealing than is their absolute value. All ratios should, however, be interpreted with caution and should not be used to support hasty conclusions.

2. *Gross profit rate.* This is the gross profit expressed as a percentage of sales. It is a measure of the effectiveness of the business's basic profit earning activity.

3. *Expenses to sales.* Expenses may be expressed as a percentage of sales, either in total or individually. This gives a measure of the efficiency of the administrative process.

4. *Current and liquidity ratios.* These are the ratios which current assets and liquid assets respectively bear to current liabilities. The ratios measure the business's short term ability to pay its way.

5. *Gearing.* This is calculated as the ratio of loan finance to total finance. For this purpose preference capital is regarded as loan capital. It is a structural ratio which can be used to gauge the business's vulnerability to financial risk.

6. *Period of credit.* This is a measure relating debtors and credit sales. It represents the average period of credit taken by customers. It has a bearing on the credit control effectiveness of the business.

7. *Stock turnover.* This measures the number of times in a

financial period that average stock is exhausted and replaced. An optimum stock turnover will avoid the wastefulness of overstocking without incurring the cost of running short of supplies.

8. *Asset turnover.* This relates net assets to sales turnover. It is a measure of how hard the business's resources are being worked.

9. *Return on capital.* This expresses profit as a return on proprietor's capital. It gives an indication of what is being earned by the investment.

10. *Earnings per share.* SSAP 3 requires that companies publish this figure which is after tax profit divided by the number of shares in issue. It conveys to a shareholder the actual (as opposed to distributed) return on his capital.

11. *Dividend cover.* This shows how many times the actual dividend could have been met by current profits. It is a measure of the security of the dividend.

12. *Asset cover.* This shows the value of assets underlying an individual share in a company. It may be compared with the current market price of the share but is of dubious value when used alone.

13. *Price/earnings ratio.* This relates the current market price of a share to the earnings per share. It may be seen as a measure of how expensive the share is and can be compared with similar values calculated for other companies.

14. *Dividend and earnings yields.* These measures relate distributed and total profit respectively to the current share price to give a percentage return on capital.

QUESTIONS

1. Your company has suffered a drop in its gross profit rate from 28 per cent last year to 22 per cent this year. You have been asked to investigate. List the possible explanations which would need to be considered.

2. Below is the summarised balance sheet of Roulette plc at 31st December.

Share capital (£1 shares)	£1,000,000	Fixed assets	£1,230,000
Profit and loss account	400,000	Current assets	720,000
Loan capital	200,000		
Current liabilities	350,000		
	£1,950,000		£1,950,000

In the year just past the company earned a profit after tax of £175,000 and paid dividends totalling 12p per share. The current share price is £1.60. Calculate and discuss some ratios likely to be of interest to a potential purchaser of shares.

3. To what extent do you agree with the following statements?

(*a*) X plc has asset cover for its shares of £2.20 each. The current market price of its shares is, however, only £1.80. A purchase now would, therefore, be a bargain.

(*b*) Smith's accounts show that his business earns 15 per cent per annum on the capital it employs. Smith has £50,000 on deposit at the bank earning 10 per cent per annum. He ought to use this money to expand the business.

(*c*) Y plc has administrative costs which amount to 8 per cent of its sales. The corresponding figure for Z plc is 12 per cent. Y is therefore more efficiently administered.

(*d*) A plc has a current ratio of 4 and B plc has a current ratio of 3. A is, therefore, in a stronger financial position.

4. Below appear the summarised accounts of Monte Carlo plc for two consecutive years. You are asked to comment on them, making use of ratios as appropriate.

MONTE CARLO PLC

TRADING AND PROFIT AND LOSS ACCOUNTS FOR THE YEAR ENDED 31ST DECEMBER

	Year 1 (£000s)	Year 2 (£000s)
Sales	3,742	4,897
Less Cost of sales	2,955	3,739
Gross profit	787	1,158
Less Administrative and other expenses	298	326
Net profit before tax	489	832
Less Taxation	210	398
Net profit after tax	279	434
Dividends	150	200
Retained profit	129	234

BALANCE SHEETS AT 31ST DECEMBER

	Year 1 (£000s)		Year 2 (£000s)	
Fixed assets		2,986		3,148
Current assets	4,358		3,998	
Less Current liabilities	2,916	1,442	1,984	2,014
		4,428		5,162
Financed by:				
Share capital		3,000		3,500
Revenue reserves		548		782
Loan capital		880		880
		4,428		5,162

5. "A set of accounts becomes meaningful only when ratio analysis is applied to it." Discuss, drawing attention to the dangers of ratio analysis as well as to its merits.

CHAPTER 15

Published Accounts of Companies

OBJECTIVES

In this chapter we shall deal with the following important topics:

(a) legal requirements for the publication of accounts by companies;
(b) the balance sheet;
(c) the profit and loss account;
(d) the directors' report;
(e) the auditors' report.

1. INTRODUCTION

One of the important obligations imposed on limited companies by law is that they should publish regular accounting reports on their activities. The minimum information which these must contain is laid out in detail in a number of Acts of Parliament of which the most recent, and the most important, is the Companies Act 1981. It is important that the main requirements should be understood and this will be the subject of this chapter. The special exemptions given to small and medium sized companies and those given to banking, insurance and shipping companies will be ignored. We shall also omit some of the more obscure provisions which operate only in special circumstances. We shall thus be looking at the shape of published company accounts as they will most commonly be encountered.

2. THE COMPANIES ACTS

The operation of limited companies is governed by Companies Acts of 1948, 1967, 1976, 1980 and 1981. Together these include, of course, many matters relating to companies which are not directly reflected in their accounts. The main accounting requirements are now contained in the latest of these Acts although there are unrepealed portions of the others which still apply. One of the objectives of the Companies Act 1981 was to incorporate into UK law the provisions of the EEC Fourth Directive and, for this reason, it represents a very considerable advance on the disclosure requirements which had existed before. It should be noted that since, at the time of writing, the Act is still in the course of being implemented, companies may continue for a short period to produce accounts governed by the old rules. This transitional arrangement need not, however, concern us.

It is emphasised that what follows concerns the requirements imposed on companies by law. A typical set of accounts will also contain material required under Accounting Standards and may also contain information which a company chooses to give voluntarily. It will be helpful to consider our subject under a number of headings.

General

A company must prepare accounts annually. These must be sent to every shareholder and debenture holder of the company, must be laid before the company at the Annual General Meeting and a copy must be filed with the Registrar of Companies. This latter copy is available for public consultation.

The statutory accounts consist of:

(*a*) a balance sheet;
(*b*) a profit and loss account;
(*c*) a directors' report;
(*d*) an auditors' report.

Each of these statements must contain specified information, often in a specified form. Some of the required detail is permitted to be given in the form of notes, rather than having to be embodied in the statements themselves, and additional notes are required to give information which would not otherwise appear in conventionally constructed accounting statements.

For every figure appearing in the accounts the corresponding value, determined on a consistent basis, for the immediately preceding year must be given.

Specific requirements

True and fair view

The Companies Act 1981 (as did earlier Acts) imposes an overriding obligation on a company that its published accounts should give a "true and fair view" of its progress and position. It follows that mere slavish adherence to the detailed disclosure requirements is not enough if a true and fair view is not thereby given. A company must give extra information or the same information in a different form if that is necessary in order to ensure that a true and fair view is conveyed.

Accounting principles

Four fundamental accounting "principles", which readers will recognise as two of the "concepts" and two of the "principles" which we looked at in Chapter 2, are given formal legal status by the 1981 Act. These are:

(*a*) going concern;
(*b*) consistency;
(*c*) prudence;
(*d*) accruals.

These principles must normally be applied. If they are departed from for any reason that fact, and the reason for it, must be given.

Valuation

Certain principles of valuation are now given the force of law. These are:

(*a*) Fixed assets having limited useful lives must be depreciated systematically over the period of those lives. (The provision of depreciation, though usual, was not obligatory before 1981.)

(*b*) Current assets must be valued at the lower of cost or net realisable value, taking them item by item.

(*c*) Goodwill (except that arising on consolidation) must be written off over a period not exceeding its useful life.

(*d*) Fictitious assets, such as preliminary expenses, share issue expenses and research costs, must not be shown as assets on the balance sheet.

(*e*) Development costs may be shown as an asset in the balance sheet only in appropriate circumstances.

(*f*) Historical cost will be the normal basis of valuation but current cost valuations are permitted, where appropriate, for the majority of assets.

3. REQUIRED STATEMENTS

Balance sheet

Two possible balance sheet formats are allowable. These are the double column (horizontal) and single column (vertical) formats. The latter will probably be that most commonly used and this is the one which is illustrated below. The headings used and their lettered references correspond to those appearing in Schedule 1 of the companies Act 1981. Whichever format is selected the same information must be given.

A: CALLED UP SHARE CAPITAL NOT PAID

This item, though important, will be relatively uncommon. As we have seen in Chapter 10, a company may make an issue of shares on the basis that certain parts of the agreed issue price are paid after the initial application for the shares. Although normally this will not extend beyond allotment, a company may occasionally choose to delay calling up its capital for some time. This might happen where a project takes time to develop and not all the capital is needed at the beginning. Where a company calls up part of its share capital and the shareholder has not yet paid this amount this debt due to the company must be shown on the balance sheet. It may either be shown as the first item or, alternatively, included amongst current assets.

B: FIXED ASSETS

I. INTANGIBLE ASSETS

(*a*) *Development costs:* in appropriate cases the costs involved in developing a project may be shown as an intangible fixed asset in the balance sheet. Where they appear they must be written off against the revenues flowing from the project over a suitable period.

(*b*) *Concessions, patents, licences, trademarks and similar rights and assets:* these may only be included if acquired by the company for valuable consideration (i.e. purchased) or if created by itself.

(*c*) *Goodwill:* this should be included only if acquired for valuable consideration. It should be written off over a period not exceeding its useful economic life. This does not apply to goodwill arising on consolidation.

(*d*) *Payments on account for intangible assets:* this heading allows for payments made for the part-acquisition of items which would otherwise appear under one of the three former headings.

II. TANGIBLE ASSETS

(*a*) Land and buildings.

(*b*) Plant and machinery.

(*c*) Fixtures, fittings, tools and equipment.

(*d*) Payments on accounts and assets in course of construction.

All tangible assets having limited useful lives must be systematically depreciated over those lives. The amount appearing in the balance sheet, i.e. gross value less aggregate depreciation to date, may be based on either historical cost or current cost.

III. INVESTMENTS

The investments included under this heading are those which it is intended should be held on a long-term basis. There is another heading for investments under current assets. There are seven required categories. They are:

(*a*) shares in group companies (i.e. holding, subsidiary and fellow subsidiary companies);

(*b*) loans to group companies;

(*c*) shares in related companies (i.e. associated companies);

(*d*) loans to related companies;

(*e*) other investments other than loans;

(*f*) other loans; and

(*g*) own shares. The Companies Act 1981 allows a company, under certain safeguards, to hold its own shares. This was previously illegal.

Investments may be shown at cost or market value or some other appropriate value.

C: CURRENT ASSETS

I. STOCKS

There are four required categories. They are:

(*a*) raw materials and consumables;

(*b*) work in progress;

(*c*) finished goods and goods for resale;

(*d*) payments on account.

Stocks will normally be valued at cost but may be valued at current cost. Where there is a material difference between the balance sheet value and the replacement value, this must be disclosed for each category separately. Where net realisable value is lower than the value which would otherwise be used, then the former should be substituted.

II. DEBTORS

The headings are:

(*a*) trade debtors;

(*b*) amounts owed by group companies;

(*c*) amounts owed by related companies;

(*d*) other debtors;

(*e*) called up share capital not paid (unless already shown under heading A);

(*f*) prepayments and accrued income. (This may alternatively be shown under a separate heading following current assets.)

Any amounts appearing under the above headings which are due for payment after more than one year from the balance sheet date must be shown separately.

III. INVESTMENTS

Investments included under current assets are those where the intention is to hold them temporarily. The three categories are:

    (*a*) shares in group companies;
    (*b*) own shares;
    (*c*) other investments.

Investments may be valued at historical cost or at current cost.

IV. CASH AT BANK AND IN HAND

D: PREPAYMENTS AND ACCRUED INCOME

This is an alternative position for this item if it is preferred not to include it with current assets. As with debtors, any amount falling due after more than one year must be separately stated.

E: CREDITORS

Creditors for amounts falling due within one year of the balance sheet date.

    The headings are:
    (*a*) debenture loans;
    (*b*) bank loans and overdrafts;
    (*c*) payments received on account, if not shown elsewhere (some may appear as deductions from work in progress);
    (*d*) trade creditors;
    (*e*) bills of exchange payable;
    (*f*) amounts owing to group companies;
    (*g*) amounts owing to related companies;
    (*h*) other creditors including taxation and social security;
    (*i*) accruals and deferred income. (This may alternatively be shown under a separate heading further on.)

F: NET CURRENT ASSETS

This figure is a subtotal computed from the figures for total current assets and total current liabilities, i.e. $C + D - E$.

G: TOTAL ASSETS LESS CURRENT LIABILITIES

This is the total for the top half of the balance sheet, i.e. $A + B + F$.

    The balance sheet is ruled off at this point before it continues with the headings below.

H: CREDITORS

Creditors for amounts falling due more than a year after the balance sheet date. The required subheadings are the same as for main heading *E*.

I: PROVISIONS FOR LIABILITIES AND CHARGES

The three categories are:
  (*a*) pensions and similar obligations;
  (*b*) taxation, including deferred taxation;
  (*c*) other provisions.

J: ACCRUALS AND DEFERRED INCOME

Those not shown under E or H, Creditors.

K: CAPITAL AND RESERVES

I.   CALLED UP SHARE CAPITAL
II. SHARE PREMIUM ACCOUNT
III. REVALUATION RESERVE
This arises where current cost valuations have been included in the balance sheet but not otherwise. Appropriate alternative titles may be used for this reserve.

IV. OTHER RESERVES
  (*a*) *Capital redemption reserve:* this is a capital reserve arising when a company redeems its own shares. The creation of this reserve is one of the conditions under which such redemption is allowed.
  (*b*) *Reserve for own shares:* this arises when a company acquires a holding in its own shares. Again it is a statutory requirement when such acquisition takes place.
  (*c*) *Other reserves.*

V. PROFIT AND LOSS ACCOUNT
This section of the balance sheet will then be totalled and should agree, of course, with the first section totalled at G.

Notes
Certain information in amplification or extension of that given in the balance sheet will appear in the form of notes. Some of the more important items are as follows.
  (1) *Movements of fixed assets.* For all fixed assets, including investments, movements must be shown. This will include changes in the balance due to additions, disposals and transfers and also

revisions in value. The effect of movements on cumulative depreciation as well as cost or valuation must be shown in the case of depreciating assets.

(2) *Investments.* For each category of investment there must be shown separately listed (i.e. on a Stock Exchange) investments. The market value of each category of listed investment must be given.

(3) *Share capital.* There must be shown the authorised share capital and the number and nominal value of each class of share issued. Details of any allotments made during the year are also required. Where the company holds any of its own shares their nominal value must be stated.

(4) *Debentures and loan stocks.* Details of any allotments of debentures or loan stocks made during the year must be shown.

(5) *Movements on reserves.* All movements on reserves must be detailed.

The profit and loss account

As with the balance sheet there are alternative formats prescribed for the profit and loss account. Again the style may be either vertical or horizontal giving two alternative shapes to the account. There is also, however, a more important division according to the classification of the required information. Since, in the end, the same package of information is required each classification requires different supporting notes according to the information which it gives or leaves out. Both permitted classifications are described below but the vertical form of presentation is, in each case, presumed. Again, the headings and their numbering correspond to those appearing in Schedule 1 of the Companies Act 1981.

Format 1.

(1) *Turnover.* This is the figure measuring the total activity of the business during the year. For a trading company it corresponds to "Sales".

(2) *Cost of sales.* This will include any necessary amount for depreciation.

(3) *Gross profit.* This is Turnover less Cost of sales.

(4) *Distribution costs.* This includes all the expenses associated with selling and distributing the business's product. Again it will include any necessary amount for depreciation.

(5) *Administrative expenses.* This includes any necessary amount for depreciation.

(6) *Other operating income.*

(7) *Income from shares in group companies.*

(8) *Income from shares in related companies.*

(9) *Income from other fixed asset investments.*

(10) *Other interest receivable and similar income.*

(11) *Amounts written off investments.* There must be shown separately:

(*a*) provision made for temporary diminution of value (this is a permissible provision);

(*b*) provision made for permanent diminution of value (this is a mandatory provision);

(*c*) any amounts written back in respect of provisions no longer required (such writing back in such circumstances is obligatory).

(12) *Interest payable and similar charges.* Amounts payable to group companies must be shown separately.

(13) *Tax on profit or loss on ordinary activities.*

(14) *Profit or loss on ordinary activities after taxation.* This is a subtotal of all matters dealt with so far.

(15) *Extraordinary income.*

(16) *Extraordinary expenditure.*

(17) *Extraordinary profit or loss.* This is the difference between items (15) and (16).

(18) *Tax on extraordinary profit or loss.*

(19) *Other taxes not shown under other headings.*

(20) *Profit or loss for the financial year.* There must then be shown Appropriations under two headings:

(*a*) amounts transferred to or withdrawn from reserves; and

(*b*) aggregate amount of dividends paid and proposed.

Format 2.

(1) *Turnover.*

(2) *Change in stocks of finished goods and in work in progress.*

(3) *Own work capitalised.*

(4) *Other operating income.*

(5) (*a*) *Raw materials.*

(*b*) *Other external charges.*

(6) *Staff costs.* These must be shown under three headings:

(*a*) wages and salaries;

(*b*) social security costs;

(*c*) other pension costs.

(7) (*a*) *Depreciation* and other amounts written off tangible and intangible fixed assets.

(*b*) *Exceptional amounts written off current assets.*

(8) *Other operating charges.* Items (9) to (22) of Format 2 are identical to items (7) to (20) in Format 1. Appropriations are also to be shown as in that case.

Notes

Certain information in amplification or extension of that given in the profit and loss account will appear in the form of notes. Some of the more important items are:

(1) *Turnover.* A breakdown of turnover must be given both by classes of business and by geographical area.

(2) *Staff costs.* If Format 1 is used the information on staff costs incorporated in Format 2 must be given as a note.

(3) *Depreciation.* If Format 1 is used a note must disclose the aggregate amount of depreciation charged. (This is incorporated in Format 2.)

(4) *Interest payable.* There must be shown separately interest payable on:

    (*a*) bank loans and overdrafts and other loans wholly repayable within five years; and

    (*b*) any other loans.

(5) *Directors' emoluments.* A considerable amount of information is required to be given in respect of directors' emoluments. The following headings must be used distinguishing in each case between amounts receivable in respect of services as directors and amounts receivable in respect of other offices:

    (*a*) aggregate emoluments;

    (*b*) directors' and past directors' pensions (except those payable from contributory funds);

    (*c*) compensation paid to directors or past directors for loss of office;

    (*d*) prior year adjustments.

Directors' emoluments must also be shown in terms of the numbers of directors lying in brackets on a scale divided in multiples of £5,000. The chairman's remuneration must be stated separately as must the remuneration of the highest paid director if other than the chairman.

(6) *Auditors' remuneration.* This must include both fees and expenses paid to auditors in respect of their duties.

(7) *Highest paid employee's emoluments.*

(8) *Hire of plant and machinery.*

(9) *Rents from land.*

General notes

There are certain other matters relating to the accounts which must be given in notes. The most important of these are as follows.

(1) *True and fair view.* If the true and fair view requirement has caused the company to depart from any other requirement of the Act, particulars must be given.

(2) *Accounting policies.* The accounting policies adopted in preparing the accounts must be stated. Matters included will be:

(*a*) depreciation;

(*b*) translation of foreign currency;

(*c*) departures from the generally accepted accounting principles presumed by the Act.

(3) *Departures from historical cost.* The fact and extent to which current cost accounting has been used must be disclosed.

(4) *Subsidiaries and associated companies.* Details must be given of all subsidiaries and other companies in which the company holds more than 10 per cent of any class of share or where the investment makes up more than 10 per cent of the investing company's assets.

(5) *Contingent liabilities.* A contingent liability is one which depends on the happening or non-happening of some future event. Where such a liability exists and is not provided for in the accounts there must be shown:

(*a*) its amount (estimated if necessary);

(*b*) its legal nature;

(*c*) details of any security provided in connection with it.

(6) *Financial commitments.* There must be shown:

(*a*) the amount of any contract for capital expenditure not provided for in the accounts;

(*b*) the amount of any capital expenditure authorised by the directors but not yet contracted for nor provided for in the accounts;

(*c*) other material financial commitments not provided for in the accounts.

(7) *Recommended dividend.* The aggregate amount of any recommended dividend must be disclosed.

Directors' Report

The third major statement making up the statutory accounts of a limited company is the Directors' Report. Its main contents are:

(*a*) a fair review of the development of the company's business during the financial year and of its position at the end of the year;

(*b*) the amount recommended by the directors to be paid as a dividend;

(*c*) the amounts to be transferred to reserves;

(*d*) the directors' names including the names of any persons who were directors for any part of the year;

(*e*) the principal activities of the company during the year and any significant changes in those activities;

(*f*) an indication, as precisely as practicable, of any difference between the balance sheet value and market value of any interests in land held by the company;

(*g*) details of any issues of shares or debentures during the financial year;

(*h*) details of any interest of a director in any contract with the company;

(*i*) particulars of directors' transactions with the company during the year;

(*j*) directors' interests in any shares or debentures of the company (unless given as a note to the accounts);

(*k*) details of important events affecting the company which have occurred after the date of the balance sheet;

(*l*) an indication of likely future developments in the company's business;

(*m*) an indication of the company's involvement in research and development;

(*n*) details of the company's acquisitions of its own shares;

(*o*) details of political contributions which are individually in excess of £200;

(*p*) details of charitable contributions where these total more than £200.

Auditors' Report

The auditors' report is usually quite brief and formal. An auditor must report on:

(*a*) whether the accounts have been properly prepared and are in accordance with the requirements of the Companies Acts 1948 to 1981;

(*b*) whether the balance sheet gives a true and fair view of the state of the company's affairs at the end of its financial year;

(*c*) whether the profit and loss account gives a true and fair view of the company's profit or loss for the financial year;

(*d*) whether the Directors' Report is consistent with the accounts.

In the event that the auditor is dissatisfied on any of these or other matters he will report in some detail on the sources of his dissatisfaction. This gives rise to what is known as a "qualified" report which may be much longer than the unqualified report normally given.

SUMMARY

1. Companies are required by law to produce annual accounts for their shareholders and debentureholders. Each of these must receive an individual copy of the accounts and a copy must also be

filed with the Registrar of Companies. This latter copy is available for public consultation.

  2. The accounts must consist of:
  (*a*) balance sheet;
  (*b*) profit and loss account;
  (*c*) directors' report;
  (*d*) auditors' report.

  3. The form and content of these statements, so far as legal requirements are concerned, are governed by the Companies Acts 1948 to 1981. The 1981 Act is by far the most comprehensive and important of these.

QUESTIONS

  1. Prior to the coming into force of the Companies Act 1981 the provision of depreciation was a matter left to the discretion of the directors of the company. Summarise the present rules regarding the provision of depreciation and its disclosure.

  2. The Companies Act 1981 sets out four basic accounting principles which are normally to be followed. State these principles, explain them and relate them to fundamental accounting concepts.

  3. Rearrange the profit and loss account given below so that, so far as possible, it complies with the legal requirements for publication. What information not given here would also be required?

STICK AND CARROT PLC

PROFIT AND LOSS ACCOUNT FOR THE YEAR ENDED 31ST DECEMBER 19—

	Debits	Credits
Dividend received from subsidiaries		£123,411
Income from other fixed asset investments		118,390
Sales		8,942,167
Stock at 31st December		75,862
		9,259,830
Administrative expenses	£767,082	
Amount written off investments	9,660	
Auditors' remuneration	15,000	
Depreciation: Administrative £31,440		
Distribution 42,160		
	73,600	
Directors' emoluments	80,000	
Distribution costs	520,716	
Dividends, paid and proposed	250,000	
Interest payable	15,472	
Purchases of stock	6,665,593	
Stock at 1st January	82,146	
Taxation	487,663	
		8,966,932
Retained profit		£292,898

4. Summarise the information required by the Companies Act 1981 concerning share capital, stating where each item might be expected to appear.

5. State what you think is meant by the expression "true and fair view" and assess the importance of the concept in legal company reporting requirements.

CHAPTER 16

The Measurement of Profit

OBJECTIVES

In this chapter we shall deal with the following important topics:

(*a*) the importance of measuring profit;
(*b*) economic income under certainty;
(*c*) economic income under uncertainty;
(*d*) current cost accounting.

1. INTRODUCTION

This chapter has a very important bearing on fundamental accounting theory and the nature of the financial reporting process. It will also lead us in to a discussion of important developments in accounting practice which have been impelled by the need for accounting to give explicit recognition to the phenomenon of inflation. The basic problem we are to discuss here, however, is the computation and reporting of business income or profit and it will be helpful if we first of all disregard the problem of inflation and look at the ideas in a non-inflationary context.

Profit is the most important measure of business performance. This derives from the proprietorship concept of accounting. Under this business activity is seen to consist of the assembly and dispersal of economic resources with the objective that the amounts dispersed in one particular direction (that of the proprietor) should exceed by as much as possible the amounts assembled from that source. Profit is not necessarily the only measure of business performance nor is it necessarily the most suitable in all circumstances. From a practical point of view, however, its importance has clearly been established by its history.

By law every company must produce an annual profit and loss account which seeks to report the income of the immediate past year. Its level and any changes in level from a previous year are frequently the subject of comment either by the directors of the company itself or by outside commentators. Because dividends are, in the long run, closely linked to profits and since, presumably, again in the long run the investor is interested in the positive cash flow arising from his investment profit provides a measure of performance of high relevance to the shareholder.

Since companies which do not make profits or which make actual losses usually eventually fail (because of the depletion of capital exacerbated by the closure of access to new capital) the security and rewards of employment with that business are also related to profit. Profit is used by the taxing authorities as a measure of ability to bear tax and it is used by price investigating bodies to determine whether fair prices are being charged. These are, therefore, a number of very practical explanations for the importance of the profit figure.

If we look at theoretical analysis, too, there is substantial justification for affording a central position to a consideration of profit. Economists have for long made wide and successful use of the concept of the profit-maximising entrepreneur. He cannot, in practice, hope to maximise profit if he is not able to measure it.

2. DEFINITION OF BUSINESS INCOME

Before we can attempt to decide how best to measure business income we need to decide exactly what we mean by that term. A search of the literature of economics will throw up a number of possibilities which vary in their appeal to logic or to susceptibility to practical techniques for measurement. One with considerable appeal and apparently very much in line with fundamental accounting concepts is that set out by Hicks in his book "Value and Capital". His definition of the income of a period is that it is that amount which could be consumed in the period and still leave its recipient as well off at the end of the period as he was at the beginning. In other words it firmly takes the position that capital must be maintained before any distributable surplus, i.e. profit, can be deemed to arise. This is very much in line with accounting practice and with company law.

Here is a simple instance of what is meant. X plc has traded for one calendar year from 1st January to 31st December. No fresh capital has been introduced during that period and no dividends have been paid.

Net assets at 31st December valued at	£52,000
Net assets at 1st January valued at	40,000
The profit for the year was therefore	£12,000

If there had been capital additions or dividends during the year these would have had to be allowed for. Thus if a dividend totalling £8,000 had been paid the figures would be:

Net assets at 31st December valued at	£44,000[1]
Net assets at 1st January valued at	40,000
Retained profit	4,000
Dividend	8,000
The profit was therefore (as before)	£12,000

(1) Depleted by the amount paid out as dividend.

This fits in with our theoretical idea. The big practical problem, however, is in the matter of the year end valuations and how these are done. The method used is obviously critical to the amount of profit which will be reported. So far we have resolved the problem by valuing assets at what they had cost but we need now to appreciate that this is only one method and that, beyond the objectivity on which we have commented, it may not hold any particular merit.

We shall now look at two alternative models of profit measurement. The first of these is useful for the theoretical insights which it offers but is of doubtful practical interest. The other has important and interesting practical implications. These are the models producing "Economic Income" and "Current Cost Income".

3. ECONOMIC INCOME UNDER CONDITIONS OF CERTAINTY

A method of valuation used in analyses for the purposes of financial decision making is based on discounted cash flow. This merely says that the present value of an asset is equal to the future net cash inflows from operating it discounted to allow for the time which must elapse before those inflows accrue. This means that cash inflows more distant in time are seen as less valuable than more immediate ones. It has to be assumed here that the reader is familiar with the discounted cash flow method of project evaluation. It underlies our first income calculation model described below.

We shall assume a world of complete certainty so that the cost of capital is known and uniform and the future returns arising from the ownership and use of any assets can be precisely predicted. To simplify the analysis we will use as our example a business which owns only one asset. This has a life of three years and promises the returns indicated in the second column of the table below. The cost of capital is 10% per annum. The table also shows the value of the asset at the beginning of Year 1 and at the end of Years 1 and 2. It has no value at the end of Year 3.

Year	Cash inflow	Value beginning year 1		Value at end year 1		Value at end year 2	
		Disc. fact.	Pres. val.	Disc. fact.	Pres. val.	Disc. fact.	Pres. val.
1	£8,000	0.909	£7,272				
2	7,000	0.826	5,782	0.909	£6,363		
3	5,000	0.751	3,755	0.826	4,130	0.909	£4,545
			£16,809		£10,493		£4,545

As we are assuming a situation of complete certainty we may take it that the valuations derived above conform also to the market value of the asset at the stated points in time. They are the valuations which would be used by management to decide as to whether to invest in, or stay invested in, the project in question.

We are now in a position to use these valuations to determine profit.

Year	Value of assets at beginning	Value of assets at end[1]	Income[2]
1	£16,809	£18,493	£1,684
2	10,493	11,545	1,052
3	4,545	5,000	455
			£3,191

(1) This includes the cash flow for the year.
(2) Assumed distributed or invested in other projects not our concern here.

It will be interesting to compare these figures for income with their historical cost counterparts. To compute these we will assume that the asset cost £16,809, its net present value at the time of purchase. It will be written off over the three years of its life on a straight line basis.

Year	Value of assets at beginning	Value of assets at end	Income
1	£16,809	£19,206	£2,397
2	11,206	12,603	1,397
3	5,603	5,000	(603)[1]
			£3,191

(1) The figure in brackets denotes a loss.

It should be noted that, in total, the two income models produce the same value for income. The year by year comparisons however, show wide variations.

The economic income model has two merits. Firstly, the income figure itself represents a constant rate of return on capital and this is at the known rate for the cost of capital (differences on the figures we have calculated are due purely to rounding off). Secondly, the asset is always valued in the balance sheet at what it is actually worth to the business and at its market value. Unfortunately, under conditions of certainty, this does not add anything to our knowledge of the situation. It does, however, show up historical cost calculations in a rather unfavourable light.

4. ECONOMIC INCOME UNDER CONDITIONS OF UNCERTAINTY

We now approach the real world a little more closely to see how our model responds to a situation of uncertainty. One difficulty which exists is that under uncertainty there will be different costs of capital according to the perception of risks by the supplier of capital. Another is that there will be different expectations about future cash flows from any project. This is what makes economic income a highly subjective quantity. We shall avoid some of the difficulties here by assuming that we are taking one particular viewpoint in the process of determining income, let us say that of the directors of the company.

At the beginning we will take it that our company owns the same asset as before with the same expectations about the future and the same cost of capital. It will, therefore, again have a present value of £16,809. The difference between this and the previous situation, however, is that where there is uncertainty actual events are likely to diverge from what was expected. We will suppose that during year 1 this happens in two ways. First the cash inflow is £7,000 instead of the expected £8,000. Secondly, possibly because of this disappointing result, the directors take a more pessimistic view of the future than they did previously and revise their expectations for years 2 and 3 to £6,000 and £4,000 respectively. For simplicity we will, however, assume that the cost of capital remains at 10 per cent per annum. We are left, however, with the double problem that not only do actual cash inflows vary from expectation but that the expectation about the future itself varies as that future approaches. The economic value of an asset at any point in time thus varies according to when we choose to do the calculation. This can easily be demonstrated.

VALUE OF ASSET AT BEGINNING OF YEAR 1 BASED ON INFORMATION AVAILABLE AT END OF YEAR 1

Year	Predicted cash flow	Discount factor	Present value
1	£7,000[1]	0.909	£6,363
2	6,000	0.826	4,956
3	4,000	0.751	3,004
			£14,323

(1) Known actual return for year 1.

We have already seen that the same asset valued at the beginning of year 1 on the information then available was £16,809. It has, therefore, suffered a loss during the year due solely to the changes in expectation and before any actual consumption of the asset has taken place. The amount of this loss is £16,809 − £14,323 = £2,486. Such a loss (or gain if such is the case) is termed a "windfall'. This implies that, although a component of overall economic income, it cannot be attributed to management activity. It happens due to extraneous factors beyond management control.

Let us now suppose that the year 2 cash flow proved to be £7,500 and that the expectation for year 3 held at the end of year 2 was, in consequence, raised to £6,000.

VALUE OF ASSET AT BEGINNING OF YEAR 2 BASED ON INFORMATION AVAILABLE AT BEGINNING OF YEAR 2

Year	Predicted cash flow	Discount factor	Present value
2	£6,000	0.909	£5,454
3	4,000	0.826	3,304
			£8,758

VALUE OF ASSET AT BEGINNING OF YEAR 2 BASED ON INFORMATION AVAILABLE AT END OF YEAR 2

Year	Predicted cash flow	Discount factor	Present value
2	£7,500[1]	0.909	£6.818
3	6,000	0.826	4,956
			£11,774

(1) Known actual return for year 2.

There is a windfall gain of £11,774 − £8,758 = £3,016 in year 2.

Finally we will suppose that the actual return in year 3 was £6,500.

VALUE OF ASSET AT BEGINNING OF YEAR 3 BASED ON INFORMATION AVAILABLE AT BEGINNING OF YEAR 3

Year	Predicted cash flow	Discount factor	Present value
3	£6,000	0.909	£5,454

VALUE OF ASSET AT BEGINNING OF YEAR 3 BASED ON INFORMATION AVAILABLE AT END OF YEAR 3

Year	Actual cash flow	Discount factor	Present value
3	£6,500	0.909	£5,909

There is a windfall gain of £5,909 − £5,454 = £455.

The complete story is now given in the table below.

Year	Asset value at beginning £16,809	Asset value at end[1]	Operating income	Windfall gain/(loss)	Total Income
1	14,323	£15,758	£1,435	(£2,486)	(£1,051)
2	11,774	12,954	1,180	3,016	4,196
3	5,909	6,500	591	455	1,046
			£3,206	£985	£4,191

(1) This includes annual cash inflow.

There has been produced for us a total income, i.e. the amount which could be distributed to leave the business as well off at the end of the year as it was at the beginning (or which, in the case of a loss, must be made up be the introduction of new capital). This is divided into two parts which we have termed operating income and windfall gain (or loss) respectively. We may, perhaps, legitimately regard operating income as a measure of management performance during a period and the windfall element as a measure of the effect of exogeneous factors not under the control of management. This is, of course, merely one possible interpretation. Another would be that windfall gains or losses represent management ineffectiveness as it shows an inability to perceive and adapt to future events.

Let us now summarise the state of the discussion so far. In an ideal situation, i.e. where there is complete management control over events and therefore complete certainty, ideal economic income provides a conceptually satisfying measure of business performance, although we have to concede that, in these circumstances, such measurements are of little value to us. If we invest money with a building society at an agreed rate of interest of, say, 10 per cent per annum (to quote an analogous situation) no useful information is produced by a constant monitoring of our rate of return on capital. This is known without such monitoring. Where the economic income idea is transferred to a situation where uncertainty exists we can argue that much more useful information is produced. It tells us something about:

(a) the divergence of current cash flow from expectation; and

(b) the distinction between the effects of a divergence of this period's cash flow and of expectations about future period's cash flows.

There is one major difficulty to which we referred briefly at the beginning but which we must now bring into the full light of day. This is that, since any form of economic income calculation under uncertainty depends upon a subjective view of the future, it will depend as much on by whom the view is formed as it will on the real situation itself. The information may be valuable in enabling management to inform itself. It is the responsibility of management to form a view of a situation and then respond accordingly. It does not follow, however, that economic income is a useful basis on which management should inform others.

Here is a simple example to illustrate this point. Suppose that a friend asks you to enquire for him as to the price of tickets for a theatre. You discover that they cost £5 each and decide that they would be too expensive for you to be able to afford to go yourself. The view "too expensive" is a useful one in enabling you to decide whether or not to buy the tickets. It will not, however, be a useful way in which to report to your friend. He must relate the price to his own circumstances. He may want to see the show more than you do or he may earn more. He must, therefore, not be told "too expensive" but be told "£5 each".

If the basic economic income concept can be modified in order to make it more objective it would become much more useful for external reporting. This brings us to the use of current values in accounting.

5. CURRENT COST ACCOUNTING

In a market economy there is a presumption that asset prices represent the best available estimates of economic values. This notion is based on the view that, out of the whole spectrum of subjective valuations which may exist, market forces will ensure equilibrium at a consensus value. It does not mean that all will agree on this valuation and indeed the fact that they do not is an essential motivator to exchange. Current market value has the advantage for accounting purposes that it is objectively determined. Although emerging as a consequence of the influence of a large number of subjective views it is itself a verifiable fact. It may therefore be reasonable for us to hope that a method of accounting based on current market values may be a compromise between historic cost and economic value many of the desirable characteristics of each. We shall now examine this proposition.

We will suppose that the single asset owned by the business (to use the same simplified situation as before) has a market value when bought (i.e. cost) of £15,000. Over its three year life it is assumed to decline evenly in value so that the straight line method of depreciation would be applied to it. The gross replacement value of the asset, however, increases over its life. The gross replacement value is defined as the replacement price of a brand new asset. Derived from it is the net replacement value which is the replacement value of a partly depreciated asset. Note that we do not use the secondhand value of the partly used asset as its current value.

The table below gives the relevant figures.

Year	Gross replacement value	Net replacement value
0	£15,000	£15,000 (full GRV)
1	£16,500	£11,000 ($\frac{2}{3}$ GRV)
2	£17,700	£5,900 ($\frac{1}{3}$ GRV)
3	£18,600	Nil

The calculation of total year by year income is shown below.

Year	Opening value of asset	Closing value of asset[1]	Income of year
1	£15,000	£19,000	£4,000
2	11,000	12,900	1,900
3	5,900	5,000	(900)
			£5,000

(1) This includes cash flow of year. The cash flows are £8,000, £7,000 and £5,000, as in our original example.

This income is made up of two components. These are (a) the current surplus of cash flow over the current value of the part of the asset consumed (current operating profit) and (b) the gain in market value of the portion of the asset still held during the year (holding gain). The terms current operating profit and holding gain are those used by Edwards and Bell in their book "The Theory and Measurement of Business Income" in 1961 and relate to the operating income and windfall gains of the economic model. The total of current operating profit and holding gain they termed business income.

These elements can be analysed by preparing accounts on the basis shown below.

	Year 1	Year 2	Year 3
Cash inflow	£8,000	£7,000	£5,000
Less Depreciation[1]	5,500	5,900	6,200
Current operating profit	2,500	1,100	(1,200)
Add Holding gain[2]	1,500	800	300
Total Business Income	£4,000	£1,900	(£900)

(1) The depreciation is, in each year, one third of the gross

replacement value of the asset at the time the depreciation takes place (deemed here to be at the year end). Thus:

$$\text{Year 1 } \tfrac{1}{3} \times \text{£16,500} = \text{£5,500}$$
$$\text{Year 2 } \tfrac{1}{3} \times \text{£17,700} = \text{£5,900}$$
$$\text{Year 3 } \tfrac{1}{3} \times \text{£18,600} = \text{£6,200}$$

(2) This is the increase in the gross replacement value times the fraction of the asset still held (i.e. 1, $\tfrac{2}{3}$, $\tfrac{1}{3}$ respectively). Thus:

$$\text{Year 1 } 1 \times (\text{£16,500} - \text{£15,000}) = \text{£1,500}$$
$$\text{Year 2 } \tfrac{2}{3} \times (\text{£17,700} - \text{£16,500}) = \quad \text{£800}$$
$$\text{Year 3 } \tfrac{1}{3} \times (\text{£18,600} - \text{£17,700}) = \quad \text{£300}$$

Since this model is useful only if the information it gives extends our understanding of the situation the interpretation of current operating profit and of holding gain respectively is important.

Current operating profit is a measure of the results achieved by current operations. It matches against revenues the *current* (as opposed to historic) cost of the resources consumed in producing it. Arguably it therefore produces a more intelligible report on the outcome of those operations. Holding gains may be variously interpreted. They may be seen as windfall gains resulting from factors not under the control of management and for which they cannot properly be held accountable. If, however, management is regarded as pursuing a purchasing and stocking policy having regard to market conditions, it may be seen as a measure of the success of that area of management. Finally, and this is a more recent idea, it may be seen as a measure of the effects of inflation on the business.

SUMMARY

1. The measurement of profit has become important through the pre-eminence which profit has acquired as a measure of business performance, as a measure of taxable capacity and as a measure of ability to pay dividends.

2. Income is most usefully defined as that amount which may be spent whilst leaving the enterprise as well off at the end of a period as it was at the beginning. This is the so-called capital maintenance concept.

3. In conditions of perfect certainty "economic" income provides a satisfactory model for profit measurement. It does not, however, add anything to the existing knowledge of the situation which it describes.

4. Economic income under uncertainty has the disadvantage of relying on subjective valuations. It does, however, separate operating income from windfall gains thus providing some basis for judging management success as opposed to fortune.

5. The current cost model attempts to combine something of the conceptual advantages of the economic income model with the objectivity of historic cost. Its original proponents were Edwards and Bell who proposed the analysis of total business income into components termed current operating profit and holding gains.

QUESTIONS

1. The investment of £18,462 in a certain project is expected to produce net cash inflows over three years of:

Year 1   £8,000
Year 2 £10,000
Year 3   £6,000

The project thus yields a return of 15 per cent per annum on the investment. Determine predicted profits for each year (*a*) on the basis of historic cost and (*b*) on the basis of the economic income model, and compare.

2. The project referred to in Question 1 is operated for three years with the following results.

Year 1: actual return £8,500 (Revised expectations for Year 2 £11,000 and Year 3 £6,500).

Year 2: actual return £10,500 (Revised expectation for Year 3 £5,000).

Year 3: actual return £6,000.

Determine at each year end the profit for the year using the economic income model adapted for uncertainty. Take 15 per cent per annum as an appropriate discount rate.

3. A machine is purchased for £15,000 which is to be written off evenly over its four year life. From this information and that given in the table below calculate the profit for each year using (*a*) the historic cost model and (*b*) the current cost model. Comment on the usefulness of the information produced under each.

	Cost of replacement new machine at year end	Net cash inflow
Year 1	£16,000	£5,000
Year 2	£18,000	£6,000
Year 3	£22,000	£4,000
Year 4	£22,500	£3,000

4. What are the deficiencies of the historic cost method of accounting which lead us to seek alternatives?

5. Discuss the concept of profit explaining why it is so difficult, in practice, to measure profit. What would you expect to be the consequences of an inaccurate measurement of profit?

CHAPTER 17

Inflation in Financial Accounting

OBJECTIVES

In this chapter we shall deal with the following important topics:

(*a*) inflation as an accounting problem;
(*b*) current purchasing power;
(*c*) current cost accounting;
(*d*) SSAP 16.

1. INTRODUCTION

By inflation is meant that process which leads to a steady reduction in the purchasing power of the unit of currency. It manifests itself by a general and sustained increase in the level of prices. Although inflation can be observed readily enough, measuring it gives rise to quite a difficult problem. All practical measures of inflation involve the calculation of index numbers but these are all based on only a selection of prices and so none is of completely general application. The general index of retail prices is widely regarded as the best all-purpose measure of general inflation and when we refer, in this chapter, to an index without qualification this is the one that we mean.

If the index in a particular period rose from 100 to 120 we shall interpret this as meaning that on average goods and services have become 20 per cent more expensive in terms of money. Another way of looking at this, and in the present context a more informative one, is to say that the £ has lost 20 per cent of its value. The index does not need to take any particular starting value and a move from 200 to 240 or from 180 to 216 would also be general price increases of 20 per cent with exactly the same implications.

Inflation attacks one of the fundamental concepts of accounting, that of money measurement. We have already seen that it is not always easy in practice to convert real resources into monetary valuations on a consistent basis. Where money itself constantly changes in value this adds a new dimension to that problem. £100 worth of stock bought when the index stood at 100 is not the same in real terms as £100 worth of stock bought when the index stood at 120. This is because at the latter date the money would have bought only as much stock as would have cost £83.33

(100/120 × 100) at the former date. Nevertheless the different consignments of stock will be recorded as equal in value in a balance sheet prepared on a conventional basis.

This difficulty in accounting measurement has been tolerated for many years but it is impossible to believe that it would have been so tolerated in any other field of measurement. Great pains are taken to ensure that our weights and measures are kept constant and accurate. Heavy penalties are imposed on those who would seek to undermine this principle. We rightly take the standards of measurement for granted as not to be able to do so would cause great and obvious inconvenience. If centimetres were gradually becoming shorter and kilograms lighter we should apparently (but not actually) all be growing both taller and heavier. A suit measured on one occasion would never fit a man measured on another occasion and interpretations which, for example, doctors might place on weight changes would be invalidated. One person might seem to be bigger than another merely because they were weighed and measured later. A direct comparison may show quite a different position.

2. CURRENT PURCHASING POWER

One way of dealing with the changing value of the currency unit is to abandon strict money measurement and measure all value in terms of the purchasing power of the £ at a specified date. All other values are then converted to this by the application of ratios derived from indices. The favoured version of this method is what is known as the current purchasing power method in which all values are quoted in terms of the purchasing power of the £ at the accounting date.

Here is an example of how this works.

X plc was formed with an issued share capital of £10,000 on 1st January when the price index stood at 100. On the same date 8,000 units of stock were bought for £1 each. By 30th June the general price level had risen by 10 per cent so that the index stood at 110. 7,500 units of stock were sold for £2 each and a further 10,000 bought for £1.50 each. By 31st December the index had risen a further 10 per cent to 121. 1,000 units of stock were sold at £3 each and 5,000 bought at £2 each. Accounts are to be prepared at 31st December in current purchasing power form.

Under historic cost all valuations are determined by transactions. These transactions obviously take place at whatever was the price level at that date. Current purchasing power is a modification of this principle and translates the transaction values in terms of what they would have cost if paid for in the (less valuable) £s of

31st December. This is not the same as what they would have cost if bought at 31st December. Let us examine this further. Using indices we can say that £1 of 30th June is equivalent to £1.10 of 31st December and £1 of 1st January is equivalent to £1.21 of 31st December. Thus stock bought at 1st January for an actual £8,000 would, theoretically, have cost £9,680 (£8,000 × 1.21) if it could have been bought then with the less valuable £ of 31st December. If it had actually been bought at 31st December, however, when its price had increased as well as when money had become generally less valuable, it would have cost £16,000 (£2 × 8,000).

Below we show historic cost accounts with, alongside, their translation into current purchasing power accounts.

PROFIT AND LOSS ACCOUNT FOR THE YEAR ENDED 31ST DECEMBER

		Historic cost		*Current purchasing power at 31st December*		
Sales:	7,500 × £2	£15,000		£15,000 × 1.1	£16,500	
	8,000 × £3	24,000	£39,000	£24,000 × 1	24,000	£40,500
Less cost of sales[1]						
	8,000 × £1	£8,000		£8,000 × 1.21	£9,680	
	7,500 × £1.50	11,250	19,250	£11,250 × 1.1	12,375	22,055
			£19,750			£18,445

(1) First in, first out, leaving stock of:

	Historic cost		*Current purchasing power*
£2,500 × £1.50	£3,750	× 1.1	£4,125
5,000 × £2	10,000	× 1	10,000
	£13,750		£14,125

BALANCE SHEET AT 31ST DECEMBER

	Historic cost		*Current purchasing power at 31st December*	
Stock	£13,750		£14,125	
Cash	16,000			16,000
	£29,750			£30,125
Represented by:				
Capital	£10,000	× 1.21		£12,100
Retained profit	19,750		£18,445	
Less Loss on holding cash			420[1]	18,025
	£29,750			£30,125

(1) The loss on holding cash is an interesting item which arises only because these accounts seek to reveal the effects of inflation. This is not limited to the removal of distortions within the profit and loss account and balance sheet but extends also to revealing profits or losses due to inflation. These are caused when a business has monetary liabilities (loans and creditors) or monetary assets (debtors, bank balances and cash) respectively. Here it is calculated as follows.

Cash holding throughout year = £2,000 (can be verified by preparing a cash account)

Degree of inflation = 21%

Loss due to inflation = 21% of £2,000 = £420.

3. CURRENT COST ACCOUNTING

Current cost accounting was introduced in the last chapter as an alternative to historic cost accounting seeming to promise certain advantages. These were not particularly related to the matter of inflation but it was hinted at the end of that discussion that there might be some bearing on this problem too. As a method of accounting for inflation (as opposed to any other advantages or functions which it might have) current cost accounting stands or falls on the view that it is inherently less vulnerable to inflationary distortions than is historic cost.

The argument can be very simply presented through the medium of an illustration. Mr King bought 20 tons of coal for £50 per ton on 1st January. He held it in stock until 30th June when its market value was £60 per ton. The complete consignment had thus improved in money value by £200. Historic cost accounting would not reveal this. Current cost accounting would reveal it as a holding gain. If this holding gain is interpreted as being attributable to inflation it is a money gain only. It should be credited to a capital reserve thus adjusting the proprietor's money investment in the business so as to maintain its real value. If it is a gain arising from a change in the demand for or supply of coal then the holding gain is a profit resulting from the management's luck or judgment in buying at a favourable time and should be credited to a revenue reserve thus being regarded as distributable. We will complete the example by assuming that King sold the coal on 30th June for £75 per ton and prepare accounts accordingly.

(a) *Historic cost.*

PROFIT AND LOSS ACCOUNT FOR THE SIX MONTHS ENDED 30TH JUNE

Sales 20 × £75	£1,500
Less Cost of sales 20 × £50	1,000
Profit	£500

BALANCE SHEET AT 30TH JUNE

Capital	£1,000	Cash	£1,500
Profit (available for distribution)[1]	500		
	£1,500		£1,500

(1) If King withdraws this £500 he will leave his *money* capital of £1,000 intact. If there has been inflation, however, this will have less purchasing power than it did when first invested.

(b) *Current cost accounting* (assuming no general inflation).

PROFIT AND LOSS ACCOUNT FOR THE SIX MONTHS ENDED 30TH JUNE

Sales		£1,500
Less Current cost of sales 20 × £60		1,200
Current operating profit		300
Add Holding gain: current value of coal	£1,200	
Less Cost	1,000	
		200
Business income		£500

The balance sheet is the same as in (a)

(c) *Current cost accounting* (as inflation accounting).

PROFIT AND LOSS ACCOUNT FOR THE SIX MONTHS ENDED 30TH JUNE

Sales	£1,500
Less Current cost of sales	1,200
Profit	£300

BALANCE SHEET AT 30TH JUNE

Capital	£1,000	Cash	£1,500
Capital reserve	200		
	1,200		
Profit (available for distribution)	300		
	£1,500		£1,500

If distribution is limited to £300, the retained capital is precisely enough to finance the next round of transactions by purchasing, at the current price, a further 20 tons of coal. It does not necessarily maintain the general purchasing power of the capital. The interpretation of the holding gain is crucial in current cost accounting and the way must be left open to a judgment that part of it is due to inflation (and thus only an apparent gain necessitating the creation of a capital reserve) and part is due to skilful or lucky buying (and thus is a real gain properly available for distribution).

4. HISTORY OF INFLATION ACCOUNTING IN THE UNITED KINGDOM

The route to a workable system of accounting for inflation in the United Kingdom has been a slowly trodden road the end of which has not yet been reached. It will be worth our while to recall progress briefly as, apart from its contribution to understanding the accounting technicalities, it is a fascinating example of the interplay which must exist between the theoretical merits of the techniques which are proposed and the opinions and feelings of those preparing and using the information which they produce. It demonstrates very clearly that there can be no such thing as ultimate truth in accounting.

Although inflation is often regarded as being a relatively modern problem it has existed for a very long time (extending over centuries) but has for most of that time been at relatively modest rates. Thus Recommendations of Accounting Principles N12 (1949) and N15 (1952) of the Institute of Chartered Accountants in England and Wales, whilst commenting on the distortions caused to accounts by inflation, were nevertheless able reasonably to say that it could safely be ignored.

Following the formation of the Accounting Standards Steering Committee (now the Accounting Standards Committee whose work is more fully explained in Chapter 18, Section 3) inflation accounting was at a fairly early stage put on its programme of work and this led to the eventual publication of ED 8 which was translated into a Standard, (P)SSAP 7 "Accounting for changes in the Purchasing Power of Money" issued in May 1974. The (P) stood for provisional and SSAP 7 is the only Standard to have been so designated. The reason for this will appear presently. The Standard was based on the current purchasing power method of accounting. The index prescribed for the adjustments was the General Index of Retail Prices (and its precursors for earlier years) and supplementary adjusted statements to accompany the main, historical cost based, accounts were required. Before ED 8 had reached the end of the period allowed for comment the Secretary of State for Trade and Industry had announced the setting up of an independent Committee of Enquiry to consider the whole question of accounting for inflation. In view of the subject's potential implications in the fields of financial reporting, company law and taxation, the government's intervention was, perhaps, not surprising. This explains why, pending the findings of the Committee, the Standard had to be regarded as provisional.

The Committee of Inquiry reported in September 1975 (The Sandilands Report named after the Committee's chairman, Sir Francis Sandilands) and came down firmly in favour of current cost accounting, thus rejecting current purchasing power and rendering (P)SSAP 7 obsolete. It was recommended, furthermore, that current cost accounting should be the basic form of accounting rather than being the subject merely of supplementary statements and the profession was left to formulate a Standard incorporating these ideas.

This led to the issue by the Accounting Standards Committee of the now infamous ED 18 (published November, 1976). It is probably fair to say that this exposure draft placed the profession in a state of shock. Although it proclaimed (para. 7) that "the essence of the CCA system is simple" and asserted (para. 5) "CCA will provide management, and the users of published accounts, with more realistic information", neither of these views seemed to be taken by accountants generally. ED 18, at over 150 pages inclusive of appendices, was far longer than had been any other Standard (before or since) and it was probably only imperfectly understood by many people. It prescribed that reporting entities should maintain their records and prepare their annual accounts on a full current cost basis. The revaluations which this required (i.e. holding gains) were then to be shown in an Appropriation Account and such part of them as the directors determined were then to be transferred to a Revaluation Reserve (i.e. capital reserve to maintain the purchasing power of capital). The exposure draft dealt with a good many problems including taxation and deferred taxation, depreciation, goodwill and group accounts. It introduced new and unfamiliar terminology such as gross and net current replacement cost, backlog depreciation and economic value.

ED 18 never became a Standard. A revolt by the membership of the Institute of Chartered Accountants in England and Wales culminated in the passing, at a special meeting in July, 1977, of the resolution "That the members of the Institute of Chartered Accountants in England and Wales do not wish any system of current cost accounting to be made compulsory". Since ED 18 did imply compulsion it was effectively dead.

From the wreckage of ED 18 and from the comments made upon it during the exposure period, the pieces were picked which would eventually form the Standard which is now in force, SSAP 16.

5. SSAP 16 CURRENT COST ACCOUNTING

SSAP 16 provides for current cost information to be included in annual accounts alongside historical cost information. It does not, that is, require the abandonment of historical cost in favour of current cost.

To the profit calculated according to conventional historic cost principles it requires a number of adjustments. These are described below before an example is given to show how they work in practice. The adjustments are:

(*a*) *Cost of sales adjustment.* This is a deduction from historic cost profit equal to the difference between historic cost of sales (already charged) and current cost of sales.

(*b*) *Depreciation adjustment.* This is a deduction equal to the difference between historic cost depreciation (already charged) and depreciation calculated on a current cost basis.

(*c*) *Monetary Working Capital Adjustment.* This is an adjustment, special to SSAP 16, which would not be encountered in current cost accounting as such. It was introduced in deference to the argument that, where inflation exists, more money capital is inevitably tied up in monetary working capital (i.e. debtors less creditors) because of the higher level of prices at which business is being conducted. The figure is determined by applying an appropriate index to net monetary working capital. This index should have regard to the constituents of the items concerned, their age and the extent to which they have been affected by price changes. Although here listed third of these three adjustments, the monetary working capital adjustment is usually coupled with that in respect of cost of sales in recognition of the fact that both are concerned with components of overall working capital.

The figure arrived at after the three adjustments just described is the current cost profit of the business. The revaluation surpluses arising from the adjustments represent the amount of historic cost profit which must be retained to maintain the purchasing power of the company's capital. This is done, as before, by transferring it to a capital reserve which, in the terminology of SSAP 16, is called the Current Cost Reserve. Current year's adjustments are, of course, added to any existing balance on Current Cost Reserve arising out of the activities of previous years.

As described above the Current Cost Reserve serves to maintain the purchasing power of *all* capital invested in the company. It may be argued, however, that only equity capital, as opposed to loan capital, need be so maintained. This is because loan capital is ultimately repayable at its face value in money terms. One final adjustment, known as the gearing adjustment, is therefore made. This serves to abate, by writing back to revenue, a proportion of the current cost adjustments already made. The abatement stands in the same proportion to the total of current cost adjustments as loan capital stands to the total of loan and equity capital. The profit figure following this adjustment is termed the current cost profit attributable to shareholders. Because it is assumed that rates of interest are likely to contain a factor to allow for inflation, interest payable on loan capital is extracted from its normal position in the profit and loss account and coupled with the gearing adjustment.

Here is an example to illustrate, in a simple case, the principles of SSAP 16. Maximus plc started in business on 1st January with the balance sheet given below (as this is the starting date of the business the historic cost and current cost balance sheets are identical).

MAXIMUS PLC

BALANCE SHEET AT 1ST JANUARY

Share capital	£20,000	Fixed assets	£20,000
Loan capital (10% p.a. interest)	5,000	Current asset	
		Stock	5,000
	£25,000		£25,000

During the ensuing year the following took place:

(a)

HISTORIC COST STOCK ACCOUNT

Opening stock	£5,000
Add Purchases	50,000
	55,000
Less Closing stock	8,000
Historic cost of sales	£47,000

(b) The current cost of sales for the year was £52,500 and the current cost of the closing stock was £8,300.

(c) Sales for the year totalled £66,500.

(d) Debtors and creditors at the year end stood at £7,500 and £5,000 respectively. They had averaged approximately these figures throughout the year. A suitable index for the computation of the monetary working capital adjustment had risen by 5 per cent during the average life of debtors and creditors.

(e) The interest on the loan capital was paid during the year and a dividend totalling £7,500 was paid to the shareholders.

(f) The fixed assets, if purchased at the end of the year, would have cost £25,000. Depreciation at the annual rate of 20 per cent is to be deemed to have taken place evenly over the year.

MAXIMUS PLC

STATEMENT TO COMPLY WITH SSAP 16

Historic cost profit before interest[1]		£15,500
Less Current cost operating adjustments:		
Cost of sales[2]	£5,500	
Monetary working capital[3]	125	
Working capital	5,625	
Depreciation[4]	500	
		6,125
Current cost operating profit		9,375
Gearing adjustment[5]	(991)	
Interest payable on loan capital	500	491
Current cost profit attributable to shareholders		9,866
Dividend		7,500
Retained profit		£2,366

Note that taxation, which would normally appear, has been ignored in this example. There are no adjustments to make in respect of it.

CURRENT COST BALANCE SHEET AT 31ST DECEMBER

Share capital	£20,000	Fixed assets[7]		£20,000
Current cost reserve[6]	9,434	Current assets		
Profit and loss account	2,366	Stock[7]	£8,300	
	———	Debtors	7,500	
	31,800	Cash[8]	6,000	
			———	21,800
Loan capital	5,000			
Current liabilities				
(creditors)	5,000			
	———			———
	£41,800			£41,800

Calculations

(1) *Historic cost profit.*

Sales		£66,500
Less Cost of sales	47,000	
Depreciation	4,000	
	———	
		51,000
		———
		£15,500

(2) *Cost of sales.*

Current cost of sales	£52,500
Less Historic cost of sales	47,000
	———
Cost of sales adjustment	£5,500

(3) *Monetary working capital.*

Average debtors	£7,500
Less Average creditors	5,000
	———
	$£2,500 \times 5\% = £125$

(4) *Current cost depreciation.*

20% of average gross replacement cost:

$20\% \times (20,000 + 25,000)/2$	£4,500
Less Historic cost depreciation	4,000
	———
	£500

(5) *Gearing adjustment*

Opening loan and equity capital	£25,000
Add Historic cost profit	15,500
Asset revaluations	4,300
	44,800
Less Interest and dividends	8,000
Closing loan and equity capital	£36,800

Average loan and equity capital is $(25,000 + 36,800)/2 =$ £30,900

Loan capital is constant at £5,000

Gearing adjustment is $5,000 \div 30,900 \times £6,125 = £991$

(6) *Current cost reserve.*

Current cost adjustments	£6,125	
Gearing adjustment	991	
		£5,134
Year end stock revaluation (£8,300 − £8,000)		300
Year end fixed assets revaluation		
(£20,000 − £16,000)		4,000
		£9,434

(7) *Current cost valuations.*

(8) *Cash.*

From Sales	£66,500	
Less Debtors	7,500	
		£59,000
To Purchases	£50,000	
Less Creditors	5,000	
		45,000
		14,000
Interest and dividends		8,000
Year end cash balance		£6,000

SUMMARY

1. Inflation is a term applied to the phenomenon whereby there is a long term decline in the purchasing power of money. It can be measured by means of the movements in a price index.

2. Inflation gives rise to problems in accounting because of the money measurement concept.

3. Current purchasing power accounting seeks to accommodate inflation by abandoning money measurement and restating values in terms of the purchasing power of money at the accounting date. It not only removes the distortions caused by inflation but also measures and reports the gains and losses caused by inflation acting on monetary liabilities and assets.

4. Current cost accounting is an alternative approach to the problem which has found favour in practice. Its use is justified by the belief that the current cost model is inherently less vulnerable to inflationary distortions than is historic cost.

5. SSAP 16 embodies a variant on current cost accounting. It requires certain adjustments to be made to historic cost profit to determine current cost profit and a further adjustment to determine current cost profit attributable to shareholders. In the first of these stages adjustments are made for cost of sales, depreciation and monetary working capital. In the second a gearing adjustment is made.

QUESTIONS

1. On 1st January 19— Rogers set up in business as a retailer with a capital of £10,000. On the same date he purchased 100 units of stock at a price of £80 per unit. On the 30th June, 80 units were sold for £120 each and a further 60 purchased at £100 each. On 31st December, 50 were sold for £150 each and 75 bought for £120 each. A general index of retail prices stood at 100 on 1st January, 110 on 30th June and 121 on 31st December. Show final accounts for Rogers under the three different conventions of historic cost, current purchasing power and current cost.

2. Pear plc commenced trading on 1st January with an issued share capital of £100,000. The following transactions took place during the company's first year of trading.

1st January   Purchased fixed assets for £60,000.
               Purchased stock for resale—10,000 units at
               £3.50 each.
31st March   Sold 9,000 units of stock for £10 each.
               Purchased 10,000 units of stock for £5 each.

30th June   Sold 10,000 units of stock for £12 each.
                   Purchased 8,000 units of stock for £6 each.
30th September Sold 5,000 units of stock for £15 each.
                   Purchased 2,000 uni.s of stock for £8 each.
31st December Purchased 1,000 units of stock for £10 each.

If replaced new at 31st December the original fixed assets would have cost £75,000. They should be depreciated on the straight line basis over an expected life of ten years.

Prepare a profit and loss account for the year ended 31st December and a balance sheet at that date:

(a) on an historical cost basis; and
(b) on a current cost basis.

3. Big Fiddle plc commenced business on 1st January—with the balance sheet appearing below.

	(£000s)			(£000s)
Share capital	2,000	*Fixed assets*		
10% Debentures	500	Building		1,500
Current liabilities	500	Equipment		1,000
				2,500
		Current assets		
		Stock	400	
		Cash	100	
				500
	3,000			3,000

(a) During the ensuing year the following purchases and sales took place.

	Stock purchases		Sales
	(£000s)	Price index	(£000s)
1st quarter	840	105	787.5
2nd quarter	880	110	825
3rd quarter	920	115	1,150
4th quarter	960	120	1,800

All sales are at *current* cost + 25 per cent. Stock purchases were made in even quantities over the year but sales had a seasonal pattern.

(b) The building had a value of £2,000,000 on 31st December 19—.

(c) The gross replacement cost of the equipment on 31st

December 19— was £1,200,000. Depreciation was at the rate of 20 per cent per annum.

(*d*) Debenture interest for the year was paid. Dividends totalling £200,000 were also paid.

(*e*) Administrative expenses totalling £250,000 were paid in the year.

(*f*) At 31st December 19— debtors and creditors were each £500,000.

Prepare accounts for the company on an historic cost basis and on a current cost basis. Prepare also a statement for issue with the historic cost accounts which will enable the company to comply with the requirements of SSAP 16.

4. "SSAP 16, whatever its merits, does not address itself to the problem of general inflation as it affects accounts." Do you agree? What alternative system might be advocated which would take account of general inflation?

5. Inflation undermines the meaning of figures produced under the historic cost system. Explain, with special reference to:

(*a*) the calculation of profit;
(*b*) asset valuation;
(*c*) the relationship between equity and loan capital.

CHAPTER 18

Accounting Standards

OBJECTIVES

In this chapter we shall deal with the following important topics:

(*a*) the initiation of Standards by the Statement of Intent of 1969;
(*b*) the composition and procedures of the Accounting Standards Committee;
(*c*) the Standards so far issued.

1. INTRODUCTION

An examination of a representative collection of published company accounts will show that there is a considerable degree of uniformity amongst them both in terms of the nature of the information which they contain and in terms of the form in which it appears. Company legislation is one obvious source of such uniformity. The necessity to present a "true and fair view" requires a conformity to what is generally accepted as so doing by the commercial and financial community. The prescription by statute of minimum levels of required information guarantees the inclusion of a number of items in standard form. The requirement that published accounts be audited by the members of specified professional bodies ensures that practices approved of by those bodies will thrive at the expense of those not approved.

Accounting Standards are a more recent influence on uniformity of presentation and amount to a formalisation of the influence which the accountancy profession has always had on the form of financial statements. In this chapter we shall describe the standard setting process and look, in outline, at the requirements of the standards which have been published so far. First, though, we ought to consider the arguments which led to the establishment of standards in the first place.

The direct ancestors of Accounting Standards were the Recommendations on Accounting Principles issued for the guidance of its members by the Institute of Chartered Accountants in England and Wales (ICAEW). The first of these appeared in 1942 and the last in 1969. Recommendations were made on a wide variety of different matters and they provided useful guidance to members involved in the preparation of accounts or responsible for their audit. By the late 1960s a number of factors had drawn public attention to the inadequacy of accounting methods in some important circumstances. Inflation was gathering pace and this of itself revealed some important general deficiencies. Probably more significant, however, were the spectacular failures of companies like Rolls-Royce and Handley-Page where no weakness had been indicated by recent accounts prepared and audited in accordance with the generally accepted principles of the time. It became clear in these cases and in others that the treatment of certain potentially controversial items had been shown by subsequent events to have been misleading. Indications seemed to be that a lesser amount of discretion in treating such items coupled with greater disclosure of the methods used would have been more revealing.

2. STATEMENT OF INTENT ON ACCOUNTING STANDARDS

In December 1969 ICAEW issued a statement entitled "Statement of Intent on Accounting Standards in the 1970s". This embodied the Institute's intention to advance accounting standards in several ways. These were as follows.

(a) *Narrowing the Areas of Difference and Variety in Accounting Practices.* The firm principle was thus established that more uniformity of treatment would be imposed on those responsible for preparing published financial reports.

(b) *Disclosure of Accounting Bases.* In areas of subjectivity, where judgment had to be relied on, the principle was established that the basis used in arriving at figures should be fully disclosed.

(c) *Disclosure of Departures from Established Accounting Standards.* Where a company chooses to depart from a Standard it was to be required to disclose fully that it had done so.

(d) *Wider Exposure for Major Proposals on Accounting Standards.* It was to be a feature of the standard setting process that controversial areas should be fully and widely debated before a definitive standard was set.

(e) *A Continuing Programme* for encouraging improved Accounting Standards in Legal and Regulatory Measures.

3. ACCOUNTING STANDARDS COMMITTEE

We will now look at the present position, ten years on, to see how accounting standards are made and what is the nature of those which have so far come into existence.

Standards are now promulgated concurrently by the six main accountancy bodies based in the British Isles. The work is initiated and directed by the Accounting Standards Committee (ASC) on which the participating bodies are represented as follows.

	Number of members
Institute of Chartered Accountants in England and Wales	12
Institute of Chartered Accountants of Scotland	3
Institute of Chartered Accountants in Ireland	2
Association of Certified Accountants	2
Institute of Cost and Management Accountants	2
Chartered Institute of Public Finance and Accountancy	2
Total membership	23

The Committee formulates a long-term programme of work which is devised in consultation with a specially formed Consultative Group convened by the Committee and consisting of representatives drawn from the fields of finance, commerce, industry and government and other persons concerned with financial reporting. Within the programme of work determined by ASC each Standard is developed, at a varying pace depending upon its subject matter, by passing through a number of stages each of which is briefly described below.

(*a*) *Research*. The first stage is a research study commissioned by ASC and usually undertaken by a firm of professional accountants or by a group of academics. This study gathers all available information on the topic and will include a review of practices in other countries and of current thinking on the matter.

(*b*) *Drafting sub-committee*. For each Standard a special drafting sub-committee is formed to translate the findings of the research into the form of a draft practical standard.

(*c*) *Internal exposure*. The draft produced by the drafting sub-committee is circulated to the Technical Committees of the participating accountancy bodies including those committees in the regions and comments are then considered by the sub-committee. The draft may be amended in the light of the comments. The draft standard is then received by the ASC which will normally engage in further consultations of its own before agreeing to issue the draft publicly.

(*d*) *Exposure Draft*. The first general publication of any standard is in the form of an Exposure Draft. These are consecutively numbered as issued (ED 1, ED 2, ED 3, etc.). The number bears no relationship to the number which will be given to the eventual standard. Comments are invited by a stated deadline from any interested parties. When all of these have been received they are considered by ASC and amendments, where considered desirable, are made to the draft.

(*e*) *Statement of Standard Accounting Practice.* As a final stage the standard, now with its own identifying number in the series SSAP 1, SSAP 2, etc. is recommended to the Councils of the participating bodies. If approved by them all (which is usual) it is then simultaneously issued to all their respective members.

4. STATEMENTS OF STANDARD ACCOUNTING PRACTICE

It is important to be clear about the status of Accounting Standards. They apply to all financial accounts intended to give a true and fair view of financial position and profit or loss although their most important field of application by far is in the annual accounts published by limited companies. They do not have the legal force of an Act of Parliament, so that in theory no company is absolutely bound by them. They are, however, made mandatory so far as the members of the participating bodies are concerned in their capacities as preparers of accounts or as auditors. These people, who comprise the vast majority of those actually concerned in the production of published accounts, are obliged under threat of disciplinary action from their professional body, to observe standards. Although this has not yet been tested in court, it is also possible that a company not complying with a standard could be deemed not to have given a true and fair view and thus to have acted illegally. In practice, Standards are observed in almost all cases and the exceptions are made for persuasive reasons, persuasively and publicly argued.

We will now briefly review all standards in force at the time of writing. For the sake of completeness those discussed fully elsewhere in the book are included but reference is then made to where the more extended treatment may be found. It should be noted that the brief descriptions of Standards given here are outlines intended to convey the spirit underlying each. Any detailed application requires reference to the original standards which are published by the member bodies of the ASC.

SSAP 1

Accounting for the Results of Associated Companies. Issued January 1971. Effective in respect of reports relating to accounting periods commencing on or after 1st January 1971. This standard deals with the case where a company has a substantial interest in another company which is nevertheless not sufficiently large to give control and thus to make that company a subsidiary. In broad terms a substantial interest is defined as one not less than 20 per cent of equity rights. The main effect of the standard is that the investing company takes into its profit and loss account its full proportion of the associated company's profit or loss for a period and not merely that amount which is distributed by way of dividend. In the investing company's balance sheet its investment in the associated company is valued at cost plus the appropriate proportion of the associated company's post acquisition retained profits and reserves.

SSAP 2

Disclosure of Accounting Policies. Issued November 1971. Effective in respect of reports relating to accounting periods commencing on or after 1st January 1972.

An important theme of this book has been that an understanding of accounting statements requires a knowledge of the concepts and principles which were used in their formulation. This Standard requires that a company set out its accounting policies relating to areas where these would not otherwise be apparent as an aid to this process. It singles out four fundamental accounting concepts which it says have such general acceptance that their use will not require special mention. These are:

(*a*) the going concern concept;
(*b*) the accruals concept;
(*c*) the consistency concept; and
(*d*) the prudence concept.

The kinds of policies where differences between reporting entities may occur and which might be expected to need explanation in compliance with SSAP 2 are such matters as depreciation, valuation of stocks and work in progress and treatment of intangible items.

SSAP 3

Earnings Per Share. Issued February 1972. Effective in respect of reports relating to accounting periods commencing on or after 1st January 1972.

The calculation of earnings per share under the definition adopted in this Standard has been explained and exemplified in Chapter 14, page 205. This Standard makes it mandatory for a company to calculate EPS and to publish the figure (together with the corresponding figure for the previous year) on the face of the profit and loss account.

SSAP 4

The Accounting Treatment of Government Grants. Issued April 1974. Effective in respect of reports relating to accounting periods commencing on or after 1st January 1974.

The Industry Act 1972 empowers the government to make grants to industry in certain defined circumstances. These grants may be in respect of either revenue expenditure or capital expenditure. Grants towards revenue expenditure are clearly properly taken to the profit and loss account of the period in which the relevant expenditure takes place (i.e. reducing it by the amount of the grant). This Standard deals with grants towards capital expenditure and it requires that they be credited to revenue over the useful life of the assets to which they relate. This is achieved either by reducing the recorded cost of the asset (and thus the annual depreciation charge) or by creating a deferred credit and transferring a portion of this to the profit and loss account each year.

SSAP 5

Accounting for Value Added Tax. Issued April 1974. Effective in respect of reports relating to accounting periods commencing on or after 1st January 1974.

This has been dealt with in Chapter 11, Section 2. Its effect is that value added tax not borne by the company (the usual case) is excluded from the accounts. Both revenues and expenses are shown net of VAT.

SSAP 6

Extraordinary Items and Prior Year Adjustments. Issued April 1974. Effective in respect of reports relating to accounting periods commencing on or after 1st January 1974. Extraordinary items are defined as those events leading to a profit or loss to the business which lie outside the ordinary scope of its activities. Examples might be the disposal of a substantial group of fixed assets or the writing off of an intangible asset rendered worthless by an unexpected development. Prior year adjustments arise when an error or a change in accounting policies means that an amendment has to be made in the current year which actually relates to the events of a previous year. The Standard requires that extraordinary items should be shown separately in the profit and loss after the results of the business's ordinary activities have been ascertained. Prior year adjustments should also be disclosed but should be dealt with by means of an adjustment to the balance brought forward on the profit and loss account (i.e. the retained profit).

SSAP 7

Accounting for Price Level Changes. This was the Standard dealing with the preparation of current purchasing power adjusted accounts and it has now been withdrawn.

SSAP 8

The Treatment of Taxation under the Imputation System in the accounts of companies. Issued August 1974. Effective in respect of reports relating to accounting periods commencing on or after 1st January 1975. The contents of this Standard have been dealt with in Chapter 11, Section 4.

SSAP 9

Stocks and Work in Progress. Issued May 1975. Effective in respect of reports relating to accounting periods commencing on or after 1st January 1976.

The normal basis for preparing a profit and loss account, as we have seen, is that the costs of stocks consumed are matched against the revenues which they ultimately produce and any balance of stock in hand is carried forward and recorded in the balance sheet. This standard requires that such stocks carried forward are valued on the basis of cost or net realisable value whichever be the lower. This is, of course, also in conformity with the principle of conservatism. The Standard also deals with the method of valuation of work in progress on long-term contracts. These are defined as those where the work is undertaken over a period extending over several accounting periods. Strict application of the normal matching principle would mean that no profit would be reported on such contracts until they had been fully completed. For a company, such as one engaged in civil engineering work, which was frequently involved in such contracts this could lead to misleadingly erratic reported profits. The Standard allows work in progress on long-term contracts to be valued at cost plus accrued profit, thus allowing interim recognition of the profit in stages as the contract proceeds. The principle of conservatism (and the Standard) requires that an ultimate profit on the project should be confidently foreseen before this treatment is put into practice.

SSAP 10

Statements of Source and Application of Funds. Issued July 1975. Effective in respect of reports relating to accounting periods commencing on or after 1st January 1976. The contents of this Standard are set out and fully explained in Chapter 12, Section 2.

SSAP 11

Accounting for Deferred Taxation. This Standard has been superseded by SSAP 15 and is now withdrawn.

SSAP 12

Accounting for Depreciation. Issued December 1977. Effective in respect of reports relating to accounting periods commencing on or after 1st January 1979. Chapter 7 described a number of methods which are used to calculate depreciation. This Standard does not advocate any specific method and companies are therefore free to choose the method or methods which they think to be appropriate. The Standard, however, requires that depreciation should be calculated and provided in respect of all assets having a finite useful life and that the method used should allocate cost less residual value fairly over that period. It also requires that, where an opinion is formed that the remaining useful life of an asset differs from what had previously been expected, then the remaining book value should be written off over the revised remaining life. Similarly, if a revaluation of a partly depreciated asset occurs the new value should be depreciated over the remaining useful life. In neither case does the Standard require any amendment to earlier years' accounts. Disclosure of the depreciation method used and the rate applied are required.

SSAP 13

Accounting for Research and Development. Issued December 1977. Effective in respect of reports relating to accounting periods commencing on or after 1st January 1978.

Research and development expenditure, commonly abbreviated to R & D, presents a special problem when it comes to matching the expenditure against revenue since anything other than a wholly arbitrary allocation is often difficult. The Standard clarifies practice by requiring the following.

(a) Fixed assets acquired to provide facilities for R & D are to be treated as other fixed assets, i.e. written off over their useful lives.

(b) Pure research expenditure, not associated with any definable project, is to be charged to revenue in the year in which it occurs.

(c) Development expenditure is also to be written off immediately except where all of the following conditions apply: (i) it is associated with a clearly definable project; (ii) the project is reasonably certain to proceed to a successful conclusion; (iii) the project will produce revenue against which the expenditure can be matched; and (*iv*) adequate resources to ensure completion of the project are reasonably believed to be available.

SSAP 14

Group Accounts. Issued September 1978. Effective in respect of reports relating to accounting periods commencing on or after 1st January 1979. The matter of group accounts is dealt with in Chapter 13. This Standard formalises the practices set out there.

SSAP 15

Accounting for Deferred Taxation. Issued October 1978. Effective in respect of reports relating to accounting periods commencing on or after 1st January 1979.

This Standard has been dealt with in the chapter on taxation, Chapter 11, Section 5.

SSAP 16

Current Cost Accounting. Issued March 1980. Effective in respect of reports relating to accounting periods commencing on or after 1st January 1980.

This is a very important Standard which is fully described in Chapter 17.

SSAP 17

Accounting for Post Balance Sheet Events. Issued August 1980. Effective in respect to reports relating to accounting periods commencing on or after 1st September 1980.

Post balance sheet events are those occurring after the date of the balance sheet but before the accounts have been finalised (which is signalled by approval to the accounts being given by the board of directors). Two kinds of post balance sheet events are identified in the Standard. These are known as adjusting events and non-adjusting events. Adjusting events are those which provide more evidence on situations known to exist at the balance sheet date and which now enable a fairer view to be given. Where adjusting events occur the indicated adjustments should be made to the figures in the accounts. Non-adjusting events are those which concern conditions which have arisen since the balance sheet date at which time they did not exist. Such events do not require adjustment to the original figures in the accounts but disclosure (by means of a note) is required where:

(*a*) the event is such that non-disclosure would impair a proper understanding of the accounts; or where

(*b*) the event is the completion of a transaction begun before the balance sheet date which has the effect of substantially altering the position revealed by that balance sheet.

SSAP 18

Accounting for Contingencies. Issued August 1980. Effective in respect to reports relating to accounting periods commencing on or after 1st September 1980.

A contingency is a situation existing at the balance sheet date whose outcome will be determined by the occurrence or non-occurrence of some future event. If the effect of a contingency is such that a loss, although not yet incurred, will probably be incurred and the amount of that loss can be reasonably closely estimated, then provision should be made for the loss. Where a loss is improbable or its amount cannot be estimated with reasonable accuracy, the contingency should be disclosed (i.e. noted). Where the effect of the contingency is that a gain is probable, this should be disclosed (but not taken credit for in the profit and loss account). If a gain is possible but improbable the contingency should not be disclosed.

SSAP 19

Accounting for Investment Properties. Issued November 1981. Effective in respect to reports relating to accounting periods commencing on or after 1st July 1981.

Investment property is property acquired for its investment potential, i.e. rental income and capital appreciation, rather than for occupancy by the company. The effect of this standard is to relieve the investing company of the obligation otherwise imposed by SSAP 12 to provide depreciation on such property.

5. CONCLUSION

The brief review which we have conducted should give a feel for the kind of things with which Accounting Standards concern themselves. There is no common theme binding them together except that each deals with some area of controversy. By and large the Statement of Intent which preceded the issue of Standards seems to have been carried out in all its major elements. There has certainly been substantial debate on areas of difference which, but for the standard making process, would not have taken place. There has also been a continuation of the trend towards consistency of treatment in published reports. The Companies Act 1981 shows that some principles, previously the subject of Standards, are entering legislation.

We should not conclude this chapter without a brief reference to

International Standards. The International Accounting Standards Committee was formed in 1973 having representatives from the accountancy professions of nine countries. These were, in alphabetical order, Australia, Canada, France, Germany, Japan, Mexico, The Netherlands, the United Kingdom, the Republic of Ireland and the United States of America. Most large companies now have multi-national dimensions and investment is made across national boundaries. This makes it important that there should be as much international standardisation of reporting practices as possible.

At the time of writing the IASC has issued thirteen standards. IASs and SSAPs sometimes concern similar matters and, where they do, care is taken to ensure compatibility. Compliance with an SSAP ensures compliance with an IAS where one exists covering the same area.

SUMMARY

1. Accounting Standards have had a considerable influence on the form and content of published accounts in the 1970s.

2. They date from an initiative taken by the Institute of Chartered Accountants in England and Wales in 1969 when it issued its Statement of Intent on Accounting Standards in the 1970s. This Statement set out the following plans:

(*a*) to narrow areas of difference and variety in accounting practices;

(*b*) the disclosure of accounting bases;

(*c*) wider exposure for major proposals on Accounting Standards; and

(*d*) a continuing programme for encouraging improved accounting standards in legal and regulatory measures.

3. Standards are created under a programme guided by the Accounting Standards Committee which has members representing the six main bodies of qualified accountants in the United Kingdom.

4. The process of standard forming may be itemised as follows:

(*a*) research;

(*b*) drafting by sub-committee;

(*c*) internal exposure;

(*d*) exposure draft;

(*e*) statement on Standard Accounting Practice.

5. Standards are mandatory on the members of the participating professional bodies. Non-compliance may be the subject of disciplinary proceedings.

QUESTIONS

1. What were the main components of the Statement of Intent issued by the Institute of Chartered Accountants in England and Wales in 1969? To what extent do you think these have been realised?

2. Standards have been criticised as being too pragmatic and lacking in any consistent theoretical basis. Illustrate this view by reference to some actual Standards.

3. Examine critically the requirements of SSAP 12 (Depreciation).

4. Outline the main steps whereby an accounting problem is identified for consideration and then translated into a finished Accounting Standard.

5. Discuss the contention that the existence of Standards inhibits experiments in financial reporting and thus discourages advantageous developments.

CHAPTER 19

Future Directions for Financial Accounting

In this chapter we shall deal with the following important topics:

(*a*) the Corporate Report;
(*b*) value added statements;
(*c*) human resources accounting;
(*d*) forecast reporting;
(*e*) social accounting;
(*f*) disaggregation;
(*g*) interim reports.

1. INTRODUCTION

The seventies has been a decade of considerable development in the field of financial reporting. Perhaps the most obvious outward sign of this development has been the construction and promulgation of Accounting Standards and the debate, sometimes fierce and always lively, which these have set in train. In many ways, however, as evidenced in the literature of the academic as much as the practice of the professional, new horizons have been glimpsed and a scene has been set for considerable future development of techniques which today, in many areas, are primitive and ill defined. It is likely that by this time next century our present day style company reports will seem to be as quaint and dated to posterity as the accounting records of the Victorians now seem to us. In this, our final chapter, we shall review briefly some of the potential which exists. In the nature of the situation it will not be possible to draw any firm conclusions and we must content ourselves with sketching out the areas, describing the problems involved and the likely benefits of new techniques and to pointing out the few preliminary ideas which seem to offer promising lines of development.

2. THE CORPORATE REPORT

The starting point for our consideration of future developments ought to be a discussion paper published in 1975 under the title

"The Corporate Report". It was commissioned by the Accounting Standards Steering Committee (now Accounting Standards Committee) and produced by a working party under the chairmanship of Derek Boothman. The terms of reference of the working party were headed by the requirement to "re-examine the scope and aims of published financial reports in the light of modern needs and conditions".

The great significance of "The Corporate Report" is that it represents the first occasion in the United Kingdom when such an objective had been addressed. Its format, that of a discussion paper, emphasised that no intention existed to prescribe a revolutionary new style of reporting. The idea was to set out some basic ideas with a view to initiating debate.

In the event the debate has not developed at the rate which might have been hoped. This could be attributed to two factors. The first is that "The Corporate Report" was prepared with very considerable haste. The working party began its task in October 1974 and the finished report was available only nine months later. The document bears many signs of this haste. It is extremely brief. Its one hundred pages contain only about half that number of original text whilst the rest is taken up with summaries, summaries of summaries and illustrative appendices. Many of the ideas presented are, therefore, insufficiently developed and the document also contains a number of important contradictions. Secondly "The Corporate Report" had to compete for attention with two other reports of great importance to the accountancy profession which were published at about the same time. One of these was the Sandilands Report (on Accounting for Inflation—September 1975) and the other was the Solomons Report (on Education and Training for the Accountancy Profession—1974).

"The Corporate Report" begins by setting out a basic philosophy for financial reports. In its own words this is that "there is an implicit responsibility to report publicly (whether or not required by law or regulation) incumbent on every economic entity whose size or format renders it significant". This is a statement of very wide ranging implications. It is a reporting responsibility embracing many entities besides those which are traditionally required to report other than to themselves. It would include, for example, unincorporated businesses such as partnerships and also non-profit making organisations such as professional associations. There is also a direct challenge to the proprietorship concept of accounting since there is not seen any prime responsibility to report to the owners—the responsibility is to report publicly, i.e. to society in general. Financial matters are not seen as the only concern of such reports for which economic significance is the underlying rationale. Finally the philosophy appears to anticipate that reporting entities should not necessarily see themselves as reporting in compliance only with laws but as freely offering information out of respect for a social ideal.

In a further onslaught on the proprietorship concept "The Corporate Report" identifies seven distinct groups of users of reports. These are so comprehensive that it is hard to imagine anyone who could not claim membership of one or other of them in respect to any particular entity. They are:

(*a*) The Equity Investor Group; i.e. existing and potential shareholders;

(*b*) The Loan Creditor Group, e.g. debenture holders;

(*c*) The Employee Group, i.e. existing, potential and past employees;

(*d*) The Analyst-adviser Group, i.e. those with a professional responsibility to advise other groups (examples are investment analysts, stockbrokers and trade union officers);

(*e*) The Business Contact Group, i.e. customers, suppliers and competitors;

(*f*) The Government;

(*g*) The Public.

Having identified these user groups the report attempts to analyse separately their requirements but seems to come to the conclusion that these are all very similar and that general purpose, rather than specialised, reports are the proper objective.

In a third section the fundamental objective of a corporate report is stated to be "to communicate economic measurements of and information about the resources and performance of the reporting entity". Desirable characteristics of the reports will be that they are (*a*) relevant, (*b*) understandable, (*c*) reliable, (*d*) complete, (*e*) objective, (*f*) timely and (*g*) comparable.

Certain statements additional to those now forming part of annual accounts are proposed. These are:

(*a*) a statement of value added;

(*b*) an employment report;

(*c*) a statement of money exchanges with government;

(*d*) a statement of transactions in foreign currency;

(*e*) a statement of future prospects;

(*f*) a statement of corporate objectives.

Some of these are discussed more fully later on in the chapter.

Interestingly, in the light of future developments which have actually taken place, "The Corporate Report" takes some space to advocate the adoption of a system of current cost accounting in place of historical cost. It concludes by pointing to some likely areas for future research even though it is not positively recommending developments in those areas. They are:

(a) public sector accounting;
(b) social accounting;
(c) disaggregation; and
(d) multi-column reporting.

Current value accounting was also included on this list.

3. VALUE ADDED STATEMENTS

A value added statement is a complete denial of the proprietorship concept underlying the conventional profit and loss account. It views the company as a wealth producing entity and sees it as having a number of groups (often referred to as stakeholders) having a legitimate claim on the wealth which accrues to it. A measure of the wealth is the difference between the value of the goods or services which the company supplies (i.e. its sales) and the value of its bought-in goods and services (i.e. amounts paid to the businesses which supply it). The term "value added" thus refers to the value which a company, by its own efforts, adds to the value of its inputs. The stakeholders amongst whom this value is to be shared are seen as the shareholders and other providers of capital, the employees, the government (representing the community at large) and the future of the business itself. Here is a very simple example in which we look first at the conventionally constructed (summarised) profit and loss account for Silk plc for a certain year.

		(£000s)
Sales		22,500
Less Cost of sales	9,250	
Wages	2,570	
Interest on debentures	1,000	
Depreciation	3,290	
		16,110
Profit before taxation		6,390
Taxation		4,500
Profit after taxation		1,890
Dividends		1,500
Retained profit		390

A value added statement for Silk plc appears as follows.

Sales		22,500
Less Cost of sales		9,250
Value added		13,250
Applied to: Employees	2,570	
Providers of capital		
Interest	1,000	
Dividends	1,500	
Government	4,500	
Maintenance and expansion of assets		
Depreciation	3,290	
Retained profit	390	
		13,250

As will be seen the value added statement is merely a redrafting of figures from the profit and loss account. In that sense, therefore, it conveys no more information than was conveyed before. There is, however, a fundamental difference in the implication of the format from which certain advantages might flow. It could be argued, for example, that this style would give employees a feeling of greater involvement in the operations of the company so that they become more co-operative. It could also be claimed that value added is of itself a more suitable measure of the success of a company's activities than is profit as conventionally determined.

4. HUMAN RESOURCES ACCOUNTING

It is fairly widely acknowledged that a business's human resources are at least as important to its success as are its physical resources. Thus a business with a dedicated and harmonious management team is likely to succeed where one operated by disillusioned executives seeking only an opportunity for personal escape will fail. Again, a well blended, happy workforce will be efficient where a disgruntled one will be inefficient. It might thus fairly be argued that any set of accounts which omits this factor, and currently almost all do, is omitting a very important component of the business's position. If this is excused on the basis that human resources are a non-financial factor and therefore no concern of the accountant, it can be pointed out that there are very considerable financial implications. Apart from the effects on profitability of the quality of the workforce the costs of staff recruitment, training and welfare are often very significant.

There are several benefits which might be expected to flow from accounting for human resources. One is that the true costs and benefits of improving its quality by, for example, a careful recruitment and training policy, could be assessed. Another is that short term profitability might be shown up in a different light if achieved at the cost of creating worker dissatisfaction by short-time working and redundancies or by reducing expenditure on staff facilities.

Although there are as yet no well-developed techniques in the field of accounting for human resources one or two lines of thought seem to emerge from the literature. One is that the human resource itself should be omitted from the accounts as at present on the principle that this is not owned but is only hired by the business. The cost of that hiring is recorded as wages and salaries and, as such, appears as an item in the profit and loss account. What might be shown in respect of the human resource, however, is the business's investment in its workforce. This would include expenditure on recruitment (advertising and interviewing), training (courses and the unproductive learning period passed through by each new employee) and development (time spent in on-the-job preparation for promotion). Such expenditure could, by the keeping of appropriate records, be capitalised and then written off over the estimated "life" (i.e. period in the employ of the company) of the employee. This could be established on an average, actuarial, basis for different grades of employee. A senior executive would cost more to recruit and train than a junior clerk but might be expected to stay for longer. Unexpired costs under the headings referred to would appear in the balance sheet as the amount invested in current personnel and on which the business would be expected to earn an adequate return as with other invested resources. The amount written off each year (representing the advance of the workforce towards its ultimate leaving date) would be debited (like depreciation) in the profit and loss account. Such a system might be expected to show very clearly the trade-off between recruitment and training costs and labour turnover and enable targets to be set for the optimum levels of each. Here is an example of the application of this method.

Humanity plc recruited Smith as a clerk in its accounts department at a salary of £5,000 per annum. Experience shows that an employee at that grade will work at only 50 per cent efficiency for his first six months as he settles down in the job and learns how to do it. He will stay with the company, on average, for three years. Recruitment costs of such personnel average £1,000 per person. The accounting treatment might be as follows:

Debited to Investment in Personnel:

Recruitment cost	£1,000
Salary attributable to learning 50% × £5,000 × half year	1,250
	£2,250

Under the conventional treatment such costs would be debited directly to the profit and loss account "lost" under the headings of advertising and salaries. Under the method now being described one third of this amount would be charged to the profit and loss account in each year and the balance would be carried forward on the balance sheet. Thus one year after Smith had been engaged £750 would be charged to the profit and loss account as expired personnel costs and £1,500 would appear on the balance sheet described as investment in personnel.

The treatment just described is firmly rooted in normal and cost based accounting methodology. Another, quite different, approach would attempt to value the business's interest in its personnel directly. Although a business does not own its workforce in the ordinary sense it has a proprietorial interest in it represented by the contracts of employment. These give each party to them definite rights as well as obligations. As a strict minimum the business's right is restricted to receiving the services of the employee (in return for payment) during a specified period of notice (which may be quite short). Realistically, however, the contract gives a probability that the employee will render services over a considerably longer period than this and the average length of service, no doubt different for different grades of employee, could be estimated. The value of the employees' services is then, on some appropriate basis, determined. Here is an example. Mr Jones is an employee earning £10,000 per annum which is, presumably, the value of the services which he renders to the company. Personnel at his grade stay with the company for, on average, five years. The expected value of Mr Jones's services in total can, therefore, be established by discounting. We will take 10 per cent per annum as being the appropriate rate of discount. The relevant expected value is £37,900 (£10,000 × (0.909 + 0.826 + 0.751 + 0.683 + 0.621)). Similar amounts calculated for all other employees would then be added to this and the grand total would appear on the balance sheet as an asset. The value would be calculated annually and, because of starters, leavers and changes in expectations about length of service, would vary. Thus if one year later Mr Jones has been promoted to a salary of £12,000 and is now expected to stay for six years his "value" has increased to £52,248 (£12,000 × (0.909 + 0.826 + 0.751 + 0.683 + 0.621 + 0.564)). The improvement of £14,348 (£52,248 − £37,900) is an increase in the value of the "asset" arising from the business's policy towards its staff. Obviously the business will not receive its employees' services without payment and therefore there must also appear in the balance sheet a liability in respect of salary payable and this will be of equal amount to the asset.

As this exercise creates an asset and a liability of equal amount it might seem that it has had no valuable effect on the balance sheet. It does, however, show:

(a) a more realistic figure for the total resources tied up in the business (thus affecting the perception of profitability);

(b) a measure of the business's obligation to its employees which always exists but is rarely measured and disclosed;

(c) a measure of changes in the human resource asset which highlight changes in the value of the stock of employment contracts consequent on expansion, contraction or changes in staff policy.

5. FORECAST REPORTS

A great weakness of present day annual accounts is that they provide information only about the past. Any user seeking to make a decision which changes his position relative to the company (e.g. a decision to become or to cease to be a shareholder) is primarily concerned with the future. He will attempt to use accounts, therefore, to predict that future. It would clearly be useful to him if company reports contained explicit forecasts and revealed future plans.

There is currently no legal requirement for companies to provide any view on their future in their annual report unless one counts a rather imprecise reference to this in the Directors' Report, although "The Corporate Report" did propose that a statement of future prospects should be required. Many companies do provide information about the future on a voluntary basis and all prepare forecasts and plans for internal purposes. The arguments normally assembled against any statutory requirement to produce information about the future include the following:

(a) any information about the future must necessarily be, to a considerable extent, speculative and subject to a high degree of error;

(b) it would be difficult for such information to be audited satisfactorily;

(*c*) information about a company's plans might be helpful to a competitor and thus detrimental to itself;

(*d*) the plans themselves might be drawn up with an eye to publication so that companies became less enterprising, setting themselves modest, easily attainable targets.

None of these points seems very persuasive and it is highly likely that the corporate report of the (distant) future will contain as much information about the next year's planned activities as it does about last year's achievements.

6. SOCIAL ACCOUNTING

It is a natural extension to the recognition sought in "The Corporate Report" of a social responsibility for economic entities that such entities should report in terms of progress towards social goals. The basic idea is one familiar for a long time to economists in a theoretical sense that the costs and benefits of the operations of a business on which its financial reports are based may differ from the costs and benefits to society at large. An apparently profitable business may impose heavy costs on the community for which it is not charged and which do not, therefore, appear in its profit and loss account. Examples of this might be the wear and tear on local roads used by heavy lorries delivering and taking away heavy goods and pollution caused to rivers or to the atmosphere by toxic waste. Conversely there may be unquantified benefits to the community. One of these might be the benefit to other businesses arising from the employment and thus wealth given to local people. Clearly reporting in a social sense should include some attempt to identify and measure costs and benefits to the community as well as private costs and benefits. Equally clearly the problem of how to do this is a difficult one and satisfactory techniques for this purpose have not yet been developed.

7. DISAGGREGATION

"The Corporate Report" mentions disaggregation as an important goal for financial reporting. The term implies that the overall picture given by financial reports is broken down so the performance of separate segments of the business may be separately judged. This breakdown might be done on the basis of type of activity, by geographical regions or by some other useful basis. It should be useful in assessing the overall risk to which the business is subject (this being a function of its diversity) as well as in obtaining a more detailed understanding of its overall performance.

The main difficulty involved in disaggregation is that of apportioning joint revenues and costs. "The Corporate Report" is so committed to the notion of disaggregation that it advocates that some arbitrary apportionments be used if necessary. It is hard to see, however, how an arbitrary apportionment which, by definition, is without logical basis, could be helpful. The principle of disaggregation seems a useful one in the further development of financial information but the precise way in which it might be achieved is still far from clear.

8. INTERIM REPORTS

Although not required by law all companies having a Stock Exchange listing are required to publish to their shareholders interim reports half way through the financial year as a condition of that listing. These interim reports are in a fairly sketchy form giving information only on certain key figures (e.g. turnover and profit) from the profit and loss account. They are unaudited.

Annual reporting has the disadvantage that many things can take place within that period of time which substantially affect the position or prospects of the company. This is the rationale for interim reporting. The difficulty of the time allocation of revenues and costs, however, great enough when accounting is done on an annual basis is even greater when the period is shorter. This fact must cast some doubt on the usefulness in practice of those interim reports. For many businesses which are seasonal in nature, the calendar year is a natural interval and a six month period is not. Nevertheless it is likely that interim reports are here to stay and they may well be developed into more frequent reporting. In this connection it is interesting to note that quarterly reporting is common in the USA.

SUMMARY

1. It may reasonably be expected that company financial reporting will continue to develop in the future as it has done in the past.

2. "The Corporate Report"—a discussion paper sponsored by the Accounting Standards Steering Committee (now the Accounting Standards Committee)—was an important attempt to "re-examine the scope and aims of published financial reports in the light of modern needs and conditions". It established a philosophy for financial reporting which recognised the importance of identifying user groups.

3. Other possibly fruitful lines of future development are:

(a) Value Added Statements;
(b) Human Resource Accounting;
(c) Forecast Reporting;
(d) Social Accounting;
(e) Disaggregation;
(f) Interim Reporting.

QUESTIONS

1. It is widely acknowledged that information about the future would be valuable to users of accounts. What are the arguments against requiring by law the publication of detailed budgets?

2. Diligent plc is experimenting with the use of human resources accounting. In its balance sheet appears on both sides the figure of £562,187. As a liability it is described as "Human Resource Reserve" and as an asset as "Human Resources Employed". How do you think the figure was arrived at? How useful is its inclusion in the balance sheet?

3. Redraft the following profit and loss account in the form of a value added statement and comment on the usefulness of this format.

SWAN PLC

PROFIT AND LOSS ACCOUNT FOR THE YEAR ENDED 31ST DECEMBER 19—

		(£000s)
Sales		91,846
Less cost of sales		68,589
Gross profit		23,257
Less wages and salaries	7,850	
depreciation	4,210	
other administrative costs	3,186	
other distribution costs	2,473	
interest on debentures	500	
		18,219
Profit before tax		5,038
Taxation		2,492
Profit after tax		2,546
Dividends		2,000
Retained profit		546

4. "There is no place for fancy concepts in company financial reporting. Straightforward accounts of strictly financial matters are the most useful." Do you agree with this point of view?

5. "There is an implicit responsibility to report publicly incumbent on every economic entity whose size or format renders its significant" (The Corporate Report). Discuss.

Essay Topics

1. "The application of SSAP 16 (Current cost accounting) resolves once and for all the problems caused to accounting by inflation." Describe the provisions of SSAP 16 and comment on the truth of the statement.

2. The "merger" and "acquisition" methods of consolidation are not interchangeable. What are the distinguishing features of each and in what circumstances would each be appropriate?

3. Taxation in company accounts presents several special problems. Identify these and comment critically on the available methods for resolving them.

4. "A company is properly accountable only to its shareholders." Make a reasoned case either in support of or against this view.

5. "I cannot end without paying tribute to the skill and loyalty of our employees. They are the real substance of the business on which its profitability rests." (Chairman of a large public company in his annual report to the shareholders.) Suggest ways in which this "substance" might be reflected in the accounts, pointing out the conceptual and practical problems which have prevented this from becoming conventional practice.

6. Compare and contrast the conventional accounting concept of profit with alternative income concepts. Assess the value of each as a feasible and relevant measure of business performance.

7. The accountant is often told to consider the points of view of user groups of the accounts. What are user groups and why is it important to consider their needs?

8. "An accurate assessment of past income requires a perfect knowledge of the future. Given such perfect knowledge an assessment of past income becomes superfluous." Discuss.

9. "No profit and loss account containing a charge for depreciation can ever give a reliable indication of performance." Discuss.

10. Review "The Corporate Report" and assess its contribution to the debate on the scope and aims of published financial reports.

11. "Double entry book-keeping is the curse of the accounting theorist. It provides the subject with a facade of order and accuracy but behind this there lies nothing but disorder and gross approximation." Discuss this statement with particular reference to the search for basic accounting concepts.

12. A successful partnership wishes to reorganise itself into a limited company. Comment on the implications of this pointing out any specific advantages or disadvantages.

13. "We have to decide whether to expense or capitalise these development costs." (The Finance Director at a board meeting.) Discuss the nature of the decision to which he refers and the factors where appropriate.

14. The Companies Acts of 1908, 1929, 1948, 1967 and 1981 are landmarks in the development of company financial reporting. Review critically the principal disclosure requirements contained in the most recent of these.

15. "Profit is the difference between the cost of providing goods or services and the revenue derived from their sale." (Quotation from an Accounting textbook.) Is this an adequate definition?

16. What are the main components of the Statement of Intent on Accounting Standards issued in 1969? Assess the extent to which those intentions have been realised.

17. In what circumstances would you expect to find the term "goodwill" in a balance sheet? Express a view on the underlying nature of such an item and discuss critically accounting techniques for dealing with it.

18. "The understanding of a set of accounts depends to a considerable extent on the enlightened use of ratios." Explain, illustrating your answer with notes on some of the chief ratios and their usefulness.

19. Select four important basic accounting concepts. Describe them and comment on their implications. Provide a practical or theoretical justification for each.

20. Companies' statutory accounts are required to give a "true and fair view". Describe what you believe is meant by this and assess the extent to which it is an attainable ideal.

Case Studies

1. Pickwick, Copperfield and Twist are in partnership selling disposable paper products to the catering trade. Because the business involves them personally in long hours of work including a great deal of travelling, they maintain only very rudimentary accounting records and leave it largely to you, their accountant, to sort out their affairs at the end of their financial year which is 31st March.

On your advice almost all their business transactions are put through the bank so that its statements will provide an accurate record. They also file all purchase invoices and copy sales invoices, marking each when it is paid.

From the information given in the exhibits below you are required to prepare accounts for the business for the year ended 31st March 19–8.

Exhibit A

PICKWICK, COPPERFIELD AND TWIST

BALANCE SHEET AT 31ST MARCH 19–7

Capital accounts			*Fixed accounts*		
Pickwick		£70,000	Building		£80,000
Copperfield		80,000	Furniture and fittings		44,457
Twist		99,816			———
		———			124,457
		249,816			
Current accounts			*Current assets*		
Pickwick	£421		Stock	£82,662	
Copperfield	263		Debtors	111,873	
	——	684	Cash	16,969	
		———		———	211,504
		250,500			
Current liabilities		85,461			
		———			———
		£335,961			£335,961

Exhibit B

Working schedules prepared with the accounts give the following amplifications of items appearing in the balance sheet.

(a) Twist's capital account:	Original capital	£100,000
	Less Current account	184
		£99,816

(b) Current liabilities:	Trade creditors	£84,814
	Accrued electricity	526
	Accrued telephone	121
		£85,461

(c) Stock:	Goods for resale	£82,542
	Office supplies	120
		£82,662

(d) Debtors:	Trade debtors	£108,633
	Insurance paid in advance	240
	Rates paid in advance	3,000
		£111,873

Exhibit C

The partnership agreement
The agreement states that profits will be shared equally after allowing for 12 per cent per annum interest on capital and a salary of £2,000 per annum for Pickwick.

Exhibit D

A summary of the business's bank statement for the year ended 31st March 19–8 appears below.

Balance at 1st April 19–7	£16,969	Paid to creditors for goods	£445,932
Received from customers	587,987	Purchases of office supplies	946
Received from sales of furniture and fittings		Wages and salaries	37,084
(book value £1,280)		Electricity	4,819
	1,722	Telephone	1,571
		Rates	29,000
		Insurance	2,040
		Miscellaneous expenses	319
		Purchases of fixtures and fittings	18,945
		Drawings of partners:	
		Pickwick	10,800
		Copperfield	11,300
		Twist	12,300
		Extensions and improvements to buildings	20,000
		Balance at 31st March 19–8	11,622
	£606,678		£606,678

Exhibit E

Rough records show that although virtually all expenditure was made by cheque, certain amounts were regularly withheld from takings before they were paid into the bank. These amounts were £5 per week for petty cash expenditure and £100 per week for each partner for personal living expenses. (Assume a 52-week year.)

The invoice files show the following amounts unpaid at 31st March 19–8.

   (*a*) Copy sales invoices   £98,168
   (*b*) Purchase invoices   £78,241

Accruals are estimated at: Electricity   £582
                               Telephone   £140
Prepayments are: Rates   £4,000
                               Insurance   £300

After discussion with the partners it has been agreed that £21,500 is an appropriate amount to provide for the depreciation of furniture and fittings. The buildings are not to be depreciated.

2. The following trial balance was extracted from the books of Tequila plc at 31st March 19–6,

TEQUILA PLC

TRIAL BALANCE AT 31ST MARCH 19–6

Additions to land and buildings[14]	250	Creditors	982
Administrative salaries[11]	2,143	Debentures (10%)	500
Cash	1,914	Income from investments (net)[1]	56
Debtors	2,425	Net realisation of plant and machinery[15]	125
Development costs[2]	977	Profit and loss account at 1st April 19–5	351
Direct factory wages	9,291	Sales turnover	27,839
Distribution salaries	1,156	Share capital	
Dividends paid:		£1 ordinary shares	10,000
preference	80	8% £1 preference shares	1,000
ordinary[9]	500	Share premium	1,500
Expenses:		Taxation[13]	137
Administration[6,12]	326		
Distribution[7]	154		
Factory	4,563		
Furniture and fittings at 1st April 19–5[4]	2,107		
Goodwill[3]	2,000		
Interest paid on debentures[8]	25		
Land and buildings[4]	2,250		
Net additions to furniture and fittings[14]	111		
Plant and machinery at 1st April 19–5	3,883		
Purchases of raw materials	4,426		
Stocks at 1st April 19–5			
Raw materials[10]	285		
Finished goods[10]	2,934		
Trade investments[5]	571		
Work in progress at 1st April 19–5[10]	119		
	42,490		42,490

From it and the notes following you are required to prepare:

   (*a*) detailed manufacturing, trading and profit and loss accounts for the year;

   (*b*) a profit and loss account suitable for publication and complying so far as is possible on the information given, with the Companies Act 1981;

(c) a balance sheet at 31st March 19–6, suitable, as above, for publication;

(d) a set of key ratios which will give useful information to a potential investor in the company.

(N.B.: All figures in the trial balance and in the notes are given in £000s. The figures in brackets refer to the notes.)

(1) The basic rate of income tax is 30 per cent.

(2) Of the development costs, 293 is to be written off in the current year and the rest carried forward. This will be written off over three years, the expected period of benefit derived from the expenditure.

(3) Goodwill is to be written off over four years. It was acquired as part of the cash purchase of another business during the year just ended.

(4) Depreciation for the year is as follows:

Building (factory)		100
Plant and machinery (factory)		1,532
Furniture and fittings		
Administrative	238	
Distribution	107	
	——	345

(5) The trade investments are permanent investments in un-related companies. The listed investments have a book value of 186 and a market value of 215.

(6) Expenses—administration includes prepayments of 22 and is subject to an accrual of 69.

(7) Expenses—Distribution includes prepayments of 43 and is subject to accruals of 95.

(8) Provision is to be made for a half year's interest payable in respect of the debentures.

(9) It is proposed to pay a further dividend on the ordinary shares of 1,500.

(10) Stocks at 31st March 19–6 are:

Raw materials	397
Finished goods	3,054

Work in progress is valued at 367.

(11) Administrative salaries includes director's emoluments of 98.

(12) Expenses—administration includes audit fees of 25.

(13) The estimated taxation on the profits of the year is 1,959.

The balance brought forward from the previous year is in respect of an overprovision.

(14) Changes in tangible fixed assets are:

	Building	Plant and machinery	Furniture and fittings
Additions	250	1,055	726
Proceeds of sales	Nil	1,180	615
		(book value 920)	(book value 522)
Net	+250	−125	+111

3. Bell, Gong and Drum traded in partnership for many years sharing profits equally. Their balance sheet at 31st December 19–2 appears below:

BELL, GONG AND DRUM

BALANCE SHEET AT 31ST DECEMBER 19–2

Capital accounts			Fixed assets		
Bell		£175,000	Building		£200,000
Gong		175,000	Equipment		201,416
Drum		150,000			
					401,416
		500,000			
Current accounts			Current assets		
Bell	£214		Stock	£128,475	
Gong	836		Debtors	82,144	
Drum	541		Cash	14,084	
	—	1,591			224,703
Current liabilities					
Creditors and accruals		124,528			
		£626,119			£626,119

During the early part of the year 19–3, Drum decided that he should retire and various plans were discussed which would enable this to take place without requiring the closure of the business. It was eventually agreed as follows.

(a) Drum's retirement would take effect on 30th June 19–3.

(b) On that date the business would be converted into a limited company. £1 ordinary shares in the new company would be issued to Bell and Gong equal in nominal value to the capital account balance of each and Drum would receive debentures of equal nominal amount to his capital. The debentures would carry interest at the annual rate of 12 per cent and would be redeemed in annual instalments of £40,000. A first instalment (of £20,000 for a half year) would be redeemed on 31st December 19–3.

(*c*) Before the above issues were made the capital accounts would be adjusted to take account of goodwill at an agreed valuation of £240,000. This valuation was not, however, to appear on the balance sheet of the company.

(*d*) All current account balances at 30th June 19–3 would be settled in cash at that date or as soon thereafter as they could be calculated.

These matters were all implemented in line with the agreement and the legal and other costs (to be borne by the company) totalled £3,252. During the half year ended 31st December 19–3 Drum's debenture interest was paid up to date and Bell and Gong received remuneration as directors of the company of £10,000 each. They also proposed and planned to pay dividends at the rate of five per cent on their shareholdings.

Not knowing how to deal with the accounting procedures relating to the formation of the company, Bell and Gong maintained their records without a break as though the partnership had continued. All amounts paid to former partners were thus shown as drawings. The trial balance appearing below shows how the books stood at 31st December 19–3.

Administrative expenses	£52,188	*Capital accounts*	
Cash	39,573	Bell	£175,000
Costs of forming company	3,252	Gong	175,000
Debtors	78,927	Drum	150,000
Electricity	13,670	Creditors	126,486
Fixed assets	422,383	Sales	1,892,320
Insurance	8,200		
Maintenance	11,920		
Partners' drawings			
Bell	45,000		
Gong	45,000		
Drum	68,800		
Purchases	1,260,098		
Rates	13,420		
Stock at 1st January 19–3	128,475		
Wages and salaries			
Administrative	186,240		
Distribution	141,660		
	£2,518,806		£2,518,806

Note that:
(*a*) electricity accrued but not paid at the year end was £762;
(*b*) rates included an amount of £1,020 paid in advance;
(*c*) depreciation for the year amounted to £30,000;
(*d*) the dividends receivable by Bell and Gong were actually paid early in 19–4;

(e) stock at 31st December 19–3 was valued at £125,693;

(f) insurance included an amount of £1,300 paid in advance;

(g) sales for the year were not even (approximately 60 per cent took place in the first half of the year and 40 per cent in the second half), for the purposes of the accounts all costs, except those specifically relating to the company, are to be apportioned on the basis of sales;

(h) an audit fee of £5,000 has to be provided for, half of which will relate to the partnership and half to the company;

(i) a provision for taxation should be made in the accounts of the company equal to 50 per cent of the profit shown by the accounts.

4. The following are the balance sheets of Pound plc, Shilling plc and Penny plc at 31st March 19–7:

ASSETS

	Pound		Shilling		Penny	
Fixed assets						
Buildings		£50,000		£25,000		£30,000
Plant and machinery		32,463		31,862		25,674
Furniture and fittings		30,523		25,302		18,664
		112,986		82,164		74,338
Current assets						
Stock	£32,185		£18,227		£26,716	
Debtors	31,448		21,922		18,214	
Cash	16,191		5,518		7,238	
		79,824		45,667		52,168
Investments in subsidiaries						
Shilling (90% equity)		56,250				
Penny (60% equity)		72,000				
		£321,060		£127,831		£126,506

LIABILITIES

	Pound		Shilling		Penny	
Share capital						
£1 ordinary shares		£206,250		£75,000		£60,000
Profit and loss account		63,348		26,950		45,280
Current liabilities						
Creditors	£30,837		£22,131		£12,226	
Proposed dividend	20,625		3,750		9,000	
		51,462		25,881		21,226
		£321,060		£127,831		£126,506

(a) Pound acquired its holding in Shilling on 1st April 19–6 when it offered five new shares of its own for every six Shilling shares held. Ninety per cent of Shilling's shareholders accepted this offer. The balance on Shilling's profit and loss account at that date was £42,640.

(b) Pound acquired its holding in Penny for cash on 1st April 19–5. Penny's profit and loss account balance at that time was £32,600.

(c) Pound had not taken into its profit and loss account the proposed dividends due from its subsidiaries.

(*d*) Pound supplies goods to Penny at cost +50 per cent. Penny holds in stock goods received from Pound which it values at £6,000.

(*e*) Pound's sales ledger shows Penny as a debtor for £10,500. Penny's purchase ledger shows Pound as a creditor for £9,800. There is £700 cash in transit between the two companies.

Prepare a consolidated balance sheet for Pound plc and its subsidiaries on each of two alternative bases:

(*a*) the acquisition method for Penny and the merger method for Shilling;

(*b*) the acquisition method for both companies (taking into account that the shares which Pound issued when taking over Shilling were then standing in the market at £1.75 each).

5. The figures appearing below relate to Marchides plc for two consecutive years.

MARCHIDES PLC

PROFIT AND LOSS ACCOUNTS

		Year 1 (£000s)		Year 2 (£000s)
Sales		7,694		13,242
Less Cost of sales		5,379		10,045
Gross profit		2,315		3,197
Less Distribution costs	418		658	
Administrative expenses	622		843	
	—	1,040	—	1,501
		1,275		1,696
Add Income from investments		Nil		20
Profit before taxation		1,275		1,716
Less Taxation		614		824
Profit after taxation		661		892
Profits/(losses) on sales of assets		11		(25)
		672		867
Less Dividends		500		600
Retained profit		172		267

BALANCE SHEETS

	End of year 1 (£000s)	End of year 2 (£000s)
Fixed assets		
Buildings	800	1,000
Plant and machinery	643	816
Fixtures and fittings	487	725
Investments		
Shares in unrelated companies		210
	1,930	2,751
Current assets		
Stock	1,247	1,420
Debtors	1,012	1,225
Cash	210	407
	2,469	3,052
Less Current liabilities		
Proposed dividends	300	400
Taxation	614	824
Creditors	500	627
	1,414	1,851
Net current assets	1,055	1,201
Total assets less liabilities	2,985	3,952
Capital and reserves		
£1 ordinary shares	2,000	2,500
Share premium	*Nil*	200
Profit and loss account	985	1,252
	2,985	3,952

Note that:

(*a*) there was a rights issue of shares during year 2 at a price of £1.40 per share;

(*b*) all sales are on credit and take place evenly through the year; and

(*c*) changes in fixed assets are:

	Buildings (£000s)	Plant and machinery (£000s)	Fixtures and fittings (£000s)
Balances end of year 1	800	643	487
Add Additions purchased	300	416	435
	1,100	1,059	922
Less Book value of sales	–	24	52
	1,100	1,035	870
Less Depreciation	100	219	145
Balances end of year 2	1,000	816	725
Profit (loss) on sales		(7)	(18)

Prepare a Statement of Source and Application of Funds for the company for year 2.

Comment in detail on the position shown by the accounts and on any significant changes between the two years. Calculate such ratios as are useful to the analysis.

6. The following data relate to Hot Air plc for the year 19—.

(a)

	Purchases		Sales	
	Units	(£)	Units	(£)
Stock at beginning	5,200	41,600		
1st quarter	6,000	54,000	5,000	80,000
2nd quarter	5,000	50,000	7,000	126,000
3rd quarter	6,000	72,000	7,000	140,000
4th quarter	5,000	70,000	5,000	110,000

(b) Relevant price indices were:

	Plant and machinery	Furniture and fittings	General
Beginning	100	100	100
1st quarter	105	106	108
2nd quarter	110	112	116
3rd quarter	115	118	124
4th quarter	120	124	132

It may be assumed that each index applied throughout the quarter to which it relates.

(c) The company's current cost balance sheet at the beginning of the year was:

Share capital	£125,000	*Fixed assets*	
Revaluation reserve	66,300	Plant and machinery[1]	£99,200
Profit and loss account	9,800	Furniture and	
Current liabilities	49,600	fittings[2]	53,600
			152,800
		Current assets	
		Stock[3]	£41,600
		Debtors	53,800
		Cash	2,500
			97,900
	£250,700		£250,700

(1) Historic cost £72,400; CPP value £105,600.
(2) Historic cost £49,100; CPP value £51,400.
(3) Historic cost £36,400; CPP value £42,000.

(*d*) A summary of the cash account for the year appears below.

Opening balance	£2,500	Paid for supplies	£251,000
Received from sales	454,200	Wages and salaries	92,500
Sales of plant and machinery	1,000	Other expenses	15,400
Sales of furniture and fittings	800	Purchases of plant and machinery	11,200
		Purchases of furniture and fittings	8,850
		Dividends paid	31,250
		Closing balance	48,300
	£458,500		£458,500

(*e*) (Sales) and purchases of fixed assets were:

	Plant and machinery	*Furniture and fittings*
1st quarter	*Nil*	(800)[1]
2nd quarter	(£1,000)[2]	
3rd quarter	11,200	
4th quarter		8,850
HC depreciation	£15,000	£10,000
CCA depreciation	£18,000	£12,000
CPP depreciation	£17,500	£12,500

(1) Book value at year beginning HC £80; CPP £120; CCA £200.

(2) Book value at year beginning HC £400; CPP £600; CCA £500.

Prepare accounts for Hot Air plc on each of the three bases HC, CPP and CCA. Comment on the significance of the differences between them.

Index